DR. RON & MAR

The WATCHMAN on the WALL

VOLUME 3

❖

DAILY DEVOTIONS FOR PRAYING GOD'S WORD OVER THOSE YOU LOVE

❖

Printed in the USA

Cover Design & Layout by Wendy K. Walters | www.wendykwalters.com

ISBN (Hardcase):978-0-9982711-8-7

ISBN (Paperback): 978-0-9982711-9-4

ISBN (Kindle): 978-1-7327271-0-6

ISBN (ePub): 978-1-7327271-1-3

Library of Congress Control Number: 2018956434

Published By

Xaris Publications
Amarillo, Texas

To Contact the Authors:

w w w . G o d s G r e a t e r G r a c e . c o m

DEDICATION

To our children:
Stephanie and her Jonathan
and
Steven and his Rachel

Thank you for faithfully loving and serving our LORD Jesus Christ.
Thank you for being excellent parents—faithful,
prayerful watchmen of our grandchildren.
Thank you for how you love and honor us.

We love you~
Mom and Dad

Thus says the LORD:
"Call to Me and I will answer you,
and I will tell you great and mighty things,
which you do not know."

—Jeremiah 33:3

CONTENTS

$\mathcal{I}$NTRODUCTION

$\mathbb{W}$elcome fellow Watchman on the Wall to Volume 3! Through the LORD's leadership, we are excited to open another arsenal of 366 prayers from the Sword of the Holy Spirit for your use.

And take the helmet of salvation and the sword of the Spirit,
which is the Word of God. With all prayer and petition,
pray at all times in the Spirit, and with this in view,
be on the alert with all perseverance and petition for all the saints.
—Ephesians 6:17-18

We have been particularly concerned about the need for shepherding well the LORD's flock, especially those who are new believers. As you pray for your loved ones, please, include new believers in your prayers as a vital part of "all the saints" (Ephesians 6:18), praying for your church to shepherd new believers to walk with Jesus.

If the LORD permits, there will be a total of four of *The Watchman on the Wall* devotional books—to cover the entire Bible with a prayer formed from each chapter of the 1,189 chapters of God's Word. This means that over the course of the four books, there will be times when we write new prayer devotions for books previously covered. For example, *Proverbs, Hosea,* and several of the New Testament letters, which had devotions in *The Watchman on the Wall 1,* are included in this volume, with new devotions and prayers formed from the chapters. God's Word is rich with innumerable verses to pray; we hope you enjoy mining those books again for treasure verses for your loved ones.

The Watchman on the Wall 3 begins by praying the *Gospel of John.* The Christmas devotions take you to Bethlehem by way of *Ruth,* and the year ends reading and praying *Ephesians.* The months in between are filled with prayers from 31 other books of the Bible—what a great way to grow in your knowledge of God, building your faith in Him! Check out the Scripture Index on page 435 to see the books you will read and pray this year.

Whether you already prayed through *The Watchman on the Wall 1 and 2* or are starting with *The Watchman on the Wall 3,* here are a few words of encouragement and helpful tips for praying God's Word as an effective prayer warrior.

Pray the Word of God

The Bible is the greatest prayer book ever written. For 366 days, you will find treasure verses to pray for yourself and others. You will be able to say the Words confidently because they will be the very Words of God, containing His will. By the end of the year, we hope you will be in the holy habit of finding Bible verses to pray, so for the rest of your life, you can constantly pray God's Words back to Him.

Pray with God

Prayer is a gift and a privilege from the LORD. It is amazing the God of all creation not only gives you permission to talk to Him but desires to converse with you—to be in intimate, nonstop communication with you. Proverbs 3:32 says the LORD is intimate with the upright. Intimate in this verse carries within its meaning the idea of sitting on a couch with a friend, engaging in rich personal conversation. God is drawing you into that kind of relationship with Him.

Pray with Faith

Have faith as you pray that God is greater than any issue of this world, that He cares about you, and He will answer your prayers. Praying is faith. "And without faith, it is impossible to please Him, for he who comes to God must believe that He is and that He is a rewarder of those who seek Him" (Hebrews 11:6). As you pray, seek the LORD. As you go closer to Him, your faith will supernaturally grow as a result.

Pray with Context

For the devotions and prayers to be most fully understood, read the chapter, as suggested, at the beginning of each devotion. If you do so faithfully, you will read nearly 1/3 of the Bible in a year. With a few intentional exceptions, the devotions flow directly through entire books of the Bible.

Pray at a Dedicated Time

If *The Watchman on the Wall* is your primary devotional for this year, then using it in the morning helps tune you with the LORD before you walk through the rest of the day. Having your "connect with God time" at night is like a violinist tuning their violin after the concert is over. Certainly, anytime with God is good and praying throughout the day is encouraged (1 Thessalonians 5:17).

Pray Alone or With Others

If possible, and fitting for your situation, consider praying with others, perhaps a friend or family member. We heard testimonies of couples married over 50 years who began praying and reading their Bibles together for the first time with *The Watchman on the Wall*. There are also churches and Bible studies using *The Watchman on the Wall* together as a group. What a powerful team you will be! The prayers are easily modified to "we" and "us" in place of: " _____ and me."

Pray with Persistence

God calls you to be a prayer warrior for the sake of others. Isaiah 62:6-7 says God has appointed watchmen who, all day and all night, never keep silent. These watchmen on the walls of Jerusalem constantly remind the LORD to establish Jerusalem. The watchmen refuse to take any rest for themselves, and they give God no rest until He establishes and makes Jerusalem a praise in the earth. Who does God want you to constantly remind Him to establish, making their life a praise to Him?

Pray Standing Firm and Faithful

Just like the watchmen praying for Jerusalem, keep talking to God about the people He wants you to watch over in prayer (Isaiah 62:6-7). Remind God of His promises, His Word, and His Name. Refuse to take a break, continually interceding until God establishes your loved ones, making them a praise in the earth. See from your place on the Wall the glory of the LORD as He answers your prayers and changes the landscape of eternity before your eyes.

To this end also, we pray for you always,
that our God will count you worthy of your calling
and fulfill every desire for goodness and the work of faith with power,
so that the name of our LORD Jesus will be
glorified in you and you in Him,
according to the grace of our God and the LORD Jesus Christ.
—2 Thessalonians 1:11-12

Praying with you on the Wall-
Ron and Marsha Harvell

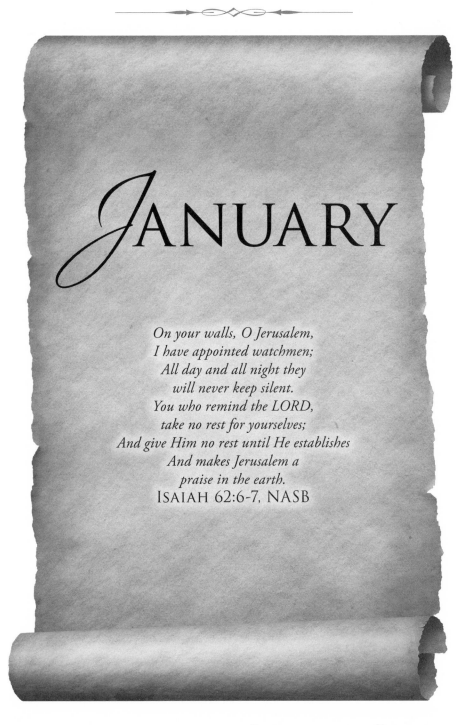

JANUARY

On your walls, O Jerusalem,
I have appointed watchmen;
All day and all night they
will never keep silent.
You who remind the LORD,
take no rest for yourselves;
And give Him no rest until He establishes
And makes Jerusalem a
praise in the earth.
ISAIAH 62:6-7, NASB

Please read John 1.

Meditate on verse 1.

> *In the beginning was the Word, and the Word*
> *was with God, and the Word was God.*

"Jesus, who are You?" When Christ lived on earth and in the years following His resurrection and ascension, many asked this question. God had the disciple John write the Gospel of John to answer it. You have the joy of starting this new year reading and praying the book of John. As you do, you will observe Jesus and the signs He performed, "so that you may believe that Jesus is the Christ, the Son of God, and that believing you may have life in His name" (John 20:31).

Who is Jesus? John wasted no time in answering the question. Jesus is:

- ❧ The Word (v. 1)
- ❧ God (v. 1)
- ❧ The Beginning (v. 2)
- ❧ The Creator (v. 3)
- ❧ Life (v. 4)
- ❧ The Light (v. 4-5)
- ❧ The Glory of the Father (v. 14)
- ❧ The Lamb of God (v. 29)
- ❧ The Messiah (v. 41)

Commit this year to contemplate and attentively observe Jesus Christ. Pray John 1:14 and 17 over yourself and those for whom you stand guard as a faithful, prayerful watchman (Isaiah 62:6-7).

> *"Word of God, You became flesh and dwelt among us.*
> *Help _____ and me see Your glory, Your*
> *glory as of the only begotten from the Father,*
> *full of grace and truth. May we know Your grace and truth,*
> *which is realized through You, Jesus Christ.*
> *In Your name, Jesus~"*

JANUARY 2

Please read John 2.

Meditate on verse 11.

> *This beginning of His signs Jesus did in Cana of Galilee, and*
> *manifested His glory, and His disciples believed in Him.*

John recorded a handful of Jesus' miracles for the purpose of you believing Jesus is the Savior and having life in His name (John 20:31). The first recorded miracle in John shows Jesus' power over creation and His power to bring permanent and obvious change. Jesus recreated over 120 gallons of water into the best wine imaginable (vs. 6-11). The picture is poignant for what Christ does with your life when you give yourself to Him. Jesus completely recreates you; your life becomes new, abundant, and the best imaginable because of the LORD Jesus Christ, your Creator, Savior, and Re-Creator.

Meditate on the miracle of Jesus changing gallons of water into wine. Ask the Holy Spirit to teach you the many parallels this miracle has to your life. Pray for Jesus to perform this miracle in the lives of those who need Him.

Pray John 2:5 over yourself and those for whom you stand guard as a faithful, prayerful watchman (Isaiah 62:6-7).

> *"LORD, whatever You say to _____ and me, let us do it.*
> *In Your name, Jesus~"*

Please read John 3.

Meditate on verse 30.

He must increase, but I must decrease.

John 3 is packed with truth to meditate on for a lifetime. You may have memorized some of these truths as a young child, like John 3:16.

In light of current events and popular worldly teaching, other truths from this chapter may become richer and richer for you. For example, if a person does not believe in Jesus, the only begotten Son of God, he has already been judged (v. 18). Those whose deeds are evil love the darkness and hate the Light—Jesus Christ (vs. 19-20). Practicing the truth is evidence of coming to Jesus, the Light (v. 21). Obeying Jesus proves that a person believes in Him (v. 36). Those who refuse to obey will not see life but will abide in the wrath of God (v. 36).

Let Christ and His Word increase more and more in you (v. 30). Jesus gives His Spirit without measure to those who believe in Him as the source of eternal life (vs. 34, 36). Let the Holy Spirit and the Word of Christ control you today.

Pray John 3:21 and 30 over yourself and those for whom you stand guard as a faithful, prayerful watchman (Isaiah 62:6-7).

"LORD, help _____ and me practice the truth.
We come to You, the Light;
let our deeds be manifested as having been wrought in God.
Christ, You must increase, but we must decrease.
For Your name's sake, Jesus~"

JANUARY 4

Please read John 4.

Meditate on what the woman said in verse 39b.

"He told me all the things that I have done."

Jesus encountered a Samaritan woman who had been married five times and was currently living with a man. The woman was amazed Jesus would even talk to her, and as their conversation unfolded, she learned Jesus knew all about her and her sordid past.

Instead of being ashamed Jesus knew all the things she had done, she was freed from her sin. Jesus' words drew her into a saving, intimate relationship with Him.

Jesus knows everything about you, and He still loves you. He offers you forgiveness and a saving relationship with Him. Let Jesus reveal past and present sins to you. Ask Him to forgive you and release you from bondage to evil. Experience the joy of walking in freedom from iniquity because you are walking in intimacy with Christ.

Pray John 4:10 and 34 over yourself and those for whom you stand guard as a faithful, prayerful watchman (Isaiah 62:6-7).

"Jesus, thank You that _____ and I can know the gift of God and be given Your Living Water, the Holy Spirit (John 7:38-39).

Give us Your appetite to say,
'My food is to do the will of Him who sent
me and to accomplish His work.'
In Your name, Jesus~"

Please read John 5.

Meditate on verses 2-3.

> *Now there is in Jerusalem by the sheep gate a pool,*
> *which is called in Hebrew, Bethesda, having five porticoes.*
> *In these lay a multitude of those who were*
> *sick, blind, lame, and withered,*
> *waiting for the moving of the waters.*

Jesus, the door of the sheep (John 10:7), stood by the sheep gate among a multitude of diseased outcasts. If these humans had been one of the lambs coming through that sheep gate, they would have been immediately rejected as not good enough for temple sacrifice. Their reality was rejection by society. Their only hope was a miraculous stirring of the waters and a quick entry into that water for healing. Jesus asked one of the sick if he wanted to be healed. When this man encountered the Living Water (John 4:10), he no longer needed to step into that Bethesda pool; Jesus immediately healed him and commanded him to walk and stop sinning (vs. 8, 14).

What a poignant picture of your life! Before Jesus, you were diseased by sin. The Lamb of God, who takes away the sin of the world (John 1:29), came to you and asked if you wanted to be healed. The Living Water washed you clean from your sin and invited you to walk with Him. As you journey with Jesus, He teaches you how to live with Him and sin no more.

As a faithful, prayerful watchman (Isaiah 62:6-7), pray John 5:24 over those who need to be healed by Jesus.

> *"LORD Jesus, may _____ hear Your Word*
> *and believe the Father who sent You,*
> *so they can have eternal life.*
> *May they not come into judgment but pass out of death into life.*
> *Because of You, the Living Water and the Lamb of God ~"*

JANUARY 6

Please read John 6.

Meditate on verse 53.

> *So Jesus said to them, "Truly, truly, I say to you,*
> *unless you eat the flesh of the Son of Man and drink His blood,*
> *you have no life in yourselves."*

John 6 contains the very familiar story of Jesus feeding over 5,000 people with only five loaves of bread and two fish, and it contains the very hard teaching of Jesus that says, "Unless you eat and drink the LORD Jesus Christ, you have no life; unless you devour Jesus, you do not have eternal life" (vs. 53-69).

Jesus' disciples were excited to do miracles in His name (Luke 10:1, 17), but the challenge of wholehearted commitment to the LORD caused many to abandon Him (v. 66).

What about you? Is Jesus Christ LORD (Almighty God and Master) of your life? Doing "church stuff" does not make you a Christian. Exchanging your life for the life of Christ makes you a Christian.

Reread John 6 and ask the Holy Spirit to give insight into understanding His Word. Being obedient to Jesus' command to eat and drink Him is the most important decision you will ever make. Please do not hesitate to do so if you haven't already.

Pray John 6:68-69 over yourself and those for whom you stand guard as a faithful, prayerful watchman (Isaiah 62:6-7).

> *"LORD, to whom shall I go?*
> *You have the Words of eternal life!*
> *I have believed and come to know that You are the Holy One of God.*
> *LORD, please draw _____ to make the same confession.*
> *In Your name, Jesus~"*

Please read John 7.

Meditate on verses 37b-39a.

> *Jesus stood and cried out, saying,*
> *"If anyone is thirsty, let him come to Me and drink.*
> *He who believes in Me, as the Scripture said,*
> *'From his innermost being will flow rivers of living water.'"*
> *But this He spoke of the Spirit, whom those*
> *who believed in Him were to receive.*

Jesus gives an amazing invitation and promise to anyone who wants to follow Him. Jesus invites you to come and imbibe deeply of Him. As a believer in Jesus, you have the privilege of soaking Him up.

When you accept Christ's invitation to come and drink of Him, He gives you His Spirit, whom He describes as a river of living water flowing inside you. The living water of the Holy Spirit vivifies, quickens, and empowers you. Incredible!

Jesus' words are a fulfillment of Isaiah 12:2-3. Say these words to your Savior:

> *"Behold, God is my salvation;*
> *I will trust and not be afraid,*
> *for the LORD God is my strength and song,*
> *and He has become my salvation.*
> *Therefore, I will joyously draw water*
> *from the springs of salvation."*

Pray John 7:37-39 over yourself and those for whom you stand guard as a faithful, prayerful watchman (Isaiah 62:6-7).

> *"LORD, I am thirsty. I come to You and drink deeply.*
> *Let the living waters of Your Spirit flow from my innermost being.*
> *LORD, please let _____ believe in You*
> *and come and drink of Your Spirit.*
> *In Your name, Jesus~"*

Please read John 8.

Meditate on verse 31.

> *So Jesus was saying to those Jews who had believed Him,*
> *"If you continue in My Word, then you are truly disciples of Mine."*

John 8 contains an interesting discussion between Jesus and some Jews who had believed Him. Jesus challenged their belief by demanding proof that they were really His followers. The proof was in the abiding; true disciples of Jesus Christ abide in His Word.

Of course, Jesus knew the heart of those who said they believed; He told them their father was the devil, and God's Word had no place in them; they did not have ears to hear His Word (vs. 37, 43-44).

What would Jesus say to you? Have you said you believe in Jesus, yet you abide in the world instead Christ and His Word? Ask the LORD to convict you of sin and give you an abiding faith that remains eternally in Him.

Pray John 8:31-32 over yourself and those for whom you stand guard as a faithful, prayerful watchman (Isaiah 62:6-7).

> *"LORD, may _____ and I continue in Your Word.*
> *Make us truly disciples of Yours.*
> *Let us know the Truth, and let the Truth make us free.*
> *Because You are the Truth, LORD Jesus~"*

Please read John 9.

Meditate on verse 5. Jesus is talking.

"While I am in the world, I am the Light of the world."

This verse may be disconcerting. If Jesus was the Light of the world while He was on earth, what happened to that Light when He ascended to the Father? Where is the Light?

Ponder these truths; Jesus is talking to his disciples, to those who follow Him:

"You are the light of the world. Let your light
shine before men in such a way
that they may see your good works and glorify
your Father who is in heaven."
—Matthew 5:14a, 16

If you are a Christian, a follower of the LORD Jesus Christ, then Christ is in you, and His light is still in the world because you are in the world. As you ponder the humbling and awesome fact that Jesus calls you the light of the world, purpose to live every moment so others will want to be in the Light and become followers of Him, too.

Pray John 9:5-7 and 37-38 over yourself and those for whom you stand guard as a faithful, prayerful watchman (Isaiah 62:6-7).

"LORD, You are the Light of the world!
Please touch the blind spiritual eyes
of _____ , so they can see You.
Jesus, thank You that I can see You and talk with You.
LORD, I believe and worship You! Please let _____ do the same.
Because You are the Light, Jesus~"

Please read John 10.

Meditate on verses 14 and 27-28. Jesus is talking.

> *"I am the good shepherd, and I know My own and My own know Me.*
> *My sheep hear My voice, and I know them, and they follow Me;*
> *and I give eternal life to them, and they will never perish;*
> *and no one will snatch them out of My hand."*

> *The LORD is my shepherd; I shall not want.*
> *—Psalm 23:1*

John 10 adds great insight into the psalmist's declaration that the LORD is his shepherd. Observe the Shepherd Jesus Christ:

- Jesus is the good shepherd (vs. 11, 14).
- Jesus lays down His life for the sheep (v. 11, 15, 17, 18).
- Jesus knows His own sheep, and His sheep know Him (v. 14, 27).
- Jesus gives His sheep eternal life, and they never perish (v. 28).
- Jesus' sheep will not be snatched out of His hand (v. 28).

As you hear and follow your Good Shepherd, know with confidence you will never perish because you have eternal life, forever carried in His hand.

As a faithful, prayerful watchman (Isaiah 62:6-7), pray John 10:27-28 over someone who needs to let the Good Shepherd give them eternal life.

> *"Good Shepherd, please let _____ hear*
> *Your voice and be known by You.*
> *May they follow You, so You will give them*
> *eternal life. I do not want them to perish.*
> *I want them to be in Your hand so no one*
> *can snatch them out of Your hand.*
> *Good Shepherd, thank You for doing all of those things for me.*
> *I shall not want in Your name, Jesus~"*

JANUARY 11

Please read John 11.

Meditate on verse 39a.

Jesus said, "Remove the stone."

Jesus commanded Martha and Mary to remove the stone, and rather than immediately obeying their LORD, Martha argued that removing the stone would be stinky. Jesus replied that obedient belief results in seeing God's glory. The sisters removed the stone, and Jesus revealed His glory (vs. 39-44). I wonder what would have happened if they had refused?

What about you? What has Jesus commanded you that you are making excuses not to obey?

"Forgive that person."

"But God, what they did to me stinks."

"Discipline your children in the fear of the LORD."

"But God, parenting is stinking hard."

"Go and serve in the ministry I have called you to do."

"But God, what if I stink at what I do."

Jesus says, "Did I not say to you that if you believe, you will see the glory of God?" (v. 40)

Pray John 11:39-40 over yourself and those for whom you stand guard as a faithful, prayerful watchman (Isaiah 62:6-7).

"LORD, You have given the command to remove the stone.
Help _____ and me stop making stinking excuses.
Help us believe! We want to see Your glory, God!
In Your name, Jesus~"

Please read John 12.

Meditate on verse 43.

For they loved the approval of men
rather than the approval of God.

John 12 contains familiar stories leading up to the crucifixion. The chapter opens with Mary lavishing love on her Savior by anointing His feet with what was probably her most costly possession. Then, in front of many dinner guests, she unashamedly wipes His feet with her hair. There was no doubt about Mary's allegiance and devotion to her LORD.

The chapter ends with Jewish rulers doing the exact opposite of Mary. They believed in Jesus, yet they refused to confess their belief because they did not want to be kicked out of the synagogue and excluded from Jewish assemblies. They were more afraid of what people thought about them than what God thought about them.

With whom do you relate from John 12? Do your words and actions make it obvious you are devoted to the LORD Jesus Christ, or do they prove that you really care more about the things of the world than the things of God?

In humility, confess and repent of areas in your life where you love man's approval more than the approval of God. Ask Him to help you make the same confession Jesus made in John 12:49-50.

"LORD, I do not want to speak on my own initiative.
Father, send me and give me a commandment
as to what to say and what to speak.
I know that Your commandment is eternal life;
therefore, the things I speak, I speak just as You have told me.
For the sake of Your name, Jesus~"

Please read John 13.

Meditate on verse 23.

> *There was reclining on Jesus' bosom*
> *one of His disciples, whom Jesus loved.*

When John wrote about reclining on the bosom of His Savior, he gave you an incredible picture of intimacy with Christ. As John couched closely with Jesus, he was able to hear His heartbeat. It is amazing that Almighty God not only allows such closeness to Him but desires you to be that close to Him!

David wrote about this kind of intimacy with God: "The secret of the LORD is for those who fear Him" (Ps. 25:14). The Hebrew word for secret literally means intimacy.[1] The LORD is intimate with and reveals His secrets to those who fear Him.

As you walk with Jesus today, lean up against His chest and hear His heart beating. Ask Him what His heartbeat is concerning issues in your life and the lives of those you love. Learn what makes Him happy, sad, joyful, and mad. Ask Him to give you His heart for what is happening in the world, so your heart beats as one with His.

Pray to obey Jesus' command in John 13:34-35. Pray it over yourself and those for whom you stand guard as a faithful, prayerful watchman (Isaiah 62:6-7).

> *"LORD, as I lean on You, help me to hear and obey You.*
> *May _____ and I love one another, even as You have loved us,*
> *that we may love one another.*
> *May all men know that we are Your disciples*
> *because we love one another.*
> *For the sake of Your name, Jesus~"*

---

1. *Retrieved from www.blueletterbible.org/lang/lexicon/lexicon.cfm?Strongs=H5475&t=NASB*

For the next four days, you have the privilege of eavesdropping on the last conversation your Savior had with His disciples before His crucifixion.

Supper was finished; Judas Iscariot has left to do his demonic deed, and Jesus is about to take the most excruciating walk of His life. But first, He has things on His heart He needs His true disciples to know; He even has you on His mind as He speaks. Therefore, every word of John 14-17 is vitally important, worthy of being meditated on and memorized. Bask in these Words and ask the Holy Spirit to teach you as you read.

Please read John 14.

Meditate on verse 14.

> *If you ask Me anything in My name, I will do it.*

Jesus says He will do anything you ask of Him if you ask in His name. Asking in the name of Jesus means to ask in the authority of His Almighty Name, according to His interests, His pleasures, His commands, and His excellencies.

Think about your prayers and what you ask of the Father in the name of Jesus. Are your requests in line with what interests Jesus and what brings Him pleasure? Do you desire what He commands in His Word and what reveals His excellent nature? "In the name of Jesus" should be said in great fear and reverence of God, desiring to ask only what is in His will and for His glory, being careful not to use His precious name in vain.

Pray John 14:26 over yourself and those for whom you stand guard as a faithful, prayerful watchman (Isaiah 62:6-7).

> *"Father, thank You for sending the Helper, the*
> *Holy Spirit, in the name of Jesus.*
> *Holy Spirit, teach _____ and me all things*
> *and bring to our remembrance all that Jesus said to us.*
> *In the name of Jesus~"*

Please read John 15.

Meditate on verses 4-6. Jesus tells you how to know for sure you really are a Christian.

"Abide in Me and I in you.
As the branch cannot bear fruit of itself unless it abides in the vine,
so neither can you unless you abide in Me.
I am the vine; you are the branches;
he who abides in Me and I in him, he bears much fruit,
for apart from Me you can do nothing.
If anyone does not abide in Me, he is thrown
away as a branch and dries up;
and they gather them and cast them into
the fire, and they are burned."

Salvation is through faith in Christ alone (Ephesians 2:8-9). Proof of your salvation is made evident by the fruit you produce because you abide and remain in Jesus.

Think about your life. Do you abide in the world, or do you abide in Christ? Do you produce fruit in keeping with the ways of the world, or do you produce fruit that proves Jesus lives and works in you?

Prior to Jesus starting this conversation with the eleven, Judas Iscariot made it obvious he did not belong to and abide in Christ. He left the group to do the work of Satan.

Jesus wants you to have the assurance of salvation. Believe in Him; live in Him; be fruitful in Him.

Pray John 15:8 over yourself and those for whom you stand guard as a faithful, prayerful watchman (Isaiah 62:6-7).

"LORD, may _____ and I bear much
fruit, and so prove to be Your disciples.
For the glory of the Father, in Your name, Jesus~"

Please read John 16.

Meditate on verses 1 and 33. Jesus is talking to you.

> *"These things I have spoken to you so that*
> *you may be kept from stumbling.*
> *These things I have spoken to you so that in Me, you may have peace.*
> *In the world, you have tribulation, but take*
> *courage; I have overcome the world."*

Jesus knew what awaited Him in the coming hours. Yet, rather than be self-absorbed, His love for you compelled Him to say things He wants you to remember, things that will keep you from stumbling and will give you peace (vs. 1, 4, 33).

You have the incredible privilege to hold those Words in your hands, read them, meditate on them, memorize them, speak them, and pray them. God's all-powerful Word changes your life and the lives of those you love.

And, not only do you have the very Words of God, Jesus gave you His Spirit of Truth, the Helper, to guide you into all truth, teaching and disclosing what His Words mean (vs. 7, 13). Amazing!

Reread John 14-16 and ask the Helper, the Spirit of Truth, to reveal why it is so important to the Savior for you to know these Words.

Pray John 16:8 and 13 over yourself and those for whom you stand guard as a faithful, prayerful watchman (Isaiah 62:6-7).

> *"Helper, convict the world, and _____, and*
> *me of sin and righteousness and judgment.*
> *Spirit of Truth, guide us into all truth and*
> *disclose to us what is to come.*
> *Make us like You, speaking not on our own initiative*
> *but what we hear in Christ's Word.*
> *In Your name, Jesus~"*

Please read John 17.

Meditate on verse 20.

I do not ask on behalf of these alone,
but for those also who believe in Me through their word.

Ponder the fact that Jesus was thinking about you and praying for you in the hours leading up to His crucifixion. Before He prayed for Himself (Luke 22:42), Jesus prayed for you:

- ✆ to have eternal life, so you can intimately know Him (v. 3).
- ✆ to be kept by the Father in His name (v. 11).
- ✆ to have His joy made full in you (v. 13).
- ✆ to not be of the world, just as Jesus is not of the world, and while you are in the world, for the Father to keep you from the evil one (v. 14-15).
- ✆ to be purified in the truth of His Word (v. 17).
- ✆ to be perfected and unified with Himself, the Father, and other Christians, just as He and the Father are one. That oneness helps the world to know and believe in Jesus (vs. 21-23).
- ✆ to be with Him so you can see His glory, the glory He gives to you (vs. 22, 24).
- ✆ to have the love of the Father in you and for Jesus, Himself, to be in you (v. 26).

Reread John 17, thanking Jesus for what He has done for you. As a faithful, prayerful watchman, pray John 17:2-3 over someone who needs to be one with the Father and the Son.

"Father, You gave Jesus authority over all flesh.
Please give _____ to Him so they
may have eternal life to know You,
the only true God and Jesus Christ whom You have sent.
In Your name, Jesus~"

JANUARY 18

Please read John 18.

Meditate on these phrases from verses 5-6 and 8. Jesus is talking.

> *He said to them, "I AM."*
> *So when He said to them, "I AM," they*
> *drew back and fell to the ground.*
> *Jesus answered, "I told you that I AM."*

Picture the scene. Jesus was in a quiet garden on the Mount of Olives praying. Suddenly, a group of over 600 men, Roman soldiers, and high-ranking officials from the temple, flood the area, carrying lanterns, torches, and weapons (Luke 22:39-47; John 18:1-3). They said they were looking for Jesus the Nazarene. When Jesus replied, "I AM," the entire mob fell to the ground! Over 600 heavily armed men immediately fell down because they were in the presence of Almighty God! I AM; the very same God who revealed Himself to Moses as I AM WHO I AM (Exodus 3:14), revealed Himself to this group of Romans and Jews, and the revelation forced them on their faces before Him.

How does Jesus affect you? Spend this day thinking about Him. And when you are so overcome by His presence, do not hesitate to fall before Him and acknowledge that He is God of you, the only I AM who has dominion over you.

Pray John 18:37 over yourself and those for whom you stand guard as a faithful, prayerful watchman (Isaiah 62:6-7).

> *"I AM, You said, 'Everyone who is of the truth hears My voice.'*
> *May _____ and I be of the truth,*
> *hear Your voice, and obey You.*
> *In Your name, Jesus~"*

*Most English translations of the "I AM" passages in the book of John add the word *He*, thinking it helps the English translation makes more sense; "I am *He*." The translators often italicize the word *He* because it is not in the original manuscripts. We want the impact of Jesus' words to be understood; therefore, we have purposely left out the italicized *He*, so you can clearly see Jesus is declaring He is God.

Please read John 19.

Meditate on verse 35.

> *And he who has seen has testified, and his testimony is true;*
> *and he knows that he is telling the truth, so that you also may believe.*

John, the beloved disciple of Jesus, stayed close to the cross when others fled. John was so close to the cross that he was an eyewitness to the prophecy fulfillment that not a bone of Christ's body was broken during the crucifixion (v. 36).

Contrast Joseph of Arimathea with John. Joseph was described as a secret disciple of Jesus because he feared the Jews (v. 38).

With whom do you most identify? Do you readily declare the truth about Jesus, so others may believe, or do you fear what people might think of you for speaking about Christ?

Ask the LORD to help you not be afraid and pray John 19:35 over yourself and those for whom you stand guard as a faithful, prayerful watchman (Isaiah 62:6-7).

> *"LORD, I have seen You in my life.*
> *Help _____ and me testify about You.*
> *May our testimony be true. Help us tell the*
> *truth, so that others may also believe.*
> *In Your name, Jesus~"*

Please read John 20.

Meditate on verses 30-31.

> *Therefore, many other signs Jesus also performed in the presence of the disciples, which are not written in this book, but these have been written so that you may believe that Jesus is the Christ, the Son of God; and that believing you may have life in His name.*

The Holy Spirit wrote this Gospel through John, the disciple, with the purpose of establishing that Jesus is the Messiah and the only Way to obtain eternal life (John 14:6). He proved it by recording a few of Jesus' innumerable miracles:

- Water to wine (John 2)
- Official's son healed (John 4)
- Man healed after 38 years (John 5)
- Feeding the 5000 (John 6)
- Walking on water (John 6)
- Blind man healed (John 9)
- Raising Lazarus (John 11)
- Resurrection from the dead (John 20)
- Materializing within a locked room (John 20)
- Breathing the Holy Spirit on the disciples (John 20)

These miracles prove Jesus is preeminent over creation, time, space, life, death, and you. As you bask in these divine truths, hear Jesus say, "Peace be with you" (v. 26).

Respond to Him with, "My LORD and my God!" (v. 28).

Pray John 20:31 over yourself and those for whom you stand guard as a faithful, prayerful watchman (Isaiah 62:6-7).

> *"Jesus, I believe that You are the Christ, the Son of God,*
> *and that by believing, I have life in Your name.*
> *Holy Spirit, please draw _____ to make the same confession.*
> *In Your name, Jesus~"*

JANUARY 21

Please read John 21.

Meditate on verse 16.

He said to him again a second time, "Simon,
son of John, do you love Me?"
He said to Him, "Yes, LORD; You know that I love You."
He said to him, "Shepherd My sheep."

Peter needed miraculous restoration. Rather than rebuke Peter for thrice disavowing Him, Jesus commanded him three times to shepherd His sheep (John 18:15-27; 21:15-17). Christ knew that caring for others was a great prescription for spiritual and emotional healing. Peter needed to tend the lambs coming to faith in Christ rather than wallow in self-condemnation and self-loathing for past mistakes.

If you are plagued by past sins and feel disqualified to serve the LORD, repent and hear Jesus say to you, "Follow Me!" (v. 19). Be quick to obey everything He asks you to do, knowing He needs you, too, to tend His flock.

Pray to obey Christ's commands in John 21:15-17, 19, and 22.

"LORD, You know that I love You.
Help me tend Your lambs; shepherd Your sheep,
and tend Your sheep as I follow You.
In Your name, Jesus~"

JANUARY 22

Please read 1 Kings 1.

Meditate on verse 6a.

> *His father had never crossed him at any time by asking,*
> *"Why have you done so?"*

Adonijah was David's fourth son (2 Samuel 3:4) who decided he wanted to be king after David. Adonijah was in the habit of making choices outside of God's will because his father never questioned his decision-making processes. If David had taught Adonijah from a young age how to hear and heed the LORD, then he probably would not have tried to usurp the throne.

Thankfully, the LORD recorded David's poor parenting techniques so you can learn from them. It takes time and energy to engage your children. Do not be a lazy parent. Talk to your children—a lot—no matter how young or old they are. Our daughter talked incessantly to her newborn son about everything going on in his world. Now that he is older, they continue to engage in rich, ongoing conversation.

Ask the "why" questions; it will open the door for deep conversations the LORD can use to help shape your children into Christlikeness.

Using 1 Kings 1:6 and 29, make a commitment to God to be a better parent. If you do not have children, pray for those who do and share this devotional with someone who needs to hear what God says about parenting. You can also pray this over any situation where you need to confront someone.

> *"As the LORD lives, who has redeemed my life from all distress,*
> *I will cross _____ and ask them, 'Why have you done so?'*
> *In the power of Your name, Jesus~"*

Please read 1 Kings 2.

Meditate on verses 2b-3.

> *Be strong, therefore, and show yourself a man. Keep the charge*
> *of the LORD your God, to walk in His ways and to keep*
> *His statutes, His commandments, His ordinances, and His*
> *testimonies, according to what is written in the Law of Moses,*
> *that you may succeed in all that you do and wherever you turn.*

This chapter contains the last words of King David to his son, King Solomon. They are wise words from a loving father who wanted to see his son firmly established in God's plans for his life (vs. 4, 12).

David's words probably echo your desires for your loved ones. You want them to be strong in the LORD. You want the males to show themselves to be men, not emasculated by the ways of the world. You want your loved ones to walk in God's truth with all their heart and soul so they can succeed in His plans for their lives.

As a faithful, prayerful watchman (Isaiah 62:6-7), pray 1 Kings 2:2b-4 and 45 over yourself and those for whom you stand guard.

> *"LORD, let _____ and me be strong. Make*
> *our men show themselves to be men.*
> *Help us keep Your charge, O LORD our God, to*
> *walk in Your ways, to keep Your statutes,*
> *Your commandments, Your ordinances, and Your testimonies,*
> *according to what is written in Your Law, that*
> *we may succeed in all that we do*
> *and wherever we turn, so that You may carry*
> *out Your promises which You spoke*
> *concerning us. Make us careful of our way to walk before You in truth*
> *with all our heart and with all our soul. Do not let us be lacking;*
> *let us be blessed and established before You forever.*
> *In Your name, Jesus–"*

Please read 1 Kings 3.

Meditate on verse 3.

> *Now Solomon loved the LORD, walking in*
> *the statutes of his father David,*
> *except he sacrificed and burned incense on the high places.*

Like most people, Solomon is a complicated fellow. This chapter sets him up as one of the wisest men who ever lived, yet it foreshadows the downfall of a man because of foolish choices.

The chapter begins with Solomon marrying an Egyptian princess for political purposes. Perhaps it was a good idea in the eyes of the world, but she and other non-Jewish women surrounding him will cause Solomon to sin against God (Nehemiah 13:26).

Solomon also had an "except" in his story. He loved the LORD, except he sacrificed on the high places (v. 3). God's law gave specific instructions for where to offer sacrifices (Leviticus 17:3-5; Deuteronomy 12:2, 13-14). These high places were formerly used for idol worship by the Canaanites and odious to the LORD.

Do you have an "except" in your life? What are you doing that follows the world's pattern rather than God's and is offensive to Him?

Ask the LORD to help you write your story with no exceptions to following His will. Pray the words from 1 Kings 3:9 and 28 over yourself and those for whom you stand guard as a faithful, prayerful watchman (Isaiah 62:6-7).

> *"LORD, please give _____ and me, Your servants,*
> *an understanding heart to judge and to discern between*
> *good and evil. Let Your wisdom, God, be in us.*
> *In Your name, Jesus~"*

Please read 1 Kings 4.

Meditate on verse 29.

> *Now God gave Solomon wisdom and very great discernment*
> *and breadth of mind, like the sand that is on the seashore.*

The lists in this chapter give you a snapshot of how great King Solomon was:

- 11 officials (vs. 2-6)
- 12 deputies (v. 7)
- 900 bushels of flour and meal, 30 oxen, and 100 sheep a day to feed his household (vs. 22-23)
- 40,000 stalls of horses (v. 26)
- 12,000 horsemen (v. 26)
- 3,000 proverbs spoken by him (v. 32)
- 1,005 songs written by him (v. 32)

And the greatest thing about King Solomon—his God-given wisdom, discernment, and breadth of mind—like the sand on the seashore. The reason he was wiser than all men was because he asked God for wisdom (1 Kings 3:9-12).

What do you ask from the LORD? It would please Him for you to pray for His wisdom for yourself and those for whom you stand guard as a faithful, prayerful watchman (Isaiah 62:6-7). Use the words from 1 Kings 4:29 to start your prayer.

> *"LORD, please give _____ and me Your*
> *wisdom and very great discernment*
> *and breadth of mind like the sand that is on the seashore.*
> *For the sake of Your name, Jesus~"*

JANUARY 26

Please read 1 Kings 5.

Meditate on verses 4-5. King Solomon is speaking.

> *"But now the LORD my God has given me rest on every side; there is*
> *neither adversary nor misfortune. Behold, I intend to build a house*
> *for the name of the LORD my God, as the LORD spoke to David my*
> *father, saying, 'Your son, whom I will set on your throne in your place,*
> *he will build the house for My name.'"*

King Solomon had a holy calling from God to govern the people of Israel and to build the temple of the LORD as planned by his father, King David. The LORD smoothed the way for Solomon to fulfill these ministries by surrounding him with people of peace who didn't cause him trouble and even supplied him with much of the building materials needed for the temple.

You, too, have a holy calling from the LORD. What has He told you to do? Are you obedient to Him? Ask Him to give you a smooth path and wisdom to know and do His will.

Pray 1 Kings 5:4-5 and 12 over the ministries God has given you and those you love, as a faithful, prayerful watchman (Isaiah 62:6-7).

> *"LORD my God, give _____ and me rest on every side;*
> *let there be no adversaries or misfortunes (evil occurrences).*
> *We intend to do in Your name, LORD God, as You have spoken.*
> *Please give us Your wisdom and Your peace.*
> *For the sake of Your Kingdom and Your name, Jesus~"*

t>222

JANUARY 26

Please read 1 Kings 5.

Meditate on verses 4-5. King Solomon is speaking.

> *"But now the LORD my God has given me rest on every side; there is neither adversary nor misfortune. Behold, I intend to build a house for the name of the LORD my God, as the LORD spoke to David my father, saying, 'Your son, whom I will set on your throne in your place, he will build the house for My name.'"*

King Solomon had a holy calling from God to govern the people of Israel and to build the temple of the LORD as planned by his father, King David. The LORD smoothed the way for Solomon to fulfill these ministries by surrounding him with people of peace who didn't cause him trouble and even supplied him with much of the building materials needed for the temple.

You, too, have a holy calling from the LORD. What has He told you to do? Are you obedient to Him? Ask Him to give you a smooth path and wisdom to know and do His will.

Pray 1 Kings 5:4-5 and 12 over the ministries God has given you and those you love, as a faithful, prayerful watchman (Isaiah 62:6-7).

> *"LORD my God, give _____ and me rest on every side; let there be no adversaries or misfortunes (evil occurrences). We intend to do in Your name, LORD God, as You have spoken. Please give us Your wisdom and Your peace. For the sake of Your Kingdom and Your name, Jesus~"*

28 | The WATCHMAN on the WALL

Please read 1 Kings 6.

Meditate on verses 11-13.

> *Now the Word of the LORD came to Solomon saying,*
> *"Concerning this house which you are building,*
> *if you will walk in My statutes*
> *and execute My ordinances and keep all My*
> *commandments by walking in them,*
> *then I will carry out My Word with you*
> *which I spoke to David, your father.*
> *I will dwell among the sons of Israel and*
> *will not forsake My people Israel."*

As you read the details of the building of the temple of the LORD, keep in mind that as a Christian, you are now the LORD's temple, and His Spirit lives inside of you (1 Corinthians 3:16). And as costly as it was for Solomon to build a temple with all of its gold, cedar, olive wood, cut stones, carvings, and engravings, the making of you into the temple of God was much costlier, for it cost God His life.

> *Do you not know that your body is a temple*
> *of the Holy Spirit who is in you,*
> *whom you have from God, and that you are not your own?*
> *For you have been bought with a price;*
> *therefore, glorify God in your body.*
> *—1 Corinthians 6:19-20*

As you ponder these truths, pray to obey God's commands from 1 Kings 6:12-13 as His faithful, prayerful watchman (Isaiah 62:6-7).

> *"LORD, as You build _____ and me into Your house,*
> *help us to walk in Your statutes and execute Your ordinances*
> *and keep all Your commandments by walking in them.*
> *As we do, please carry out Your Word which You have spoken to us*
> *to dwell among us and not forsake us.*
> *Because of Your name, Jesus-"*

Please read 1 Kings 6:37-7:51.

Meditate on verses 6:37-7:1.

> *In the fourth year, the foundation of the house of*
> *the LORD was laid, in the month of Ziv.*
> *In the eleventh year, in the month of Bul, which is the eighth month,*
> *the house was finished throughout all its parts*
> *and according to all its plans.*
> *So he was seven years in building it.*
> *Now Solomon was building his own house thirteen*
> *years, and he finished all his house.*

It is interesting that Solomon spent nearly twice as many years building his own house as he did building the LORD's house. And his house was four times larger than the temple. The temple was 2,700 sq. feet, as planned by his father, King David (1 Kings 6:2). Solomon's palace was 11,250 sq. feet (v. 2).

Scripture does not record Solomon's motives for building his house so much larger than God's. Perhaps he didn't even put much forethought into the size variation; however, Scripture records the difference, so it is worth asking the LORD what practical applications you can make because now you know the story.

What are you building in your life? How much time and money are you investing in it? What is its purpose? Whom does it benefit? Whom does it glorify? Is the LORD asking you other questions about your priorities?

Use the words from 1 Kings 7:14 to pray over yourself and those for whom you stand guard as a faithful, prayerful watchman (Isaiah 62:6-7).

> *"LORD, please fill _____ and me*
> *with wisdom and understanding*
> *and skill for doing any work You call us to do.*
> *We will come to You, King Jesus, and perform all Your work.*
> *For the sake of Your name and Kingdom, Jesus~"*

Please read 1 Kings 8. Notice the repeated word: *house*. It is used 21 times in this chapter.

Meditate on verse 11b.

... for the glory of the LORD filled the house of the LORD.

The house of the LORD no longer exists as a grand structure; it was destroyed in 70AD by the Romans and has never been rebuilt. However, there is no need for one because Christians are now the temple of the LORD (1 Corinthians 3:16). You are the house of God, and His glory fills you (Hebrews 3:6)! That is an amazing truth. As you ponder it, think about how His glory is manifested in your life and how it impacts others.

As God's temple and His servant, pray 1 Kings 8:23, 28, and 59-61 over yourself and those for whom you stand guard as a faithful, prayerful watchman (Isaiah 62:6-7).

> *"O LORD, the God of Israel and of _____ and*
> *me, there is no God like You*
> *in heaven above or on earth beneath, keeping covenant*
> *and showing lovingkindness to us, Your servants.*
> *May we always walk before You with all our heart.*
> *Please have regard to the prayer of Your servants*
> *and to our supplication, O LORD our God,*
> *to listen to the cry and to the prayers which*
> *Your servants pray before You today.*
> *And may these words of ours, with which we*
> *make supplication before You, LORD,*
> *be near to You, LORD our God, day and night, that*
> *You may maintain the cause of Your servants and the*
> *cause of Your people Israel as each day requires,*
> *so that all the peoples of the earth may*
> *know that, LORD, You are God;*
> *there is no one else. Let our hearts, therefore, be*
> *wholly devoted to You, LORD our God,*
> *to walk in Your statutes and to keep Your commandments.*
> *In Your name, Jesus-"*

Please read 1 Kings 9.

Meditate on verses 3-5a.

> *The LORD said to him, "I have heard your*
> *prayer and your supplication,*
> *which you have made before Me; I have consecrated this house*
> *which you have built by putting My name there forever,*
> *and My eyes and My heart will be there perpetually.*
> *As for you, if you will walk before Me as your father David walked,*
> *in integrity of heart and uprightness, doing according to all*
> *that I have commanded you and will keep*
> *My statutes and my ordinances,*
> *then I will establish the throne of your kingdom over Israel forever."*

As the house of the LORD (Hebrews 3:6), these verses contain great promises and exhortations for you. The LORD put His name on you forever when you became a Christian; He never takes His eyes off you, and His heart is with you perpetually. If you walk with Him in integrity, righteousness, and obedience, He will establish you.

What are you trying to accomplish? Are you doing things with the LORD, seeking His wisdom, or are you launching into projects in your own strength, calling out to God only when things don't go according to your plans?

Invite the LORD to journey with you every step of the way by praying 1 Kings 9:3-5a as His faithful, prayerful watchman (Isaiah 62:6-7).

> *"LORD, please hear my prayer and supplication*
> *which I am making before You.*
> *Consecrate, dedicate, and make*
> *sacred _____ and me as Your house*
> *which You are building by putting Your name on us forever.*
> *Let Your eyes be on us and Your heart be with us perpetually.*
> *Let us walk before You in integrity of heart and uprightness,*
> *doing according to all that You have commanded us.*
> *Help us keep Your statutes and ordinances.*
> *Establish us forever, LORD.*
> *Because of Your name, Jesus~"*

Please read 1 Kings 10.

Meditate on verse 24.

> *All the earth was seeking the presence of Solomon*
> *to hear his wisdom which God had put in his heart.*

Have you ever wished to be as wise as Solomon, to be able to answer any question presented to you, to bless people by merely letting them hear your wisdom (vs. 3, 8)? Consider these truths from God's Word:

> *The Helper, the Holy Spirit, whom the Father will send*
> *in My name, He will teach you all things and bring*
> *to your remembrance all that I said to you.*
> —John 14:26

> *All things that I have heard from My Father*
> *I have made known to you.*
> —John 15:15b

> *Let the Word of Christ richly dwell within you, with all wisdom*
> *teaching and admonishing one another.*
> —Colossians 3:16a

> *We have the mind of Christ.*
> —1 Corinthians 2:16b

If you are a Christian, you have the Word of God and the Holy Spirit teaching you; you have the mind of Christ giving you the ability to comprehend, obey, live, and share everything being made known to you. Because you have Jesus, the Holy Spirit, and the Word of Christ, you can be even wiser than Solomon. Walk in the wisdom of God and pray 1 Kings 10:24 over yourself and those for whom you stand guard as a faithful, prayerful watchman (Isaiah 62:6-7).

> *"LORD, let _____ and me live in such a*
> *Godly way that when You send people*
> *from all over the earth to seek our presence,*
> *they would hear the wisdom which You have put in our hearts.*
> *For the glory of Your name, Jesus~"*

FEBRUARY

On your walls, O Jerusalem,
I have appointed watchmen;
All day and all night they
will never keep silent.
You who remind the LORD,
take no rest for yourselves;
And give Him no rest until He establishes
And makes Jerusalem a
praise in the earth.
ISAIAH 62:6-7, NASB

Please read 1 Kings 11.

Meditate on verse 4.

*For when Solomon was old, his wives turned
his heart away after other gods,
and his heart was not wholly devoted to the LORD his God,
as the heart of David his father had been.*

Despite all the God-given wisdom of Solomon, he did not guard his heart. When Solomon disobeyed God's command to not associate with foreign women who would turn his heart to other gods, the LORD surrounded him with enemies and irreparably divided his kingdom.

God's wisdom is calling you to examine your heart. What are you holding fast that is turning your heart away from the LORD (vs. 2-3)? Do not let pride convince you God will be intolerably patient with a heart not wholly devoted to Him (vs. 4, 9). Wholeheartedly repent and pray 1 Kings 11:38 over yourself and those for whom you stand guard as a faithful, prayerful watchman (Isaiah 62:6-7).

*"LORD, help _____ and me listen to all that You command
and walk in Your ways and do what is right in Your sight
by observing Your statutes and Your commandments.
LORD, be with us and build us an enduring house.
For the sake of Your name, Jesus~"*

Please read 1 Kings 12.

Meditate on verse 15.

> *So the king did not listen to the people, for it*
> *was a turn of events from the LORD,*
> *that He might establish His word, which the LORD spoke through*
> *Ahijah the Shilonite to Jeroboam the son of Nebat.*

Solomon dies, and his kingdom quickly divides, just as God said, because Solomon led his people away from the LORD to worship the gods of his non-Jewish wives (1 Kings 11:33, 43). God told Solomon his kingdom would be given to his servant, Jeroboam, and despite Solomon's efforts to stop the prophecy, God's Word prevailed; Jeroboam became king over the ten northern tribes of Israel (1 Kings 11:11, 26-40). After being anointed, Jeroboam did not trust God to give him those tribes (1 Kings 11:38). Instead, he built two places for idol worship with a couple of golden calves in the northern part of Israel, so his followers would not worship in Jerusalem and become subjects of King Rehoboam (vs. 25-33). You can probably imagine things did not go well for Jeroboam!

Examine the events in your life. What is happening because God keeps His Word? What is happening because God punishes sin? Spend this day being honest with yourself and God, confessing, repenting, and desiring to walk wholeheartedly with Him.

Pray 1 Kings 12:24 over yourself and those for whom you stand guard as a faithful, prayerful watchman (Isaiah 62:6-7).

> *"LORD, help _____ and me obey*
> *You when You say to not go up*
> *and fight against _____.Help us to discern*
> *what events have come from You.*
> *Let us listen to Your Word, LORD, and return to You*
> *and go Your way, according to Your Word.*
> *In Your name, Jesus~"*

FEBRUARY 3

Please read 1 Kings 13.

Meditate on verses 16-18.

He said, "I cannot return with you, nor go with you, nor will I eat
bread or drink water with you in this place. For a command came
to me by the Word of the LORD, 'You shall eat no bread, nor drink
water there; do not return by going the way which you came.'"
He said to him, "I also am a prophet like you,
and an angel spoke to me by the word of the LORD, saying,
'Bring him back with you to your house that
he may eat bread and drink water.'"
But he lied to him.

What a powerful and timely story about obeying the Word of the LORD and not being deceived by false prophets!

The man of God was given specific instructions from God about what to do and where to go. He passed the first test and did not give in to the temptation to go home with King Jeroboam (vs. 7-9). The man of God, however, failed the second test and believed the self-proclaimed prophet who declared an angel spoke to him a word from the LORD (v. 18). Instead of standing firm on God's Word, the man of God obeyed the false prophet. The result—God killed him (v. 26).

Do not be tempted to take God's Word lightly and turn from it to fulfill your sinful desires. Do not be tempted to believe a self-declared prophet who proclaims a word contrary to God's Word (Galatians 1:8-9; 1 John 4:1).

Use 1 Kings 13:17 to pray to be obedient to the Word of the LORD.

"LORD, the command has come
to _____ and me by Your Word:
'You shall....'
Help us obey completely.
In Your name, Jesus~"

Please read 1 Kings 14.

Meditate on verses 7-10a.

> *Go, say to Jeroboam, "Thus says the LORD God of Israel,*
> *'...you have not been like My servant David, who kept My*
> *commandments and who followed Me with all his heart,*
> *to do only that which was right in My sight;*
> *you also have done more evil*
> *than all who were before you... and have*
> *cast Me behind your back—*
> *therefore behold, I am bringing calamity on the house of Jeroboam.'"*

Jeroboam, king of the ten northern tribes, called Israel, sinned against God, casting Him behind his back. God destroyed Jeroboam and his family.

Rehoboam, king of Judah (the southern tribes of Judah and Benjamin), committed the abominations of the world instead of pleasing God (vs. 21-24). The King of Egypt attacked and continually warred with Rehoboam (vs. 25-30).

As you read 1 and 2 Kings, observe how God hates and does not tolerate sin. Learn from these kings of Judah and Israel; sin brings war to your soul and impacts everyone around you. But, remember, if you are a Christian, you have the heart of Christ to keep God's commandments, follow Him, and do what is right in His sight.

Pray 1 Kings 14:8-9 over yourself and those for whom you stand guard as a faithful, prayerful watchman (Isaiah 62:6-7).

> *"LORD, make _____ and me like Your servant*
> *David and like You, LORD Jesus Christ,*
> *to keep Your commandments and follow You with all our hearts,*
> *to do only that which is right in Your sight. Let us do no evil.*
> *Do not let us make for ourselves other gods to provoke You to anger.*
> *Do not let us cast You behind our backs.*
> *Because of Your name, Jesus~"*

Please read 1 Kings 15.

Meditate on verse 3.

> *He walked in all the sins of his father, which*
> *he had committed before him,*
> *and his heart was not wholly devoted to the LORD*
> *his God, like the heart of his father David.*

What a horrible epitaph! Abijam, king of Judah, lived his life committing all the sins of his father, King Rehoboam, because he did not have a heart completely devoted to God. After reigning for three years, his son Asa became king of Judah (v. 9). He was described as doing "what was right in the sight of the LORD" (v. 11).

You are also introduced to two kings of Israel in this chapter: Nadab, the son of King Jeroboam, and Baasha, who killed Nadab and all of Jeroboam's family (vs. 25-29). Both kings were described as doing "evil in the sight of the LORD" (vs. 26, 34).

The LORD wants these stories to be much more than history lessons. Pay careful attention to the actions and attitudes of these kings of Israel and Judah, noticing God's actions and attitudes toward them. As you read, ask the LORD to keep you and your loved ones from walking in the sins these men committed that made the LORD so angry.

Use the words from 1 Kings 15:3 and 11 to pray over yourself and those for whom you stand guard as a faithful, prayerful watchman (Isaiah 62:6-7).

> *"LORD, do not let _____ and me walk*
> *in any of the sins of our fathers*
> *which they committed! Let our hearts be*
> *wholly devoted to You, LORD.*
> *Let us do what is right in Your sight.*
> *For the sake of Your name, LORD Jesus~"*

FEBRUARY 6

Please read 1 Kings 16.

Meditate on verse 34.

In his (Ahab's) days, Hiel the Bethelite built Jericho; he laid
its foundations with the loss of Abiram, his firstborn, and
set up its gates with the loss of his youngest son, Segub,
according to the Word of the LORD, which
He spoke by Joshua the son of Nun.

This chapter records interesting facts about some of Israel's evil kings. A chariot commander became king after killing a drunk king; he reigned only seven days before killing himself (vs. 8-10, 15-18). An army commander then became king and fathered Ahab, one of the evilest kings in Israel's history (vs. 16, 25-30).

As if these wicked kings were not tragic enough, the chapter ends with Jericho being rebuilt in defiance to God's Word and at the expense of children losing their lives.

Then Joshua made them take an oath at that time, saying,
"Cursed before the LORD is the man who
rises up and builds this city Jericho;
with the loss of his firstborn, he shall lay its foundation,
and with the loss of his youngest son, he shall set up its gates."
—Joshua 6:26

The Bible does not say if the children were sacrificed as part of pagan dedicatory rituals or died due to cruel child labor practices; what you do know is Abiram and Segub died because their father, Hiel, disobeyed God.

Examine your life. Are you obeying God's Word? Are others being sacrificed by your behaviors? Learn well from these stories and determine not to repeat sins from the past.

Pray the opposite of 1 Kings 16:30-31 over yourself and those you love as a faithful, prayerful watchman (Isaiah 62:6-7).

"LORD, do not let _____ and me do evil in Your sight.
Make us even holier than those who were before us.
Let us not treat any sin as a trivial thing.
Let us serve and worship only You.
In Your name, Jesus~"

Please read 1 Kings 17.

Meditate on verse 1.

> *Now Elijah the Tishbite, who was of the*
> *settlers of Gilead, said to Ahab,*
> *"As the LORD, the God of Israel lives, before whom I stand,*
> *surely there shall be neither dew nor rain*
> *these years, except by my word."*

The opening words of this chapter introduce you to Elijah fearlessly delivering a message from the LORD to one of the most evil kings in the history of Israel, King Ahab. With just a few words, you know several things about Elijah; although he is in the presence of an earthly king, his allegiance lies with his heavenly King. You also know he fears the LORD more than he fears man as he boldly speaks the Truth of God to wicked King Ahab.

For the next week, you will learn more about Elijah, a mighty man of God who fearlessly spoke God's Word. As you read, notice his actions and attributes and ask the LORD to help you emulate his Godly qualities.

Pray 1 Kings 17:24 over yourself and those for whom you stand guard as a faithful, prayerful watchman (Isaiah 62:6-7).

> *"LORD, may others know that _____ and I are people of God*
> *and that Your Word, which is in our mouths, is truth.*
> *Help us boldly speak Your Word of Truth.*
> *In Your name, Jesus~"*

FEBRUARY 8

Please read 1 Kings 18.

Meditate on verse 3.

> *Ahab called Obadiah who was over the household.*
> *Now Obadiah feared the LORD greatly.*

Three years of severe famine passed between 1 Kings 17:1 and 1 Kings 18:1, when God told Elijah to return to evil King Ahab. He was met by Obadiah, a God-fearing man who risked his life doing great exploits for the LORD despite being the servant of two of the most notorious monarchs in Israel's history, King Ahab and Queen Jezebel (vs. 3-16). Obadiah described himself as fearing the LORD from his youth (v. 12).

What a difference it makes when a person learns and chooses to fear God rather than man from the time they are young! Obadiah knew he could be killed for telling Ahab he had seen Elijah, yet he trusted God and obeyed the prophet.

What is the LORD asking you to do? Out of awe, reverence, and holy fear of God, are you obeying Him? Does fear of what others might think or how they might react keep you from wholeheartedly following the LORD? "If the LORD is God, follow Him" (v. 21)!

As a faithful, prayerful watchman (Isaiah 62:6-7), use the words from 1 Kings 18:3, 12, and 21 to pray for yourself and those you love to be like Obadiah.

> *"LORD, may _____ and I fear You greatly.*
> *Let _____ fear You from their youth.*
> *Do not let us hesitate between two opinions.*
> *LORD, You are God; we will follow You.*
> *In Your name, Jesus–"*

Please read 1 Kings 19.

Meditate on verse 13b. The LORD is speaking.

"What are you doing here, Elijah?"

Instead of a victory party after God won the showdown on Mt. Carmel, Elijah was attacked by the enemy and running for his life (vs. 2-3).

Can you relate? Often after doing great things in God's name, one can be exhausted and even attacked by Satan and those not as excited about what the LORD has done. God does not want you to be afraid, but He does want you to do some of the things Elijah did in that difficult and exhausting situation. Consider these practical steps:

- Find a quiet place and rest (vs. 4-5).
- Eat nourishing food and drink lots of water (v. 6).
- Rest some more and eat again (vs. 6-8).
- Read God's Word and listen to Him speak directly to you (v. 9).
- Talk to God, being honest about your feelings and everything that is happening to you (v. 10).
- Let the Holy Spirit gently breathe new life into your sails and go in the strength of the LORD (vs. 12-13, 15).

God's Word is so practical! Thank Him for giving you the story of Elijah and pray 1 Kings 19:9, 12-13, and 15 over yourself and those for whom you stand guard as a faithful, prayerful watchman (Isaiah 62:6-7).

"LORD, thank You that Your Word has come to _____ and me.
We hear Your question: 'What are you doing
here?' Help us answer honestly.
Holy Spirit, gently blow into our lives and speak to us.
When You say, 'Go,' let us obey completely.
In Your name, Jesus~"

Please read 1 Kings 20.

Meditate on verse 13.

> *Now behold, a prophet approached Ahab king of Israel and said,*
> *"Thus says the LORD, 'Have you seen all this great multitude?*
> *Behold, I will deliver them into your hand today,*
> *and you shall know that I am the LORD.'"*

Twice the LORD miraculously saved King Ahab and the Israelites from a besieging Ben-hadad, king of Aram (Syria). God acted for His renown, so the Israelites and the Syrians would know He is LORD and God over everything (vs. 13, 28). Sadly, after the victories, King Ahab made a covenant with his enemy, Be-hadad, rather than destroy him as the LORD commanded (vs. 34, 42). God promised Ahab that he and his people would die because of Ahab's disobedience (v. 42). Isn't it interesting that the Israelites are still plagued by enemies in Syria to this day? I wonder what would be different in the Middle East if Ahab had obeyed God.

Total obedience is a big deal to God! Do not take His miracles for granted and do not be tempted to disobey Him even in little things. Destroy completely any sin that remains in your life.

Use the words from 1 Kings 20:28 to pray over yourself and those for whom you stand guard as a faithful, prayerful watchman (Isaiah 62:6-7).

> *"LORD, You are God of the mountains,*
> *and You are God of the valleys.*
> *You have given _____ into my hand.*
> *Let me be obedient to do what You say,*
> *so I and others will know You are the LORD.*
> *In Your name, Jesus~"*

Please read 1 Kings 21.

Meditate on verse 20.

Ahab said to Elijah, "Have you found me, O my enemy?"
And he answered, "I have found you because you have sold yourself
to do evil in the sight of the LORD."

Evil King Ahab and wicked Queen Jezebel really did it this time! Coveting, pouting, uncaring, lying, murdering, stealing—those two committed all of these sins in one callous fell swoop against Naboth, a man simply minding his own business, caring for what his family had given him (vs. 1-16). God saw the whole thing—you can't hide anything from Him—and He confronted Ahab about all of the wicked abominations, declaring that he, Jezebel, and those belonging to them would die and be eaten by either the dogs or the birds (vs. 17-26). But then the unbelievable happened; Ahab humbled himself before the LORD, and God saw that, too! Ahab's punishment was lessened because of God's mercy (vs. 27-29).

What is your response to this story from God's Word? Do you think, "Are you kidding me, God? Why would you relent in punishing such an evil person?" Or, are your thoughts, "O LORD, there is hope for me, for I, too, am selfish and pouting and uncaring... LORD, please forgive and have mercy on me"?

Use the words from 1 Kings 21:20 and 29 to pray over yourself and those for whom you stand guard as a faithful, prayerful watchman (Isaiah 62:6-7).

"LORD, please find _____ and me doing what pleases You.
Let us never sell ourselves to do evil in Your sight!
Let us always humble ourselves before You.
Please do not bring evil in our days.
Please let no evil come to our house or the house of our children.
In Your name, Jesus~"

Please read 1 Kings 22.

Meditate on verses 13-14.

> *Then the messenger who went to summon*
> *Micaiah spoke to him saying,*
> *"Behold now, the words of the prophets are*
> *uniformly favorable to the king.*
> *Please let your word be like the word of one*
> *of them and speak favorably."*
> *But Micaiah said, "As the LORD lives, what the*
> *LORD says to me, that I shall speak."*

King Ahab surrounded himself with 400 false prophets who told him what he wanted to hear. They even said the word "Lord," but they were not prophets of the LORD, and they did not prophesy in His name (vs. 6-7). Micaiah, a true prophet of God, was hated by King Ahab because he prophesied evil and not good for this king described as doing "evil in the sight of the LORD more than all who were before him" (v. 8; 1 Kings 16:30).

There are still people, similar to King Ahab, who surround themselves with false preachers and teachers who condone rather than condemn their sins. They claim God has changed His mind with the times, and certain sins are now permissible. Do not be deceived! The LORD did not change His mind, and His Word has not changed. Refuse to listen to ear-tickling teachers preaching false doctrine (2 Timothy 4:3). Be a fearless Micaiah, who spoke God's Word even as he was taken to prison for telling the Truth (vs. 26-28).

Pray 1 Kings 22:14 and 43 over yourself and those for whom you stand guard as a faithful, prayerful watchman (Isaiah 62:6-7).

> *"LORD, as You live, what You have said I will speak!*
> *May _____ and I not turn aside from Your ways;*
> *let us do what is right in Your sight.*
> *Take away the high, prideful places in our lives.*
> *In Your name, Jesus~"*

Please read 1 Kings 22:51-53 and 2 Kings 1.

Meditate on verse 16.

> *Then he said to him, "Thus says the LORD, 'Because you*
> *have sent messengers to inquire of Baal-zebub, the god*
> *of Ekron—is it because there is no God in Israel*
> *to inquire of His Word? Therefore, you*
> *shall not come down from the bed*
> *where you have gone up but shall surely die.'"*

King Ahaziah, the son of evil King Ahab and wicked Queen Jezebel, walked in the ways of his parents, serving and worshiping Baal, causing Israel to sin, and provoking the LORD God to anger (1 Kings 22:51-53). When he suffered a serious fall, he sought the idol Baal for answers concerning his wellbeing. Three times God declared that Ahaziah would die because he consulted Baal instead of the LORD. "So Ahaziah died according to the Word of the LORD" (v. 17a).

Examine your life. Where do you turn for advice and consultation? The LORD wants you to seek Him and His will for your life. Read His Word and learn what He has already declared to be His will. Talk to Him about everything and listen to the Holy Spirit and the Godly people He sends to guide you in every detail of your life.

Use the words from 2 Kings 1:16 to pray over yourself and those for whom you stand guard as a faithful, prayerful watchman (Isaiah 62:6-7).

> *"LORD, You are God in my family;*
> *therefore, I am inquiring of Your Word.*
> *Please do not confine us to our beds; please let us live.*
> *In Your name, Jesus~"*

Please read 2 Kings 2.

Meditate on verse 9.

When they had crossed over, Elijah said to Elisha,
"Ask what I shall do for you before I am
taken from you." And Elisha said,
"Please, let a double portion of your spirit be upon me."

Elisha was appointed and anointed by God to be Elijah's successor as a prophet of the LORD (1 Kings 19:16). As the time approached for Elijah to be taken up to heaven, Elisha refused to leave him, wanting to soak up every moment with this great man of God. The last thing Elisha requested of Elijah was to receive a double portion of his spirit, which of course was controlled and empowered by God's Spirit. God granted his request, and Elisha was immediately able to do great things in the LORD's name and for His glory (vs. 14-15).

What is your attitude about being with Jesus? Cry out to Him, "As You live, LORD, I will not leave You!"

So Jesus said to the twelve, "You do not want to go away also, do you?"
Simon Peter answered Him, "LORD, to whom shall we go?
You have words of eternal life."
—John 6:67-68

Use the words from 2 Kings 2:9 and 21 to pray over yourself and those for whom you stand guard as a faithful, prayerful watchman (Isaiah 62:6-7).

"LORD, please let a double portion of Your
Spirit be upon _____ and me.
Purify us, LORD, with the living water
of Your Spirit (John 7:38-39).
Let there no longer be death or unfruitfulness in us.
For the sake of Your name, Jesus~"

Please read 2 Kings 3.

Meditate on verse 12.

> *Jehoshaphat said, "The Word of the LORD is with him (Elisha)."*
> *So, the king of Israel and Jehoshaphat and the*
> *king of Edom went down to him.*

After the death of King Ahaziah, Jehoram, his brother, became king in his place (2 Kings 1:17). Jehoram, another descendant of evil King Ahab and wicked Queen Jezebel, ruled over God's beloved nation of Israel. Jehoram did evil in the sight of the LORD, but at least he wasn't as bad as his father and mother because he removed Ahab's sacred pillar to Baal (v. 2). Pray for your descendants to do better than you as they walk with the LORD. And be diligent to walk well with God, so your children's walks can be amazing!

The chapter continues with God doing the impossible on behalf of Israel, Judah, and Edom in the fight against Moab. As prophesied by Elisha, the LORD miraculously filled a valley with water to refresh those He was fighting for, yet He made it appear as blood for those He was fighting against. It is important to be on the side of the LORD! Pray toward that goal by using the words from 2 Kings 3:12 and 15 as a faithful, prayerful watchman (Isaiah 62:6-7).

> *"LORD, keep _____ and me in Your Word,*
> *so Your Word is always with us.*
> *Let Your hand come upon us for good.*
> *In Your name, Jesus-"*

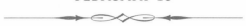
Please read 2 Kings 4.

Meditate on verse 44.

> *So he set it before them, and they ate and had some left over,*
> *according to the Word of the LORD.*

Notice the five miracles in 2 Kings 4 and how they foreshadow Christ and what He does in your life.

- ❧ The Miracle of the Oil – God gives the Holy Spirit without measure and pours His love into hearts of Christians (John 3:34; Romans 5:5).
- ❧ The Miracle of a Son – "Behold the virgin shall be with child and shall bear a Son" (Matthew 1:23).
- ❧ The Miracle of Resurrection – Jesus said to her, "I AM the resurrection and the life" (John 11:25).
- ❧ The Miracle of Removing Death from the Pot – "O death, where is your victory? O death, where is your sting? Thanks be to God, who gives us the victory through our LORD Jesus Christ" (1 Corinthians 15:55, 57).
- ❧ The Miracle of the Bread of the First Fruits – Jesus said, "I AM the living bread that came down out of heaven." "In Christ, all will be made alive, but each in his own order: Christ the first fruits, after that those who are Christ's at His coming" (John 6:51; 1 Corinthians 15:22-23).

Pray 2 Kings 4:42 over yourself and those for whom you stand guard as a faithful, prayerful watchman (Isaiah 62:6-7).

> *"LORD, You are the Bread of the first fruits.*
> *Thank You for giving Yourself to* _____ *and*
> *me to eat in order to live in You.*
> *For the sake of Your name, Jesus~"*

Please read 2 Kings 5.

Meditate on this phrase from verse 13.

Wash and be clean.

Leprous Naaman was given the miraculous opportunity to be cured of his terrible disease. The instructions from Elisha were simple: "Go and wash in the Jordan seven times, and your flesh will be restored to you, and you will be clean" (v. 10). At first, Naaman furiously rebelled, but thankfully, he had a change of heart and mind, and the healing hand of God touched and restored him.

Naaman's cleansing is a picture of your salvation through faith in Jesus Christ.

> *He saved us, not on the basis of deeds which*
> *we have done in righteousness,*
> *but according to His mercy, by the washing of*
> *regeneration and renewing by the Holy Spirit.*
> —Titus 3:5

There are people in your life who need to accept God's invitation to "wash and be clean," so they can experience the miraculous restoration of the Holy Spirit. Pray for them, using the words from 2 Kings 5:13-14, as their faithful, prayerful watchman (Isaiah 62:6-7).

> *"LORD, please let _____ want to*
> *be washed and cleaned by You.*
> *Let them obey according to Your Word. Restore*
> *them and make them clean.*
> *In Your name, Jesus~"*

FEBRUARY 18

Please read 2 Kings 6.

Meditate on verses 5-6 and 31.

> *But as one was felling a beam, the axe head fell into the water;*
> *and he cried out and said, "Alas, my master! For it was borrowed."*
> *Then the man of God said, "Where did it fall?"*
> *And when he showed him the place,*
> *he cut off a stick and threw it in there and made the iron float.*
>
> *Then he (King Jehoram) said, "May God do so to me and more also,*
> *if the head of Elisha the son of Shaphat remains on him today."*

Isn't it wonderful that a chapter about a man of God with a double bounty on his head begins with the miracle of a floating axe head? Elisha had no doubt that God who saved the head of an axe could certainly save his. And the remainder of the chapter records a man walking in the confidence of the LORD rather than running around like a chicken with his head cut off.

Be encouraged by the story of Elisha. He fully expected God to do the miraculous in his life, and God did not disappoint him. Ask the LORD to open your physical and spiritual eyes to see the marvelous things He is doing on your behalf. Walk confidently with the LORD in constant praise and thanksgiving for who He is and what He does.

Pray 2 Kings 6:16-17 over yourself and those for whom you stand guard as a faithful, prayerful watchman (Isaiah 62:6-7).

> *"LORD, do not let _____ and me*
> *fear; make those who are with us*
> *more than those who are with them (our enemies).*
> *O LORD, I pray, open our eyes that we may see!*
> *Open the eyes of us, Your servants, to see the miraculous things*
> *You are doing all around us.*
> *In Your name, Jesus~"*

Please read 2 Kings 6:32-7:20.

Meditate on 2 Kings 6:33-7:1.

> *While he was still talking with them, behold,*
> *the messenger came down to him and he said,*
> *"Behold, this evil is from the LORD; why should*
> *I wait for the LORD any longer?"*
> *Then Elisha said, "Listen to the Word of*
> *the LORD; thus says the LORD,*
> *'Tomorrow about this time a measure of*
> *fine flour will be sold for a shekel,*
> *and two measures of barley for a shekel, in the gate of Samaria.'"*

Talk about a hopeless situation! The people of Samaria were in a horrible place; so horrible, they were boiling and eating their children in order to survive (2 Kings 6:28-29). No wonder the messenger for King Jehoram questioned why he should wait any longer for the LORD to intervene. The LORD answered with, "Tomorrow..." (v. 1). Only God knows what will happen tomorrow, and for the Israelites, He was going to do the impossible on their behalf.

Do you feel like no longer waiting for the LORD? Do things appear hopeless? Be encouraged by what God did for the Israelites and never doubt what He can do for you and those you love. Be honest with the LORD about your concerns and hear Him whisper into your ear, "Tomorrow...."

Pray 2 Kings 7:1-2 over yourself and those for whom you stand guard as a faithful, prayerful watchman (Isaiah 62:6-7).

> *"LORD, help _____ and me listen to Your Word. We*
> *will hear what You say about tomorrow. We know You*
> *can make windows in heaven open on our behalf.*
> *LORD, we want to see it with our own eyes*
> *and eat from Your heavenly provision.*
> *For the glory of Your name, Jesus~"*

Please read 2 Kings 8.

Meditate on verse 18.

> *He (Jehoram) walked in the way of the kings of Israel,*
> *just as the house of Ahab had done, for the*
> *daughter of Ahab became his wife;*
> *and he did evil in the sight of the LORD.*

First, try not to let the Jehorams and Jorams frustrate you. There was King Jehoram (sometimes called Joram), son of Ahab and king of Israel. There was another King Jehoram (sometimes called Joram), son of Jehoshaphat, king of Judah, who married the daughter of Ahab. So, King Jehoram of Israel and King Jehoram of Judah were brothers-in-law.

Interestingly, Jehoshaphat did right in the sight of the LORD (1 Kings 22:43). Sadly, Jehoram did not get the same descriptor as his father because he chose to walk in the ways of his evil in-laws (v. 27).

It matters who you marry and who their family is! Pray for the people in your life making that critical choice to seek the person God wants them to marry. If you married a person who loves Jesus more than they love you, be thankful. If you married into a family who needs to know the LORD, keep your covenant marriage vows, staying faithful to your spouse and the LORD. Pray fervently for God to change the descriptor of your family to: "They walked in all the ways of the LORD."

Pray the opposite of 2 Kings 8:27 over yourself and those for whom you stand guard as a faithful, prayerful watchman (Isaiah 62:6-7).

> *"LORD, let _____ and my house be described*
> *as a house that walks in Your way.*
> *Do not let us do evil in Your sight! May*
> *our children and grandchildren*
> *marry into the houses of Your Godly ones.*
> *For the sake of Your name, Jesus~"*

Please read 2 Kings 9.

Meditate on verse 20.

> *The watchman reported, "He came even to*
> *them, and he did not return;*
> *and the driving is like the driving of Jehu the*
> *son of Nimshi, for he drives furiously."*

Have you ever said, "He drives like a wild Jehu (yay-hoo)"? Now you know from where the saying comes—this incredible passage of Scripture! This chapter proves that the Bible is definitely not boring.

It also gives you some interesting verses to pray; such as: "LORD, please stop _____ from being an evil Jezebel, so the dogs do not eat their flesh and they become dung on the face of the earth" (vs. 36-37).

Perhaps you really do have people in your life who need verses 36-37 prayed over them. It's wonderful that God's Word can be applied to every situation imaginable!

You might also choose to pray 2 Kings 9:6, asking the LORD to anoint (set apart, dedicate) you and those you love for His purposes. Pray these words because He has anointed you to be a faithful, prayerful watchman (Isaiah 62:6-7).

> *"LORD, let _____ and me hear You speak these words over us:*
> *'Thus says the LORD, "I have anointed you to …."'*
> *For the sake of Your name, Jesus~"*

Please read 2 Kings 10.

Meditate on verse 31.

> *But Jehu was not careful to walk in the law*
> *of the LORD, the God of Israel,*
> *with all his heart; he did not depart from the sins of Jeroboam,*
> *which he made Israel sin.*

Although Jehu was zealous in his exploits for God, his epitaph was similar to all of the kings of the northern kingdom, Israel: Jehu did not follow the LORD with his whole heart, and he caused others to sin.

Scripture records that Jehu committed "the sins of Jeroboam," the first king of Israel after the nation divided (v. 29; 1 Kings 12:20). What exactly were those sins that so angered God? Idolatry, ordination of anyone to be priests, devising places and ways to worship contrary to God's Word, and encouraging others to join in his ungodly behaviors are the sins of Jeroboam (1 Kings 12:25-33; 13:33-34).

The turning point in Jehu's walk with the LORD probably came when he forced Jehonadab to ride with him and see his zeal for God as he finished killing all of evil Ahab's family (vs. 16-17). The pride that comes with a need to be seen messes-up a wholehearted, humble walk with God.

Allow God to examine your heart with Jehu's story. Is your worship of God in the image of the world, or is it according His Word? Do you need others to notice what you are doing for the cause of Christ? Humble yourself before God and pray for the opposite of 2 Kings 10:31 to be true of you and those you love.

> *"LORD, let _____ and me be careful to*
> *walk in Your law with all our heart.*
> *Let us depart from sin; do not let us make others sin.*
> *For the sake of Your name, Jesus~"*

Please read 2 Kings 11.

Meditate on verse 3.

So he (Joash) was hidden with her (his aunt)
in the house of the LORD six years,
while Athaliah (his grandmother) was reigning over the land.

Unbelievably evil! Athaliah killed her grandchildren to ensure she ruled Judah instead of them (v. 1). Lust for power can drive a person to pathetic places and beastly behaviors. Thankfully, courageous Jehosheba hid baby Joash from his wicked grandmother. Their place of refuge was the temple of the LORD.

As a Christian, you also have perpetual refuge in the presence of God (Hebrews 4:14-16).

One thing I have asked from the LORD, that I shall seek:
that I may dwell in the house of the LORD all the days of my life,
to behold the beauty of the LORD and to meditate in His temple.
For in the day of trouble, He will conceal me in His tabernacle;
in the secret place of His tent He will hide
me; He will lift me up on a rock.
—Psalm 27:4-5

Pray 2 Kings 11:3, 17-18, and 20 over yourself and those for whom you stand guard as a faithful, prayerful watchman (Isaiah 62:6-7).

"LORD, hide _____ and me in Your house, in Your presence.
We covenant with You, LORD, to be Your people.
Let us tear down and thoroughly break in pieces
all altars and images not pleasing to You.
We will rejoice. Bring quiet to our lives.
Because of You, Jesus~"

FEBRUARY 24

Please read 2 Kings 12.

Meditate on verse 2-3.

> *Jehoash (Joash) did right in the sight of the*
> *LORD all his days in which*
> *Jehoiada the priest instructed him. Only the*
> *high places were not taken away;*
> *the people still sacrificed and burned incense on the high places.*

Joash became king at the age of seven. He served the LORD and his people well as long as Jehoiada, the priest, was alive to teach him. But after the death of this Godly mentor, Joash's heart turned from following the LORD (2 Chronicles 24:17-19).

It is important to be with Godly others who encourage you in your walk with Christ. Thankfully, Jesus gave you His Church, those who believe and follow Him.

And what about those "high places"? It is a repeated phrase throughout 1 and 2 Kings. These regional places of worship often combined the worship of God with false gods and were contrary to God's will (Deuteronomy 12:2-3). However, the people liked their high places, and it was easier for the priests and other leaders to let them do what they wanted rather than upsetting them and their high places.

As you ponder the high places, ask the Holy Spirit to convict you of high places in your life. Destroy your high places—any area of your life controlled by pride and disobedience to Christ and His Word.

Use the words from 2 Kings 12:2-3 and 15 to pray over yourself and those for whom you stand guard as a faithful, prayerful watchman (Isaiah 62:6-7).

> *"LORD, let _____ and me do right in Your sight all our days.*
> *Instruct us and let us instruct others about*
> *You. Let us take away all high places;*
> *let us sacrifice nothing on the high places. Make*
> *us people who deal faithfully.*
> *Because of Your name, Jesus-"*

Please read 2 Kings 13.

Meditate on verses 4a and 5a.

> *Then Jehoahaz entreated the favor of the LORD,*
> *and the LORD listened to him.*
> *The LORD gave Israel a deliverer.*

Israel and Judah were in a terrible mess because of unrelenting, sinful behaviors. Doing evil in the sight of God, following the path of the wicked, and causing others to sin is a recipe for making God angry and incurring His judgment (vs. 2-3).

As you observe God's justifiable wrath, notice His unending mercy as well. When Jehoahaz begged the LORD for His favor, He listened and gave Israel a savior (vs. 4-5). Amazing! Yet, isn't that every Christian's story?

> *But God demonstrates His own love toward us,*
> *in that while we were yet sinners, Christ died for us.*
> —Romans 5:8

Thankfully, God recorded the lives of these kings because everyone needs a deliverer; everyone needs a Savior.

Use the words from 2 Kings 13:2-5 to pray over yourself and those for whom you stand guard as a faithful, prayerful watchman (Isaiah 62:6-7).

> *"LORD, do not let _____ and me do evil*
> *in Your sight and follow the sins of others.*
> *Do not let us cause others to sin by not turning away from sin.*
> *LORD, we do not want Your anger kindled against us,*
> *so that You give us continually into the hand of our enemies.*
> *We entreat Your favor, LORD! Please listen to us!*
> *LORD, thank You for our Deliverer, Jesus,*
> *who allows us to escape from evil.*
> *In Your name, Jesus~"*

Please read 2 Kings 14.

Meditate on verses 3-4.

> *He did right in the sight of the LORD, yet not like David his father;*
> *he did according to all that Joash his father had done.*
> *Only the high places were not taken away;*
> *the people still sacrificed and burned incense on the high places.*

If you are like me (Marsha), you probably wish these verses about "high places" would just disappear. They make me uncomfortable because they are the stain on a life that could have been described as "pleasing to the LORD." These verses make me squirm because I know God repeats Himself in order to drive home things that are really important to Him. Refusing to remove "high places" is a big deal to God, and He really wants me—and you—to know it's a big deal to Him. Therefore, we must acknowledge the high places in our lives and get rid of them.

As I write this devotional, my cry is, "Oh, LORD, show me my high places! I want them gone! Forgive me, LORD, for not acknowledging and removing them sooner. I want to live a life pleasing to You."

Removal of the high places is an important part of your walk with Christ. Listen to the Holy Spirit as He reveals prideful places in your life, places that are higher in precedence than He is. Let God's power tear them down and let Him constrain you not to rebuild them again.

Use 2 Kings 14:3-4 to pray over yourself and those for whom you stand guard as a faithful, prayerful watchman (Isaiah 62:6-7).

> *"LORD, help _____ and me do right in*
> *Your sight, even better than our fathers did.*
> *LORD, take away our high places; do not*
> *allow us to sacrifice there any longer!*
> *Because of Your name, Jesus~"*

Please read 2 Kings 15.

Meditate on verse 28.

He (Pekah) did evil in the sight of the LORD;
he did not depart from the sins of Jeroboam son of Nebat,
which he made Israel sin.

If you are keeping track of the kings of Israel and Judah, you have noticed that the kings of the northern kingdom, Israel, were evil monarchs who did not depart from the sins of Jeroboam. Jeroboam, the first of those 19 kings, left an idolatrous and evil legacy that characterized the reigns of 18 more kings over the course of 200 years. This downward spiral of infectious sin eventually hit rock bottom when Assyria captured and destroyed Israel in 722 BC.

What are you doing positively or negatively that is influencing future generations? What will be your legacy? As you walk in obedience with Jesus, ask Him to make the refrain of your life the opposite of the kings of Israel. Pray not to be like kings Jeroboam, Nadab, Baasha, Elah, Zimri, Omri, Ahab, Ahaziah, Joram, Jehu, Joahaz, Joash, Jeroboam II, Zechariah, Shallum, Menahem, Pekahiah, Pekah, and Hoshea.

As a faithful, prayerful watchman (Isaiah 62:6-7), pray for yourself and those you love to not be described like Menahem in 2 Kings 15:18.

"LORD, please keep _____ and me
from doing evil in Your sight.
Let all of our days be a departure from sins.
Help us depart from all the sins of our fathers.
Do not let us make others sin!
For the sake of Your name, Jesus~"

Please read 2 Kings 16.

Meditate on verse 3.

> *But he (Ahaz) walked in the way of the kings*
> *of Israel, and even made his son*
> *pass through the fire, according to the abominations of the nations*
> *whom the LORD had driven out from before the sons of Israel.*

These 20 brief verses of 2 Kings 16 describe the evil reign of King Ahaz, possibly the worst king to rule over the southern kingdom of Judah. Instead of modeling his reign after his predecessor, King David, he walked in the way of the wicked kings of Israel, even committing the abominable act of sacrificing his child to the Canaanite god, Molech (v. 3, Leviticus 18:21; Deuteronomy 12:29-31).

Ahaz submitted himself and his people to the Assyrians and acquiesced to their heathenism by removing holy objects from the temple of the LORD and replacing them with a pagan altar patterned after one he saw in Syria. Sadly, Urijah, the priest, did not stop King Ahaz from defiling the temple, but instead, gave in to his demands. Such spiritually spineless behavior left Urijah with the epitaph of: "He did according to all that King Ahaz commanded" (v. 16).

As you read the story of King Ahaz, let God's Word convict you of areas in your life where you might be sacrificing your loved ones to the ways of the world. Ask the LORD to remove spiritual spinelessness and make you strong by His Spirit (Zechariah 4:6).

Pray to do the opposite of 2 Kings 16:16 over yourself and those for whom you stand guard as a faithful, prayerful watchman (Isaiah 62:6-7).

> *"LORD, make _____ and me Your priests*
> *who do according to all You command.*
> *For the sake of Your name, Jesus~"*

Please read 2 Kings 17.

Meditate on this phrase from verse 13.

"Turn from your evil ways and keep My commandments."

During the ninth year of Hoshea's reign (722 BC), the northern kingdom of Israel was taken captive to Assyria and ceased to exist as a nation (vs. 5-6). The LORD gave the reasons for their destruction; there could be no doubt about why they were punished. Carefully observe the list and learn from their mistakes. They:

1. feared other gods, served Baal and other idols, and worshiped the host of heaven (vs. 7, 12, 16)
2. walked in the customs of other nations (v. 8)
3. did things secretly which were not right against the LORD (v. 9)
4. built high places everywhere for themselves (v. 9)
5. sold themselves to do evil, provoking the LORD (vs. 11, 17)
6. did not listen, stiffened their necks, and did not believe in God (v. 14)
7. rejected God's statutes and covenant, forsook all His commandments (vs. 15, 16)
8. followed vanity and became vain (v. 15)
9. sacrificed their children (v. 17)
10. practiced divination and enchantments (v. 17)

> *So the LORD was very angry with Israel*
> *and removed them from His sight;*
> *None was left except the tribe of Judah.*
> —2 Kings 17:18

Thankfully, you know what makes God angry. As a faithful, prayerful watchman (Isaiah 62:6-7), use the words from 2 Kings 17:13-14 to pray to be pleasing to Him.

"LORD, You have warned _____ and
me through all Your prophets.
Let us turn from our evil ways and keep
Your commandments and statutes
which You have commanded. Help us
listen! Do not let us stiffen our necks!
We believe in You, LORD our God!
In Your name, Jesus~"

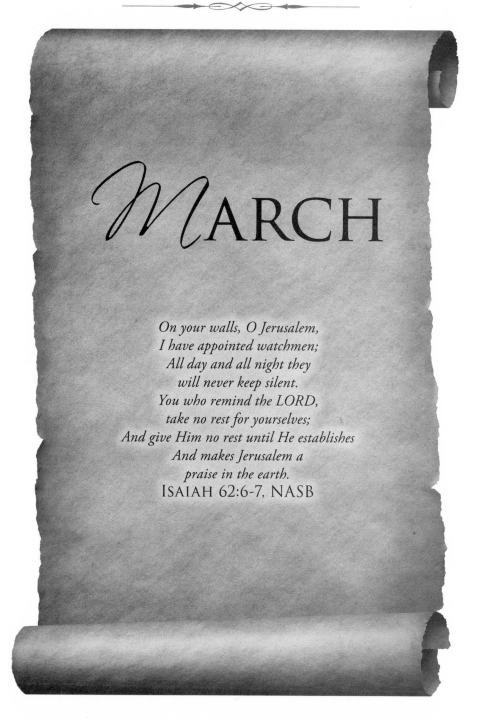

MARCH

On your walls, O Jerusalem,
I have appointed watchmen;
All day and all night they
will never keep silent.
You who remind the LORD,
take no rest for yourselves;
And give Him no rest until He establishes
And makes Jerusalem a
praise in the earth.
ISAIAH 62:6-7, NASB

Please read 2 Kings 18.

Meditate on these phrases from verses 3-7.

> *He (Hezekiah) did right in the sight of the LORD...*
> *He removed the high places...He trusted in the LORD...*
> *He clung to the LORD...The LORD was with him....*

Hooray! The high places have been removed! Finally, there is a king with the courage to do what is right in the eyes of God rather than catering to his selfish lusts and the ungodly demands of the people. Hezekiah is one of the eight good kings of Judah (Judah had a total of 19 kings and one queen). And Hezekiah is one of only two of the good kings who actually destroyed the high places. (You will read about the other destroyer of high places in 2 Kings 22.)

The rest of 2 Kings 18 tells about the destruction of Israel and the near destruction of Judah. Be sure to notice Hezekiah's strong leadership as he tells his people not to answer Rabshakeh when he tries to shake their confidence in God (vs. 17-37). It is best to ignore "Rabshakehs" in your life who want you to lose your trust in God's miraculous provision. You do not need to acknowledge their ungodly negativity.

Pray 2 Kings 18:3-7 over yourself and those for whom you stand guard as a faithful, prayerful watchman (Isaiah 62:6-7).

> *"LORD, let _____ and me do right in Your sight. Help*
> *us remove the high places and break down anything that has*
> *become an idol in our lives. We trust in You, LORD.*
> *We cling to You, LORD. Do not let us depart from*
> *following You; let us keep Your commandments. LORD,*
> *be with us; wherever we go, please let us prosper.*
> *In Your name, Jesus~"*

Please read 2 Kings 19.

Meditate on verse 14.

*Then Hezekiah took the letter from the hand
of the messengers and read it,
and he went up to the house of the LORD
and spread it out before the LORD.*

King Hezekiah took his impossible situations to God. When Rabshakeh taunted and threatened, Hezekiah entered the temple to be in God's presence (v. 1). When he received a message from Rabshakeh claiming God's Word to be deceptive, he took the letter to God, so He could read it (vs. 8-14). Hezekiah's actions were visual proof that he trusted in the LORD and clung to Him (2 Kings 18:5-6). God rewarded his faith with the miraculous defeat of the Assyrians, the salvation of Jerusalem, and the assassination of the Assyrian king, Sennachrib (vs. 31-37).

Is something or someone threatening to destroy you and those you love? Take refuge in the presence of God. Tell Him everything that is happening. Let His confident assurance and peace replace your anxious thoughts. Wait for Him to act on your behalf.

Pray 2 Kings 19:15-16 and 19 over your difficult situations as a faithful, prayerful watchman (Isaiah 62:6-7).

*"O LORD, the God of Israel and the God of my family,
You are enthroned above the cherubim. You are the
God, You alone, of all the kingdoms of the earth.
You have made heaven and earth. Incline
Your ear, O LORD, and hear;
open Your eyes, O LORD, and see; and listen to the words of those
who threaten _____ and me, which have
been sent to reproach You, the living God.
Now, O LORD our God, I pray, deliver us from the enemy's hand
that all the kingdoms of the earth may know
that You alone, O LORD, are God.
In Your name, Jesus~"*

MARCH 3

Please read 2 Kings 20.

Meditate on verse 13.

> *Hezekiah listened to them (the men from Babylon) and*
> *showed them all his treasure house, the silver and the gold*
> *and the spices and the precious oil and the house*
> *of his armor and all that was found in his treasuries.*
> *There was nothing in his house nor in all his*
> *dominion that Hezekiah did not show them.*

The LORD wants you to pay careful attention to Hezekiah's story because He recorded it three times in the Bible—2 Kings 18-20; 2 Chronicles 29-32, and Isaiah 36-39.

Pride overcame Hezekiah after the LORD heard and answered his prayers for protection from the Assyrians and healing from a mortal illness. When God in His mercy granted Hezekiah health and 15 more years of life, he stopped walking humbly with God and proudly showed off all of his God-given blessings to men who are actually Babylonian spies. The people of Judah would soon pay dearly for a king who got full of himself.

Be mindful of pride that can creep in as you experience the LORD's favor. Be diligent to have a humble and grateful heart toward God for His unmerited love and mercy, remembering to be kind and unarrogant toward others who experience God's blessings in different ways than you.

Pray 2 Kings 20:3 over yourself and those for whom you stand guard as a faithful, prayerful watchman (Isaiah 62:6-7).

> *"LORD, I beseech You to help _____ and*
> *me remember to walk before*
> *You in truth and with a whole heart. Help*
> *us to do what is good in Your sight.*
> *In Your name, Jesus~"*

Please read 2 Kings 21.

Meditate on verses 8-9. The LORD is speaking.

> *"And I will not make the feet of Israel wander anymore from*
> *the land which I gave their fathers, if only they will observe*
> *to do according to all that I have commanded them,*
> *and according to all the law that My servant*
> *Moses commanded them."*
> *But they did not listen, and Manasseh seduced them to do evil more*
> *than the nations whom the LORD destroyed before the sons of Israel.*

Sometimes God lets people wallow in their sin. It is one of the worst punishments for sinning against Him, allowing people to stay in their self-made, putrid mess rather than plucking them out. That is what the LORD did to evil Manasseh and the people of Judah. Manasseh ruled for 55 years, practicing horrific sins throughout his reign and killing so many people that Jerusalem was filled with their blood (vs. 1-7, 16). The LORD did not put a stop to the atrocities because for over 700 years, the people and their forefathers had done evil in His sight and provoked Him to anger since the day they left Egypt (v. 15).

Is the LORD allowing you and those you love to wallow in sin? If so, stop and confess everything God. Ask Him to keep your feet from wandering from His righteous path. Pray using the words from 2 Kings 21:7-9 over yourself and those for whom you stand guard as a faithful, prayerful watchman (Isaiah 62:6-7).

> *"LORD, You have put Your name on _____ and me forever.*
> *Do not let our feet wander anymore from You.*
> *Let us observe to do according to all that You have commanded*
> *and according to all Your law. Help us to listen;*
> *do not let us be seduced to do evil.*
> *For the sake of Your name, Jesus~"*

Please read 2 Kings 22.

Meditate on verse 19.

*"Because your heart was tender and you humbled yourself before
the LORD when you heard what I spoke against this place and
against its inhabitants, that they should become a desolation and
a curse, and you have torn your clothes and wept before Me,
I truly have heard you," declares the LORD.*

Have you ever received a message containing really bad news that made your heart faint and your body feel like it was sinking into the floor? That is probably how King Josiah felt as the Law of the LORD was read, and he realized he and his people were in so much trouble for disobeying God. Josiah grieved as he heard these Words:

*"The LORD will send upon you curses, confusion, and rebuke,
in all you undertake to do, until you are
destroyed and until you perish quickly,
on account of the evil of your deeds, because you have forsaken Me."*
—Deuteronomy 28:20

When God's Word so touched Josiah that he humbled himself and wept before the LORD, God took notice and heard Josiah's cries (vs. 18-19).

How does God's Word affect you? Does it give you a tender heart toward the LORD and the things that are important to Him?

Pray 2 Kings 22:18-19 over yourself and those for whom you stand guard as a faithful, prayerful watchman (Isaiah 62:6-7).

*"LORD, regarding Your Words which _____ and
I have heard, let our hearts be tender
and let us humble ourselves before You. Please
hear us as we tear our clothes
and weep before You because of the desolation and curse caused by sin.
In Your name, Jesus~"*

Please read 2 Kings 23.

Meditate on verse 2.

> *The king (Josiah) went up to the house of the*
> *LORD and all the men of Judah*
> *and all the inhabitants of Jerusalem with him,*
> *and the priests and the prophets and*
> *all the people, both small and great, and he*
> *read in their hearing all the words of*
> *The Book of the Covenant which was found*
> *in the house of the LORD.*

When the Book of the Covenant, the Word of God, was discovered in the Temple of the LORD, it radically impacted King Josiah. He wanted all of the people to hear the Words; he made covenant promises to the LORD, and he took action to remove everything idolatrous in Israel. God's Word changed Josiah's life.

How does the Bible, the Book of the Old and the New Covenant, impact you and those you love? Do you crave reading and hearing it? Does God's Word make you want to follow Him better, with all your heart, soul, and might (v. 25)? What actions are you taking to remove things in your life contrary to God's Word?

Pray 2 Kings 23:24-25 over yourself and those for whom you stand guard as a faithful, prayerful watchman (Isaiah 62:6-7).

> *"LORD, let _____ and me perform the Words*
> *of the Law which are written in Your Book.*
> *Let us turn to You with all our heart, and with*
> *all our soul, and with all our might,*
> *according to all the Law of Moses, according to all of Your Word.*
> *In Your name, Jesus~"*

Please read 2 Kings 24.

Meditate on verse 3.

> *Surely at the command of the LORD, it came upon*
> *Judah to remove them from His sight because of the sins*
> *of Manasseh, according to all that he had done.*

2 Kings 24 records the first two of three sieges of Jerusalem and deportations of the people of Judah to Babylon. God commanded they be removed from His sight because of the sins of King Manasseh. Manasseh began his reign 92 years before the Babylonian exile even started. Four kings ruled after him, yet people who weren't even alive during Manasseh's reign experienced the wrath of God because of his sins.

Do not think for a moment that God takes sin lightly, or what you do contrary to the Word of God is no big deal. Sin is deadly, and it cost God His life to pay its cost. Thankfully, if you are a Christian, you will be saved from the wrath of God through Jesus Christ (Romans 5:9). Sadly, for those who choose not to become children of God, but remain sons of disobedience, the wrath of God will come upon them (Ephesians 5:6; Colossians 3:6).

Pray for the opposite of 2 Kings 24:19-20 to be true of those you know are sons of disobedience, as their faithful, prayerful watchman (Isaiah 62:6-7).

> *"LORD, please let _____ stop doing evil*
> *in Your sight. Let them follow You*
> *so they do not experience Your anger and be cast from Your presence.*
> *In Your name, Jesus~"*

MARCH 8

Please read 2 Kings 25.

Meditate on verse 29.

> *Jehoiachin changed his prison clothes and had his meals*
> *in the king's presence regularly all the days of his life.*

2 Kings 25 records the third siege of Jerusalem, its total destruction, and the final deportation of Israelites to Babylon. It's a sad chapter, illustrating the devastation of sin. Interestingly, the last four verses of 2 Kings are like a surprise ending to a book riddled with sin and its consequences. Jehoiachin was shown mercy by the king of Babylon and released from his prison. He was given a change of clothes, so he no longer wore prison garb. The king spoke kindly to Jehoichin and allowed him to eat meals in his presence all the days of his life (vs. 27-30).

Jehoiachin's story foreshadows the salvation provided by King Jesus. When you become a Christian, you are released from your prison of sin and given Jesus' robe of righteousness to wear (Isaiah 61:10). Christ speaks kindly to you and provides for all of your daily needs (Titus 3:4-7). He even invites you to eat with Him (Revelation 3:20). What an amazing story of salvation! What an amazing God who writes His salvation message into every page of the Bible!

Pray 2 Kings 25:27-30 in thanksgiving for what Jesus has done for you.

> *"LORD, thank You for releasing me from my prison of sin.*
> *Thank You for speaking kindly to me.*
> *Thank You for changing me out of my prison clothes*
> *and allowing me to eat in Your presence*
> *regularly all the days of my life.*
> *Thank You for giving me a portion for each day all the days of my life.*
> *In Your name, Jesus~"*

As you read *1 and 2 Kings*, you learned a lot about God's character and what He expects of His people. You saw His people easily forget Him, falling into sinful behaviors that brought God's righteous judgment.

Ezekiel is the next book you will read. The scribe for this book was a young man named Ezekiel. Raised to be a priest, he found himself part of the second-wave of exiles taken to Babylon by King Nebuchadnezzar in 597 BC. The author of the book is the LORD God, and you will be reminded of that fact several hundred times as you read His Words.

Devotionals from *Ezekiel* follow the ones for *1 and 2* Kings because they give greater insight into God's perspective for what was happening during the reigns of the last several kings of Judah.

We hope you continue to grow in your knowledge of God and who you are in Him as you read and pray *Ezekiel*.

Please read Ezekiel 1.

Meditate on verses 1 and 3.

> *Now it came about in the thirtieth year, on*
> *the fifth day of the fourth month,*
> *while I was by the river Chebar among the exiles,*
> *the heavens were opened, and I saw visions of God.*
> *The Word of the LORD came expressly to Ezekiel the priest,*
> *son of Buzi, in the land of the Chaldeans by the river Chebar,*
> *and there the hand of the LORD came upon him.*

If things had gone according to plan, Ezekiel's 30th birthday would have been celebrated with him officially entering the priesthood, serving at the Temple in Jerusalem (Numbers 4:3). Instead, he sat among a bunch of Israelite exiles in Babylon as part of God's punishment for sin. Ezekiel never served in the Temple at Jerusalem because the Babylonians destroyed both city and Temple. However, God had greater things planned for Ezekiel, revealing Himself in amazing ways never before seen or heard by humans. Amazingly, you have the privilege of seeing Ezekiel's visions and hearing God's Words because Ezekiel acted as a faithful priest despite horrible circumstances, and God ensured every precious Word was recorded.

Sometimes, God surrounds His people with barrenness of exilic proportions in order to force them to look up. When they do, they see the heavens opened (v. 1). Does the LORD have you or someone you love in that place? If so, take heart as you spend the next 48 days reading the prophecies God gave Ezekiel. Pray to be like the four living creatures in Ezekiel's first recorded vision, using the words from Ezekiel 1:12.

> *"LORD, let _____ and me go straight forward;*
> *wherever Your Spirit is about to go is where we want to go,*
> *without turning as we go.*
> *Because we are following You, Jesus~"*

Please read Ezekiel 2.

Meditate on verse 2.

> *As He (God) spoke to me, the Spirit entered me and set me on my feet,*
> *and I heard Him speaking to me.*

What an amazing calling from God Ezekiel had! As God spoke to him, the Holy Spirit entered him, and he was given the command to speak God's Words to stubborn and rebellious people. No matter what those obstinate people said or did, Ezekiel was to fearlessly tell them the Word of the LORD, whether they listened or not (v. 7).

Can you imagine God talking to you and being filled with the Holy Spirit? If you are a Christian, your story is similar to Ezekiel's.

> *"It is the Spirit who gives life; the flesh profits nothing;*
> *the words that I (Jesus) have spoken to you are spirit and are life."*
> —John 6:63

> *"These things I (Jesus) have spoken to you while abiding with you.*
> *But the Helper, the Holy Spirit, whom the Father*
> *will send in My name, He will teach you*
> *all things and bring to your remembrance all that I said to you."*
> —John 14:25-26

Pray for God to give you and those you love the courage of Ezekiel to confidently speak His Word in the power of His Spirit. Pray Ezekiel 2:8 over yourself and those for whom you stand guard as a faithful, prayerful watchman (Isaiah 62:6-7).

> *"LORD, help _____ and me listen*
> *to what You are speaking to us.*
> *Do not let us be rebellious like that rebellious house.*
> *Open our mouths and let us eat what You*
> *are giving us, Your Word of Truth.*
> *In Your name, Jesus-"*

Please read Ezekiel 3.

Meditate on verse 3.

> *He said to me, "Son of man, feed your stomach*
> *and fill your body with this scroll*
> *which I am giving you." Then I ate it, and*
> *it was sweet as honey in my mouth.*

The LORD gave Ezekiel His Word and expected him to devour it, so it would fill every fiber of his being. Then, he was to tell the people every Word he had consumed. Even if they refused to listen, Ezekiel was to continue telling them the Word of the LORD. God gave Ezekiel the awesome responsibility as watchman over the house of Israel, and it was his divine duty to warn them of what God said (v. 17). If Ezekiel refused to obey God's calling, the people's blood was on his hands (v. 18).

What a sobering chapter in God's Word; do not take it lightly! God has gone to much effort to give you His Word; He expects you to consume it so it impacts every aspect of your life. He has appointed you to be a watchman over precious people in your life; He wants you to tell them and warn them about what He says in His Word—even if they are not yet listening.

Stay faithful to God's calling and pray Ezekiel 3:10-11 and 17 over yourself because you are a faithful, prayerful watchman (Isaiah 62:6-7).

> *"LORD, I hear You saying to me, _____ take into your heart*
> *all My Words which I will speak to you and listen closely.*
> *Go to your people and speak to them and tell*
> *them, whether they listen or not.*
> *I have appointed you a watchman to the house of _____ ;*
> *whenever you hear a Word from My mouth, warn them from Me.'*
> *LORD, do not let me fail You or them.*
> *In Your name, Jesus~"*

Please read Ezekiel 4.

Meditate on verses 16-17.

> *Moreover, He said to me, "Son of man, behold,*
> *I am going to break the staff of bread*
> *in Jerusalem, and they will eat bread by weight and with anxiety*
> *and drink water by measure and in horror*
> *because bread and water will be scarce,*
> *and they will be appalled with one another*
> *and waste away in their iniquity."*

God's call to be a prophet was challenging. Ezekiel became a living sermon illustration, lying in specified positions for a total of 430 days to illustrate how many years Israel and Judah lived in iniquity (vs. 4-6). He had to eat bread made of various scraps baked over cow dung to illustrate how deprived the depraved were as a result of God's punishment (vs. 9-15).

Contrast the Israelites' consumption of paltry amounts of bread and water with what Jesus offers 600 years later:

> *"I am the bread of life; he who comes to Me will not hunger,*
> *and he who believes in Me will never thirst. I am the living bread*
> *that came down out of heaven; if anyone eats of this bread,*
> *he will live forever, and the bread also which I will give*
> *for the life of the world is My flesh."*
> —John 6:35, 51

Use the words from Ezekiel 4:16-17 to thank the LORD for being the bread that was broken for you (Luke 22:19), so you will not waste away in your iniquity.

> *"LORD, You ultimately broke the staff of*
> *bread in Jerusalem on the cross.*
> *Thank You that I can eat the bread You offer*
> *without measure and without anxiety.*
> *I can drink Your living water without measure and without*
> *horror because Your bread and water are not scarce, and those*
> *who believe in You will not be appalled with one another,*
> *and we will not waste away in our iniquity.*
> *Thank You, LORD Jesus~"*

Please read Ezekiel 5.

Meditate on verse 3. The LORD is talking.

> *"Take also a few in number from them*
> *and bind them in the edges of your robes."*

Ezekiel again became a living sermon illustration when the LORD had him cut off his hair and beard and divide it into thirds (vs 1-2). The hairs represented the Israelites. One-third would die by plague or famine; one-third would fall by the sword, and one-third would be scattered to the wind as a result of disobeying God (vs. 11-12). But God would spare a remnant, a precious few tucked safely into the edge of His robe. From this remnant would come His Son, to save His people from their sin.

Sadly, the people of Ezekiel's day experienced God's wrath because they refused to obey Him. Thankfully, if you are a Christian, you are saved from the wrath of God and bound safely into His righteous robe.

> *But God demonstrates His own love toward*
> *us, in that while we were yet sinners,*
> *Christ died for us. Much more then, having*
> *now been justified by His blood,*
> *we shall be saved from the wrath of God through Him.*
> —Romans 5:8-9

Use Ezekiel 5:13 to thank God for saving you from His wrath and to pray for those who need to become Christians, so they, too, can be saved from His anger.

> *"LORD, it is only through Jesus that Your anger is spent; Your*
> *wrath is satisfied, and You are appeased. Let_____ know*
> *that You, the LORD, have spoken in Your zeal.*
> *Save them so You do not have to spend Your wrath on them.*
> *In Your name, Jesus~"*

MARCH 14

Please read Ezekiel 6. The LORD is speaking.

Meditate on verse 10.

"Then they will know that I am the LORD;
I have not said in vain that I would inflict this disaster on them."

"You (they) will know that I am the LORD" is a repeated phrase in this chapter of Ezekiel (vs. 7, 10, 13-14). The people wallowed in sin for so long, refusing to obey God's commandments, that they forgot who God is. They experienced exile, destruction, desolation, famine, plague, and death because sin lorded over them instead of the LORD.

It is a big deal to God for people to know Him. Jesus took the punishment for all of mankind's evil abominations, so every human can know He is the LORD. Thank the LORD for the precious privilege you have of knowing Him and ask Him to help you not to sin.

You therefore, beloved, knowing this beforehand,
be on your guard so that you
are not carried away by the error of unprincipled men and
fall from your own steadfastness but grow in the grace and
knowledge of our LORD and Savior Jesus Christ.
—2 Peter 3:17-18a

As a faithful, prayerful watchman (Isaiah 62:6-7), use the words from Ezekiel 6:10 to pray for those who need to know the LORD.

"LORD, let _____ desire to know You are the LORD,
so You do not have to inflict disaster on them.
Let Your Word not be in vain in their lives.
In Your name, Jesus~"

MARCH 15

Please read Ezekiel 7. The LORD is speaking.

Meditate on verse 6.

> *"An end is coming; the end has come!*
> *It has awakened against you; behold, it has come!"*

The end of Jerusalem was imminent. The people were told and retold how to please God. They were warned and warned about what displeased Him. He spared them time and time again, yet in their arrogance, they chose to idolize their abominations and their detestable things over loving and following God (v. 20).

The LORD continues to warn His people today. His message in the New Testament sounds strikingly similar to His message in the Old Testament:

> *Or do you think lightly of the riches of His*
> *kindness and tolerance and patience,*
> *not knowing that the kindness of God leads you to repentance?*
> *But because of your stubbornness and unrepentant*
> *heart you are storing up wrath*
> *for yourself in the day of wrath and revelation*
> *of the righteous judgment of God.*
> —Romans 2:4-5

God poured out His wrath on Israel over 2500 years ago. The day is coming when He will pour out His wrath on the entire earth (Revelation 16:1).

Talk to God about people you know who need to be saved from His wrath. Start the conversation with Ezekiel 7:4.

> *"LORD, I know a day is coming when Your eye will have no pity on*
> *_____, nor will You spare them, but*
> *You will bring their ways upon them,*
> *and their abominations will be among them,*
> *unless they repent of their abominations.*
> *Please let them come to know You are the LORD before it is too late.*
> *In Your name, Jesus~"*

Please read Ezekiel 8.

Meditate on verse 6.

> *And He said to me, "Son of man, do you see what they are*
> *doing, the great abominations which the house of Israel are*
> *committing here, so that I would be far from My sanctuary?*
> *But yet you will see still greater abominations."*

"Yet you will see still greater abominations" is a repeated phrase in this chapter of Ezekiel. It is hard to imagine people doing worse than disgusting wickedness, yet three times, God told Ezekiel he would see people behaving more abominably evil than they were already behaving (vs. 6, 13, 15). And in the dark, they wallowed in their abominations, convincing themselves the LORD did not see them (v. 12).

Wouldn't it be great to be able to wag your head at the evil Israelites, yet all you have to do is read a few of today's news stories to realize you are seeing "still greater abominations than these" every day.

As a faithful, prayerful watchman (Isaiah 62:6-7), confess sins and plead for others, using Ezekiel 8:17-18.

> *"LORD, I know You see all our abominations.*
> *We have committed abominations here, and if that weren't enough,*
> *we have filled the land with violence and provoked You repeatedly.*
> *We have put the twig to our nose as we snub You.*
> *LORD, please help us turn from our abominations,*
> *so You will not have to deal with us in wrath.*
> *Please let Your eye have pity on us and spare us!*
> *Please listen when we cry in Your ears with a loud voice.*
> *Because of Your mercy, Jesus~"*

MARCH 17

Please read Ezekiel 9.

Meditate on verses 8:18-9:1. The LORD is speaking.

> *"Therefore, I indeed will deal in wrath. My*
> *eye will have no pity nor will I spare;*
> *and though they cry in My ears with a loud*
> *voice, yet I will not listen to them."*
> *Then He cried out in my (Ezekiel's) hearing with a loud*
> *voice saying, "Draw near, O executioners of the city,*
> *each with his destroying weapon in his hand."*

Imagine the scenes from Ezekiel 8 and 9. The people sinned repeatedly against God with no regard for His Word, convincing themselves He did not see them. As their abominations and violence affected the entire land, the wrath of God came upon them; they cried out in the pain of their punishment. Then the LORD cried with a loud voice, and six executioners came, each with a shattering weapon to destroy the wicked. What a hopeless scene! But wait, God also summoned a man in linen to put a mark on every person whose heart grieved like His because of the abominations being committed. Those who encountered the man and were marked by him did not encounter the executioners' deathblows.

What is your attitude toward sin? Do you "sigh and groan over all the abominations which are being committed" (v. 4)? Ask God to help you see with His eyes and perceive with His heart what is happening in the world. Pray for people to repent and desire Christ and His holiness.

Pray Ezekiel 9:4 over yourself and those for whom you stand guard as a faithful, prayerful watchman (Isaiah 62:6-7).

> *"LORD, _____ and I sigh and*
> *groan over all the abominations*
> *which are being committed in the midst of our world.*
> *Put Your mark on our foreheads—we belong to You.*
> *Because of Your name, Jesus~"*

Please read Ezekiel 10.

Meditate on verse 18.

> *Then the glory of the LORD departed from the threshold of the temple
> and stood over the cherubim.*

What a sad chapter in Israel's history—God's glory departed from His
temple in Jerusalem! The glory of the LORD first filled the tabernacle
approximately 850 years earlier (Exodus 40:17, 34-35). Then, when King
Solomon built the temple in Jerusalem, the glory of the LORD filled it (2
Chronicles 7:1-3). Now, after approximately 370 years of God's glory being
in His temple, His glory leaves, and the temple will soon be completely
destroyed in 586 BC.

But God's glory will return—to a field—with sheep and shepherds—
outside Jerusalem— where He announces the coming of His Glory (John
1:14):

> *In the same region, there were some shepherds staying out in
> the fields and keeping watch over their flock by night. And
> an angel of the LORD suddenly stood before them,
> and THE GLORY OF THE LORD shone around
> them; and they were terribly frightened.
> But the angel said to them, "Do not be afraid; for behold,
> I bring you good news of great joy which will be for all
> the people, for today in the city of David there
> has been born for you a Savior, who is Christ the LORD."*
> —Luke 2:8-11

And now, as the temple of God, the Spirit of God dwells in Christians,
from whom He will never depart (1 Corinthians 3:16). What an exciting
chapter of His story you have the privilege to be part of!

Pray Ezekiel 10:4 over yourself and those for whom you stand guard as a
faithful, prayerful watchman (Isaiah 62:6-7).

> *"LORD, please let Your glory go up to _____,
> so they can become Your temple.
> As Your temple, You fill us with Your Spirit.
> Let our lives be filled with the brightness of Your glory, LORD.
> In Your name, Jesus~"*

Please read Ezekiel 11.

Meditate on verses 19-20. The LORD is speaking.

> *"And I will give them one heart and put a new spirit within them.*
> *And I will take the heart of stone out of their*
> *flesh and give them a heart of flesh,*
> *that they may walk in My statutes and keep*
> *My ordinances and do them.*
> *Then they will be My people, and I shall be their God."*

The glory of the LORD left not only the temple but the entire city of Jerusalem (v. 23). Prior to departing, the LORD gave a word of hope: He would restore a remnant and give them a heart and a spirit to obey Him and walk with Him (vs. 17-20).

Are you or someone you love in a hopeless situation? This chapter gives you great verses to pray! Pray Ezekiel 11:1-2, 5, 12, and 17-20 over yourself and those for whom you stand guard as a faithful, prayerful watchman (Isaiah 62:6-7).

> *"LORD, by Your Spirit, lift _____ and me up! Keep*
> *us from men who devise iniquity and give evil advice. Spirit*
> *of the LORD, fall upon us! You know our thoughts.*
> *We know You are the LORD! Please forgive us for not walking*
> *in Your statutes nor executing Your ordinances. Forgive us*
> *for acting according to the ordinances of the people around*
> *us. LORD, please gather us from the peoples and gather us*
> *from where we have been scattered. Help us to remove all*
> *the detestable things and abominations from our lives.*
> *Give us one heart and put a new spirit within us.*
> *Take the heart of stone out of our flesh and give us a heart of flesh,*
> *that we may walk in Your statutes and keep*
> *Your ordinances and do them.*
> *We want to be Your people, and we want You to be our God.*
> *For the sake of Your name, Jesus~"*

MARCH 20

Please read Ezekiel 12.

Meditate on verses 1-2.

> *Then the Word of the LORD came to me, saying,*
> *"Son of man, you live in the midst of the rebellious*
> *house, who have eyes to see but do not see,*
> *ears to hear but do not hear; for they are a rebellious house."*

Ezekiel again became a walking sermon illustration for the rebellious people of Israel and their king, Zedekiah. Morning, evening, and night Ezekiel carried around baggage as a message that they would indeed pack their bags and be taken to Babylon, just as the two waves of exiles before them were taken. Even King Zedekiah, the last king of Judah, would be exiled with his eyes blinded by the Babylonians (v. 13; 2 Kings 25:1-7).

As the time drew near (586 BC) for this 3rd and final exile, the people believed everything would be fine, and the exilic prophecies would prove false (v. 22). However, God promised the fulfillment of every vision (v. 23).

Some people today are still in denial of Scriptural prophetic truth. They mock the promises of Christ's return (2 Peter 3:4). Some listen to false prophets who speak destructive heresies and malign the truth (2 Peter 2:1-3). The Word of the LORD, spoken through the faithful prophet Ezekiel, still rings relevant and true today.

Ask God to make you a faithful watchman who boldly speaks His Word. Pray using the words from Ezekiel 12:22-23.

> *"LORD, let me never speak this false proverb:*
> *'The days are long, and every vision fails.'*
> *Let me boldly say, 'The days draw near as well as*
> *the fulfillment of every vision from God's Word.'*
> *In Your name, Jesus~"*

Please read Ezekiel 13.

Meditate on verses 3 and 6.

> *Thus says the LORD GOD, "Woe to the foolish prophets who*
> *are following their own spirit and have seen nothing. They*
> *see falsehood and lying divination who are saying,*
> *'The LORD declares,' when the LORD has not sent them,*
> *yet they hope for the fulfillment of their word."*

God is against those who prophesy contrary to His Word, yet claim they have a word from the LORD (v. 8). False prophets and teachers who do not counsel according to God's Word have no place among God's people (v. 9). It is against God's will and angers Him to prophesy according to one's own inspiration (vs. 13, 17).

These are harsh words spoken by God Himself against the false prophets and teachers of Ezekiel's day. And they are words to take to heart, today. God's hand is still against those who claim to have a word from the LORD, but they have not tested it with God's Word. God's wrath will tear down their lies. Do not fall prey to such people and make certain you are not one of them. Know God's Word by reading, studying, and memorizing it. Do not hesitate to stand boldly on God's Truths, confidently speaking them.

Pray to be the opposite of Ezekiel 13:22 over yourself and those for whom you stand guard as a faithful, prayerful watchman (Isaiah 62:6-7).

> *"LORD, do not let _____ and me*
> *dishearten the righteous with falsehood.*
> *Help us encourage the wicked to turn from their*
> *wicked ways and preserve their lives.*
> *Because we know You are the LORD Jesus~"*

Please read Ezekiel 14.

Meditate on verses 6-7.

> *Therefore say to the house of Israel, "Thus says*
> *the LORD GOD, 'Repent and turn*
> *away from your idols and turn your faces*
> *away from all your abominations.*
> *For anyone of the house of Israel or of the*
> *immigrants who stay in Israel*
> *who separates himself from Me, sets up his idols*
> *in his heart, puts right before his face*
> *the stumbling block of his iniquity, and then comes to*
> *the prophet to inquire of Me for himself, I the LORD*
> *will be brought to answer him in My own person.'"*

Have you ever had someone seek your advice about a bad situation caused by sinful behaviors? Have you ever been tempted to give them worldly counsel instead of Godly counsel because God's Word would tell them to stop sinning and flee from wickedness? The world advises God wants them to be happy, so whatever they need to do to make that happen is certainly okay.

God warned Ezekiel to tell the idolatrous elders, "Repent and turn from all your abominations" (v. 6).

It doesn't matter to whom you are talking; do not water down God's Word. God would have destroyed Ezekiel along with the idolaters if he had not spoken the whole truth of what God said (v. 9).

Use Ezekiel 14:6 as a prayer of repentance for yourself and those for whom you stand guard as a faithful, prayerful watchman (Isaiah 62:6-7).

> *"LORD, I repent and turn away from my*
> *idols, and I turn my face away*
> *from all my abominations. Please*
> *convict _____ to do the same.*
> *Because of Your name, Jesus~"*

Please read Ezekiel 15.

Meditate on verse 6.

> *Therefore, thus says the LORD GOD, "As the wood of the vine*
> *among the trees of the forest, which I have given to the fire*
> *for fuel, so have I given up the inhabitants of Jerusalem."*

The LORD gave another sermon illustration for the inhabitants of Jerusalem, comparing them to a vine's wood which is useful if it is producing fruit. The Israelites did not produce fruit; instead they produced and worshiped worthless wooden idols (Hosea 4:12). God was going to destroy them like the branch of a vine thrown into a fire.

God often compared His people to a vine's branches (Isaiah 5:1-7; Jeremiah 2:21). His warning to Christians sounds similar to His warning to Israel:

> *"I am the vine; you are the branches; he*
> *who abides in Me and I in him,*
> *he bears much fruit, for apart from Me you can do nothing.*
> *If anyone does not abide in Me, he is thrown*
> *away as a branch and dries up,*
> *and they gather them and cast them into*
> *the fire, and they are burned."*
> —John 15:5-6

Devote your life to fruitfulness in Christ and pray for the opposite of Ezekiel 15:7-8 over yourself and those for whom you stand guard as a faithful, prayerful watchman (Isaiah 62:6-7).

> *"LORD, _____ and I know You are the*
> *LORD. Do not set Your face against us.*
> *Do not let the fire consume us. Please do not make us desolate.*
> *Help us to act faithfully!*
> *Because You are the vine in Whom we abide, Jesus~"*

Please read Ezekiel 16. It is God's allegory symbolizing the history of Jerusalem.

Meditate on verse 6.

> *"When I passed by you and saw you squirming in your*
> *blood, I said to you while you were in your blood, 'Live!'*
> *Yes, I said to you while you were in your blood, 'Live!'"*

God's graphic story powerfully shows His involvement in every aspect of Israel's existence. She had her beginnings in Canaan (present-day Israel). The Canaanites hated her and treated her like an unwanted newborn baby. God let her live and took her to be His own. He entered into a covenant relationship with her and bedecked her as a beautiful bride. She became famous among the nations, but sadly her fame went to her head, and she played the harlot with the idolatrous people around her. Forgetting the One who gave her life, she committed heinous acts against Him and broke her covenant vows (vs. 1-59).

Incredibly, the story ends with the lavishing love and undying commitment of God:

> *"Thus, I will establish My covenant with you, and*
> *you shall know that I am the LORD,*
> *so that you may remember and be ashamed and never*
> *open your mouth anymore because of your humiliation,*
> *when I have forgiven you for all that you have*
> *done," the LORD GOD declares.*
> —Ezekiel 16:62-63

God established His everlasting covenant through the LORD Jesus Christ. His forgiveness of even heinous sins comes through Jesus, and it is available to Jerusalem, Israel, Canaanites, and you and your loved ones.

Pray Ezekiel 16:62-63 over yourself and those for whom you stand guard as a faithful, prayerful watchman (Isaiah 62:6-7).

> *"LORD, establish Your covenant with _____ and me;*
> *we know You are the LORD! Thank You for forgiving us.*
> *Because of You, Jesus~"*

Please read Ezekiel 17.

Meditate on verse 24.

> *"All the trees of the field will know that I am*
> *the LORD; I bring down the high tree,*
> *exalt the low tree, dry up the green tree,*
> *and make the dry tree flourish.*
> *I am the LORD; I have spoken, and I will perform it."*

The LORD gave Ezekiel another parable concerning the people of Israel in the first third of this chapter (vs. 1-10); He explained the parable in the second third (vs. 11-21), and He gave a great parable of promise in the last third (vs. 22-24).

The two eagles are Babylon and Egypt. The plucked twig is King Zedekiah, the last king of Judah. In the midst of Babylon (the first eagle) besieging Jerusalem and exiling the people, Zedekiah sought the help of Egypt (the second eagle). He rejected God and His covenant, seeking the help of ungodly people to fix his problems. God promised judgment for his unfaithfulness (v. 20).

Zedekiah was the last earthly king of Israel, yet there is another twig plucked and planted by the LORD. It flourishes, becoming a stately cedar, providing nourishment and protection for all who nest in its shade. This parable is a beautiful picture of Messiah, King Jesus.

Use the words from Ezekiel 17:22-24 to acknowledge the LORD Jesus.

> *"LORD, You are planted on a high and lofty mountain. You bring*
> *forth boughs and bear fruit; You are a stately cedar. People of every*
> *kind can nest under You; they can nest in the shade of Your branches.*
> *LORD, You are where _____ and I choose to dwell.*
> *Let everyone know that You are the LORD. You will*
> *bring down the high tree, exalt the low tree, dry up*
> *the green tree, and make the dry tree flourish.*
> *LORD, make us flourish! LORD, You have*
> *spoken, and You will perform it.*
> *In Your name, Jesus~"*

Please read Ezekiel 18.

Meditate on verse 23.

> *"Do I have any pleasure in the death of the*
> *wicked," declares the LORD God,*
> *"rather than that he should turn from his ways and live?"*

What an incredible Old Testament passage full of rich truths about how to have eternal life! God is speaking in the entire chapter, and He clearly reveals His heart for all people "to be saved and come to the knowledge of the truth" (1 Timothy 2:4). Each individual is accountable for his own sins; God will not punish a son for his father's iniquity (vs. 14-20). If a wicked person turns from all His sins and walks in God's righteousness, the LORD will not remember his transgressions (vs. 21-23).

Take seriously God's Words that all souls belong to Him, and "the soul who sins will die" (v. 4). Pray fervently for the souls of those you know who will die in their sins unless they repent and practice righteousness (v. 22).

Pray Ezekiel 18:30-32 over those for whom you stand guard as a faithful prayerful watchman (Isaiah 62:6-7).

> *"LORD, please draw _____ to repent and*
> *turn away from all their transgressions,*
> *so that iniquity will not become a stumbling block to them.*
> *May they cast away all their transgressions*
> *which they have committed.*
> *LORD, make them a new heart and a new spirit so they will not die!*
> *You have no pleasure in the death of anyone who dies;*
> *therefore, let _____ repent and live.*
> *In Your name, Jesus~"*

Please read Ezekiel 19.

Meditate on verse 1.

> *"As for you, take up a lamentation for the princes of Israel."*

The LORD told Ezekiel to lament the last four kings of Israel. Their reigns were evil, and God used the Babylonians to severely punish them (2 Kings 23:28-25:30). In the lament, these kings were called lions, but instead of reigning victoriously, some were caged and hauled to Babylon as if they were beasts (v. 9).

Can you imagine the weeping as the Israelites and their leaders were taken in three consecutive waves to Babylon, and the Davidic promise of an everlasting kingdom seemingly died with each shackled step? But wait—

> *One of the elders said to me, "Stop weeping; behold, the*
> *Lion that is from the tribe of Judah, the Root of David, has*
> *overcome so as to open the book and its seven seals."*
> —Revelation 5:5

Jesus Christ, the eternal King of kings and LORD of lords, reigns supreme! And while it appeared there would no longer be a scepter to rule Israel (v. 14), hear these Words of the LORD:

> *But of the Son He says, "Your throne, O God, is forever and ever,*
> *and the righteous scepter is the scepter of His Kingdom."*
> —Hebrews 1:8

Perhaps you or someone you love is in the midst of a lamenting time. Use the words from Ezekiel 19:12-14 to appeal to the Lion of Judah as a faithful, prayerful watchman (Isaiah 62:6-7).

> *"LORD, _____ and I were plucked up*
> *in fury and cast down to the ground.*
> *The east wind dried up our fruit; our strong*
> *branch was torn off so that it withered,*
> *and fire consumed it. Now we are planted in the*
> *wilderness, in a dry and thirsty land.*
> *So, we turn to You, our Strong Branch.*
> *Let Your scepter rule in our lives, LORD Jesus~"*

Please read Ezekiel 20.

Meditate on verse 31.

> *"When you offer your gifts, when you cause*
> *your sons to pass through the fire,*
> *you are defiling yourselves with all your idols to*
> *this day. And shall I be inquired of by you,*
> *O house of Israel? As I live," declares the LORD*
> *GOD, "I will not be inquired of by you."*

Israel's elders came to Ezekiel to seek the LORD for truth and information (v. 1). God refused to let them inquire of Him because they continued to appeal to their idols, sacrificing to them rather than trusting in the living God. God declared three times in this chapter, "As I live..." (vs. 3, 31, 33).

"As I live," declares the LORD GOD, "surely with a mighty hand and with an outstretched arm and with wrath poured out, I shall be king over you" (v33). The Israelites would indeed know God is very much alive!

What about you? Do your actions show that you believe God lives? Where do you turn to make inquiries? The LORD has all the answers; He wants you to turn to Him.

Pray Ezekiel 20:8-9 over yourself and those for whom you stand guard as a faithful, prayerful watchman (Isaiah 62:6-7).

> *"LORD, do not let _____ and me rebel against You; let*
> *us listen to You and cast away the detestable things of our eyes.*
> *Let us forsake our idols. Please do not pour out Your wrath*
> *on us to accomplish Your anger against us,*
> *but act for the sake of Your name,*
> *that it should not be profaned in the sight*
> *of others among whom we live.*
> *Make Yourself known through us to those around us.*
> *In Your name, Jesus~"*

Please read Ezekiel 21.

Meditate on verse 27. The LORD is speaking.

> *"A ruin, a ruin, a ruin, I will make it. This also will be no more*
> *until He comes whose right it is, and I will give it to Him."*

The LORD spoke grievous prophecies over Jerusalem. Three times He said His sword would come out of its sheath against all flesh (vs. 3-5). Three times He said He would make Jerusalem a ruin (v. 27). Three sieges of Jerusalem—three waves of exile—the LORD was indeed pouring out indignation and wrath on His people because of their iniquities, transgressions, and sins (vs. 24, 31).

In the midst of such dismal words, there is a glimmer of hope, a Messianic prophecy—Jerusalem will be ruined, ruined, ruined until He comes who has the right to rule Jerusalem (v. 27). The only hope for the ruined is the Messiah. The only hope for you and those you love is Jesus the Messiah because without Him everyone is a ruin, a ruin, a ruin.

Pray Ezekiel 21:27 in confession and commitment to the LORD as a faithful, prayerful watchman (Isaiah 62:6-7).

> *"LORD, _____ and I are a ruin,*
> *a ruin, a ruin until You come*
> *and take Your rightful place in our lives.*
> *We give ourselves to You, LORD Jesus~"*

MARCH 30

Please read Ezekiel 22.

Meditate on verses 30-31.

> *"I searched for a man among them who would build up*
> *the wall and stand in the gap before Me for the land, so*
> *that I would not destroy it; but I found no one.*
> *Thus, I have poured out My indignation on them;*
> *I have consumed them with the fire of*
> *My wrath; their way I have brought upon their*
> *heads," declares the LORD GOD.*

How important is it for you to be an unceasing prayer warrior for your family, church, community, and country? The LORD was about to completely destroy Jerusalem because no one cared enough to stand in the gap and beg God to change the hearts of their rulers, priests, and prophets. Righteous people would be destroyed with the wicked because not even they prayed for God's holiness to rule and reign in His people (Ezekiel 21:3-4; 22:30).

This is a sobering Scripture passage. Would God describe you as standing in the gap for the sake of others? Commit to pray, pray, pray as if their lives depended on it.

Pray Ezekiel 22:30-31 over yourself and those for whom you stand guard as a faithful, prayerful watchman (Isaiah 62:6-7).

> *"LORD, You have searched for someone among the people*
> *who would build up the wall of prayers and stand in the gap*
> *before You for the land, so that You would not destroy it—*
> *LORD, You have found me! Do not pour out*
> *Your indignation on _____,*
> *do not consume us with the fire of Your wrath;*
> *do not bring our way upon our heads.*
> *Instead make our way holy in Your sight.*
> *For the sake of Your name, Jesus-"*

Please read Ezekiel 23.

Meditate on verses 48-49.

> *"Thus, I will make lewdness cease from the land,*
> *that all women may be admonished*
> *and not commit lewdness as you have done.*
> *Your lewdness will be requited*
> *upon you, and you will bear the penalty of worshiping your idols;*
> *thus, you will know that I am the LORD GOD."*

The LORD does not mince words; therefore, the shocking story of Oholah and Oholibah is in the Bible to illustrate the depravity of Israel. The two sister whores allegorically depict the harlotry of idolatry committed in Samaria, the capital of the northern kingdom of Israel, and in Jerusalem, the capital of the southern kingdom of Judah. And as their adulteries spilled throughout the kingdoms, the people were infected with unfaithfulness, bringing the wrath and judgment of God on their heads.

Words within the story like: "The sound of the carefree multitude was with her, and drunkards were brought from the wilderness" (v. 42) could describe people living today. Take to heart that God will not stand for unfaithfulness toward Him; His wrath is coming. Stand in the gap for those who need to repent of their harlotries, so they can walk wholeheartedly with Him.

Pray Ezekiel 23:48-49 as a faithful, prayerful watchman (Isaiah 62:6-7).

> *"LORD, make lewdness cease from the land.*
> *Admonish us not to commit lewdness*
> *as we have done. May we repent before our*
> *lewdness is requited upon us,*
> *and we bear the penalty of worshiping idols.*
> *May we know that You are the LORD.*
> *In Your name, Jesus~"*

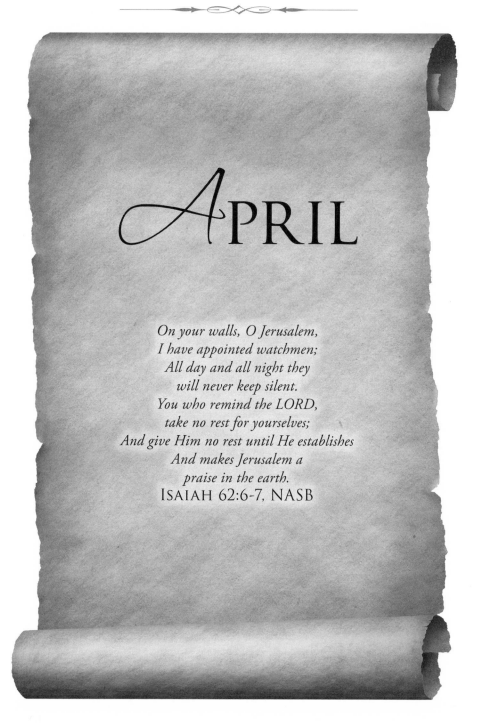

APRIL

On your walls, O Jerusalem,
I have appointed watchmen;
All day and all night they
will never keep silent.
You who remind the LORD,
take no rest for yourselves;
And give Him no rest until He establishes
And makes Jerusalem a
praise in the earth.
Isaiah 62:6-7, NASB

Please read Ezekiel 24.

Meditate on verse 13. The LORD is speaking.

> *"In your filthiness is lewdness. Because I would have cleansed you,*
> *yet you are not clean; you will not be cleansed from your*
> *filthiness again until I have spent My wrath on you."*

On the day the king of Babylon began his third and final siege of Jerusalem, God gave Ezekiel another parable (vs. 2-3). He compared the people to a rusty pot boiled so vigorously that its filthiness melted away; its rust was consumed (vs. 3-11). God gave the people every opportunity to return to Him, yet they refused; therefore, His wrath would cleanse them of their filthy sins (vs. 12-14).

Then, the LORD again made Ezekiel a living sermon illustration the day his wife died (vs. 16-18). Her death and the way Ezekiel handled it made such an impact, the people were finally ready to hear what the LORD had to say (vs. 19-24).

These words from God are sobering. Pray for those you love to repent before it is too late. Listen to God today, so He does not have to use a tragedy to get you to listen tomorrow.

Pray Ezekiel 24:13-14 in repentance, petition, and intercession over yourself and those for whom you stand guard as a faithful, prayerful watchman (Isaiah 62:6-7).

> *"LORD, in our filthiness is lewdness. Please*
> *cleanse us so You do not have to*
> *spend Your wrath on us. Relent and have pity on us.*
> *Please be sorry for us. Cleanse us so You do not have to judge us*
> *according to our ways and according to our deeds.*
> *Because of Your salvation, Jesus~"*

Please read Ezekiel 25.

Meditate on verses 6-7a.

> *For thus says the LORD GOD, "Because you have clapped your hands*
> *and stamped your feet and rejoiced with*
> *all the scorn of your soul against*
> *the land of Israel; therefore, behold, I have*
> *stretched out My hand against you."*

The LORD told Ezekiel to prophesy against Ammon, Moab, Edom, and the Philistines. God promised to punish Ammon for gloating over Israel's demise and to judge Moab for speaking ill of her (vs. 3, 6, 8). Edom and the Philistines would experience the vengeance of God for taking their own vengeance on Judah (vs. 12-17).

God deals with His nation, Israel, and He does not take lightly when others mistreat her or rejoice in her sufferings. In fact, God does not want you to take your own vengeance or rejoice in anyone's calamity.

> *Never take your own revenge, beloved, but*
> *leave room for the wrath of God,*
> *for it is written, "Vengeance is Mine; I will repay," says the LORD.*
> —Romans 12:19

> *He who rejoices at calamity will not go unpunished.*
> —Proverbs 17:5b

Pray not to do Ezekiel 25:3 and 6 over yourself and those for whom you stand guard as a faithful, prayerful watchman (Isaiah 62:6-7).

> *"LORD, may _____ and I always hear Your Word.*
> *Let us never say 'Aha!' against Israel or*
> *anyone when they are profaned,*
> *made desolate, and exiled. Do not let us*
> *clap our hands and stamp our feet*
> *and rejoice with all the scorn of our souls against Israel or anyone else.*
> *For the sake of Your name, Jesus~"*

Please read Ezekiel 26.

Meditate on verses 2-3.

> *"Son of man, because Tyre has said concerning Jerusalem,*
> *'Aha, the gateway of the peoples is broken; it has opened*
> *to me. I shall be filled, now that she is laid waste,'*
> *therefore, thus says the LORD GOD,*
> *'Behold, I am against you, O Tyre,*
> *and I will bring up many nations against*
> *you, as the sea brings up its waves.'"*

The people of Tyre, a Mediterranean coastal city on the northern border of Israel, were glad when Nebuchadnezzar conquered Jerusalem for a third time. Their trade routes with the East were now open, increasing their wealth (v.2). God was not pleased, and the same besieging Babylonians did to Tyre what they did to Jerusalem. Others would "Aha" at them.

Let the LORD examine your heart, mind, and attitudes. Are you benefiting at the expense of others? Do you take joy, even secretly, at the misfortune of someone else? Guard against such evil thinking, for it can even creep into the life of your church. "My Bible study has more attendees than theirs does. Our church will get more members when they have to close the doors of their little church." Ask the Holy Spirit to make your thoughts obedient to Him.

> *We are destroying speculations and every lofty thing raised*
> *up against the knowledge of God, and we are taking*
> *every thought captive to the obedience of Christ.*
> —2 Corinthians 10:5

Ask the LORD to let you never say the words from Ezekiel 26:2.

> *"LORD, let me **never** say about Jerusalem or anyone else:*
> *'Aha, their gateway has broken; now it has opened to me.*
> *I shall be filled, now that they are laid waste.'*
> *LORD, fill me with Your thoughts toward others.*
> *In Your name, Jesus~"*

APRIL 4

Please read Ezekiel 27.

Meditate on verses 3b and 7a.

> *O Tyre, you have said, "I am perfect in beauty."*
> *Your sail was of fine embroidered linen from Egypt*
> *so that it became your distinguishing mark.*

Tyre was a beautiful, wealthy port city on the Mediterranean Sea in southern Lebanon. The people had great trade relations with many countries and cities; over 30 of them are mentioned in this chapter. In fact, it was King Hiram of Tyre who supplied King Solomon with the cedars of Lebanon for building the LORD's temple in Jerusalem (1 Kings 5). But, Tyre not only gloated over the fall of Jerusalem, the city was filled with so much pride she claimed to be "perfect in beauty" (Ezekiel 26:2; 27:3). The LORD's response to such arrogance was:

> *"Your wealth, your wares, your merchandise,*
> *your sailors and your pilots,*
> *your repairers of seams, your dealers in*
> *merchandise and all your men of war*
> *who are in you, with all your company that is in your midst,*
> *will fall into the heart of the seas on the day of your overthrow."*
> —Ezekiel 27:27

God hates pride (Proverbs 8:13)! Ask Him to remove all arrogance from you so He can be the distinguishing mark on your life.

Use the words from Ezekiel 27:3 and 7 to pray over yourself and those for whom you stand guard as a faithful, prayerful watchman (Isaiah 62:6-7).

> *"LORD, only You are perfect in beauty!*
> *Please be the distinguishing mark on _____ and me.*
> *For the sake of Your name, Jesus~"*

Please read Ezekiel 28.

Meditate on this accusation from verse 2. The LORD is speaking to the leader of Tyre.

> *"Because your heart is lifted up and you have said,*
> *'I am a god; I sit in the seat of gods in the heart of the seas.'*
> *Yet, you are a man and not God."*

The king of Tyre was a smart, wealthy man who became so prideful he believed he was a god. God said his splendor would be defiled, and he would die at the hands of ruthless strangers (vs. 7, 10). After the LORD pronounced His judgment on the arrogant king, He told Ezekiel to take up a lament (vs. 11-19).

The lamentation speaks to the spiritual force behind this arrogant human king. Notice the many descriptors of Satan within verses 11-19. For example: "You were in Eden, the garden of God" (v. 13). "You were the anointed cherub who covers" (v. 14). "You were internally filled with violence, and you sinned; therefore, I have cast you as profane from the mountain of God" (v. 16).

It is important to learn from the human king of Tyre and the spiritual power behind him, Satan; pride eventually leads you to believe you are god of your own life. The LORD will not let such arrogance go unchecked or unpunished.

Pray for yourself and those you love to be the opposite of the king of Tyre, using the words from Ezekiel 28:2.

> *"LORD, do not let _____ and my heart be lifted up.*
> *Let us NEVER say or think we are a god*
> *or that we sit in the seat of gods.*
> *Let us never forget we are human and not God.*
> *We cannot make our hearts like Yours, God.*
> *Only You can make our hearts to love and follow You.*
> *Because of You, LORD Jesus Christ~"*

Please read Ezekiel 29.

Meditate on verses 9-10a.

> *"The land of Egypt will become a desolation and waste.*
> *Then they will know that I am the LORD.*
> *Because you said, 'The Nile is mine,*
> *and I have made it;' therefore, behold, I am against you."*

Twice in this chapter the LORD declared He was against Pharaoh because he claimed to create and own the Nile (vs. 3, 9). God does not tolerate such arrogant speech and attitudes. He promised to let the beasts and birds eat Pharaoh; then all of Egypt would know who is God (vs. 5-6).

A "this is mine" attitude is part of our sinful nature. It usually rears its ugly head by the time we turn one-year-old. The "look at what I did" attitude appears at about the same age, and left unchecked by Christ and His Word, it convinces us that we built our business, our stuff belongs to us, and we are self-made individuals—all "Pharaohish" things to think.

Let God's Word change you:

> *For by Him (Jesus) all things were created,*
> *both in the heavens and on earth,*
> *visible and invisible, whether thrones or*
> *dominions or rulers or authorities—*
> *all things have been created through Him and for Him.*
> —Colossians 1:16

Jesus Christ is the Creator of everything, and He created everything for Himself. That means if you have anything, it is only because the LORD Jesus chose to share it with you.

Humbly pray to be the opposite of Ezekiel 29:3 over yourself and those for whom you stand guard as a faithful, prayerful watchman (Isaiah 62:6-7).

> *"O LORD God, please do not be against _____ and me.*
> *Do not let us act like Pharaoh; remove the*
> *great monster that lies in each of us*
> *that says, 'My _____ is mine, and I myself made it.'*
> *Because You created everything, and everything belongs to You, Jesus~"*

Please read Ezekiel 30.

Meditate on verses 1-2a.

> *The Word of the LORD came again to me saying,*
> *"Son of man, prophesy and say, 'Thus says the LORD God.'"*

By now you may have noticed the repeated phrases "the Word of the LORD," "thus says the LORD God," and "I am the LORD" in Ezekiel. "The Word of the LORD" is used at least 60 times, "thus says the LORD God" over 125 times, and "I am the LORD" is found over 65 times within this amazing book of prophecy. God wanted there to be no doubt from where these words came. These are the very Words of God spoken to people who desperately needed to know who He is. Thankfully, God's Words were recorded for all of eternity, so you can touch them with your hands, see them with your eyes, hear them with your ears, meditate on them with your mind, speak them with your mouth, and let them saturate every fiber of your being. Every page of your Bible screams, "Thus says the LORD, 'This is the Word of the LORD declaring I AM the LORD!'"

What is your response to such a declaration? Use the words from Ezekiel 30:1-3 and 26 in prayer and total commitment to the LORD and His Word as His faithful, prayerful watchman (Isaiah 62:6-7).

> *"LORD, Your Word has come to me saying:*
> *'Thus says the LORD GOD,*
> *"Wail, 'Alas for the day!'"*
> *'For the day is near, even the day of the LORD is near;*
> *it will be a day of clouds, a time of doom for the nations.'*
> *LORD, help me tell others Your Words, so they will know*
> *that You are the LORD before it is too late.*
> *In Your name, LORD Jesus~"*

Please read Ezekiel 31.

Meditate on verses 10-11.

> *Therefore, thus says the LORD GOD,*
> *"Because it is high in stature and*
> *has set its top among the clouds, and its*
> *heart is haughty in its loftiness;*
> *therefore, I will give it into the hand of*
> *a despot of the nations; he will*
> *thoroughly deal with it. According to its*
> *wickedness, I have driven it away.*

God forewarned the prideful Egyptians of their coming destruction with a story about Assyria. He compared Assyria to a most amazing cedar of Lebanon whose beauty came from God (vs. 3-9). And while the LORD caused the cedar to grow toward the heavens, the cedar's heart grew haughty, so the LORD felled it (vs. 10-12). God used the Babylonians to humble and destroy the mighty Assyrians, and He promised the Egyptians He would do the same to them.

> *Pride goes before destruction, and a haughty spirit before stumbling.*
> —Proverbs 16:18

Heed God's warnings. Do not think you are in such a high position that it is impossible to be brought down. Commit to walk humbly with your God, recognizing it is He who makes your life beautiful (v. 9).

Pray for the LORD not to have to do verses 10-11 in your life and the lives of those for whom you stand guard as a faithful, prayerful watchman (Isaiah 62:6-7).

> *"LORD, do not let _____ and me become high*
> *in stature and set our tops among the clouds.*
> *Do not let our hearts be haughty in loftiness,*
> *so You do not have to give us*
> *into the hands of despots to thoroughly deal with us.*
> *Keep us from wickedness, so You do not need to drive us away.*
> *For the sake of Your name, Jesus~"*

Please read Ezekiel 32.

Meditate on verses 2 and 11.

> *"Son of man, take up a lamentation over*
> *Pharaoh king of Egypt and say to him,*
> *'You compared yourself to a young lion of the nations,*
> *yet you are like the monster in the seas; and*
> *you burst forth in your rivers*
> *and muddied the waters with your feet and fouled their rivers.'"*
> *For thus says the LORD GOD, "The sword of the*
> *king of Babylon will come upon you."*

Egypt was filled with pride at being one of the strongest kingdoms in the world when the LORD prophesied against Pharaoh and his realm. Egypt's strength was no match for God, who easily removes powerful empires when they get full of themselves and forget about Him. He even listed some of them in this chapter: Assyria, Elam, Meshech, Tubal, Edom, and Sidon (vs. 22-30). Egypt would join the list of the once mighty, but now shamefully fallen, who reside in Sheol, the place of the dead.

Be mindful of the temptation to get full of yourself, stopping it immediately before the LORD devastates your pride (v. 12). Pray not to be like Pharaoh, using the words from Ezekiel 32:2. Pray it over yourself and those for whom you stand guard as a faithful, prayerful watchman (Isaiah 62:6-7).

> *"LORD, do not let _____ and me*
> *compare ourselves to a young lion,*
> *yet act like a monster in our seas of responsibilities.*
> *Do not let us burst forth in the rivers where you placed us*
> *and muddy the waters with our feet and foul our rivers.*
> *For the sake of Your name, Jesus~"*

APRIL 10

Please read Ezekiel 33.

Meditate on verse 6. The LORD is speaking.

> *"But if the watchman sees the sword coming and does*
> *not blow the trumpet and the people are not warned,*
> *and a sword comes and takes a person from them,*
> *he is taken away in his iniquity; but his blood I*
> *will require from the watchman's hand."*

What a powerful chapter from God's Word!

First, the LORD does not take lightly the ministry of being a watchman. He appointed Ezekiel as a watchman over the house of Israel, and He appointed you a watchman over your house; God expects you to faithfully give your loved ones His warnings and messages (v. 7).

Secondly, what an encouraging chapter about God's forgiveness! The people knew they were rotting in their transgressions and did not think they could survive (v. 10). God's message was: "Turn from your evil ways and live! If you turn from your sin and practice justice and righteousness, none of the sins you committed will be remembered against you" (vs. 11-16). Incredible!

Thirdly, the chapter ends with a sad description of how people heard God's Word; the verses could describe some who attend church today (vs. 30-33). They hear a message but refuse to do God's Words because "their heart goes after their own gain" (v. 31). They only hear "a sensual song by one who has a beautiful voice and plays well on an instrument" (v. 32). "LORD, convict us!"

There are many verses to pray. Start by using the Words from Ezekiel 33:22-24 as a faithful, prayerful watchman (Isaiah 62:6-7).

> *"LORD, You opened my mouth; I am no longer*
> *speechless. Your Word came to me;*
> *may I speak it and pray it into the waste*
> *places where people need to hear.*
> *For the sake of Your name, Jesus~"*

Please read Ezekiel 34.

Meditate on verse 2b.

> *Thus says the LORD, "Woe, shepherds of Israel*
> *who have been feeding themselves!*
> *Should not the shepherds feed the flock?"*

The LORD told Ezekiel to prophesy against the shepherds, the priests and leaders of Israel, who did not take care of the flock of God. The people were lost sheep because their shepherds did not feed and watch over them. The LORD promised to gather the flock and care for them. Christ, the Great Shepherd, came for the sake of his sheep (Hebrews 13:20). He commissioned His disciple Peter to help feed and shepherd them (John 21:15-17). Peter then told all Christian leaders to "shepherd the flock of God among you" (1 Peter 5:2).

So, this chapter from Ezekiel applies to you. As a Christian, God has given you at least one, possibly many, lambs and sheep to feed and shepherd. Your flock might be your family, life group, friends, congregation, or coworkers. The LORD expects you to shepherd the flock until He, the Chief Shepherd, returns (1 Peter 5:4).

Ask God to make you a good shepherd by praying not to be like the shepherds described in Ezekiel 34:2 and 4.

> *"LORD, make _____ and me shepherds who feed the flock*
> *instead of only feeding ourselves. Help us to strengthen the sickly,*
> *heal the diseased, bind up the broken, bring*
> *back the scattered, and seek the lost.*
> *Do not let us dominate them with force and severity.*
> *Help us to feed them Your Word.*
> *For the sake of Your name, Great Shepherd Jesus Christ~"*

Please read Ezekiel 35.

Meditate on verse 11.

> *"Therefore, as I live," declares the LORD GOD, "I*
> *will deal with you according to your anger*
> *and according to your envy which you showed*
> *because of your hatred against them;*
> *so I will make Myself known among them when I judge you."*

The LORD pronounced judgment against Mount Seir/Edom (present-day southwestern Jordan) because of everlasting enmity with Israel (v. 5). God was against Edom (vs. 2-3), and He promised to "make Mount Seir a waste and a desolation" (v. 7). He would deal with their anger, envy, and hatred (v. 11).

Ask the LORD to search your heart for any anger, envy, and hatred. Let His Word deal with these areas of your life:

> *Walk by the Spirit, and you will not carry out the desire of the flesh.*
> *Now the deeds of the flesh are evident, which are: immorality,*
> *impurity, sensuality, idolatry, sorcery, enmities, strife, jealousy,*
> *outbursts of anger, disputes, dissensions, factions, envying,*
> *drunkenness, carousing, and things like these, of which I*
> *forewarn you, just as I have forewarned you, that those who*
> *practice such things will not inherit the kingdom of God.*
> *But the fruit of the Spirit is love, joy, peace, patience,*
> *kindness, goodness, faithfulness, gentleness, self-*
> *control; against such things there is no law.*
> *—Galatians 5:16, 19-23*

As a faithful, prayerful watchman (Isaiah 62:6-7), pray for the LORD not to have reason to accuse you and those you love of Ezekiel 35:13.

> *"LORD, please do not let _____ and me*
> *speak arrogantly against You.*
> *Do not allow us to multiply our words against You.*
> *We know You hear everything we say.*
> *Let us speak well in Your name, Jesus~"*

Please read Ezekiel 36.

Meditate on verse 23.

> *"I will vindicate the holiness of My great*
> *name which has been profaned*
> *among the nations, which you have profaned in their midst.*
> *Then the nations will know that I am the*
> *LORD," declares the LORD GOD,*
> *"when I prove Myself holy among you in their sight."*

God prophesied to the mountains of Israel, promising to rebuild the land made desolate by sin. After speaking about the land, the LORD addressed the people, explaining what He would do for the sake of His great name. The LORD would sprinkle clean water on them to cleanse them from all their filthiness (v. 25). He promised to remove their old hard hearts and give them new ones (v. 26). He would put His Spirit within them and cause them to walk in His ways (v. 27). It is incredible what the LORD does for His name's sake!

As God's Word and His Spirit touch your heart, let Him sprinkle clean water on you, washing away all your sins. Ask Him to give you His heart to replace your old hard one. Be filled with His Spirit and walk in His ways—for the sake of His great name.

Pray Ezekiel 36:9 and 25-27 over yourself and those for whom you stand guard as a faithful, prayerful watchman (Isaiah 62:6-7).

> *"LORD, please be for _____ and me, and turn to us, and*
> *cultivate our lives, and sow into us! Sprinkle clean water on us,*
> *so we will be clean. Cleanse us from all our filthiness and from*
> *all our idols. Give us a new heart and put a new spirit*
> *within us; remove the heart of stone from our flesh and give*
> *us a heart of flesh. Put Your Spirit within us and cause us*
> *to walk in Your statutes, being careful to observe Your ordinances.*
> *For the sake of Your great name, LORD Jesus~"*

APRIL 14

Please read Ezekiel 37.

Meditate on verses 4, 7, and 10.

> *Again He said to me, "Prophesy over these bones and say to them,*
> *'O dry bones, hear the Word of the LORD.'"*
> *So I prophesied as I was commanded, and*
> *as I prophesied, there was a noise,*
> *and behold, a rattling; and the bones came together, bone to its bone.*
> *So I prophesied as He commanded me,*
> *and the breath came into them,*
> *and they came to life and stood on their*
> *feet, an exceedingly great army.*

God's Word is powerful, and when Ezekiel was obedient to speak as the LORD commanded, dry bones were joined together. As the Word of the LORD continued to pour from Ezekiel's lips, breath entered the bones, bringing them to life and raising them up into a mighty army. The bones represented the whole house of Israel. In the midst of exile and destruction because of sin, they were dried up, hopeless, and completely cut off, just like those old, dry bones (v. 11). God's Word breathed life and hope into them for what the LORD was doing in their lives.

Thankfully, you have God's Words recorded in the Bible. You can touch them, read them, hear them, and speak them. They are powerful, bringing your life together and raising you up from the valley of death. Commit to reading God's Word every day and be faithful to speak His Words so those who feel dried up and disjointed can hear what God wants to miraculously do for them.

Pray Ezekiel 37:14 over those who need God's Spirit to breathe into their dry and hopeless lives.

> *"LORD, put Your Spirit within _____ so they will come to life.*
> *Place them where You want them.*
> *May they know that You, the LORD, have spoken and done it.*
> *In Your name, Jesus~"*

Please read Ezekiel 38.

Meditate on verse 23.

> *"I will magnify Myself, sanctify Myself, and make Myself known*
> *in the sight of many nations, and they will*
> *know that I am the LORD."*

In the last days, God will use Gog to bring an army from many nations against Israel to show Himself majestic to His people and the nations of the world (vs. 14-16). Picture the battle. When Gog's army arrives, the LORD's fury mounts up, and in His zeal and blazing wrath, there is a great earthquake in the land of Israel (vs. 18-19). The fish, birds, beasts, all creeping things, and all humans on the face of the earth shake at God's presence (v. 20). The LORD casts His sword against Gog; He judges him with pestilence and blood (v. 22). God rains down on Gog and his troops with hail, fire, and brimstone (v. 22). The result is: God magnifies Himself, shows Himself holy, and makes Himself known in the sight of the nations, so they know without a doubt, He is the LORD (v. 23).

Let the words of this chapter seal this truth in your heart: It is all about God. It is only about God; it is not about you or me. The LORD works for His renown; let your life be lived for that purpose.

Pray Ezekiel 38:23 as a prayer of dedication to the LORD.

> *"LORD, You will magnify Yourself, sanctify*
> *Yourself, and make Yourself known*
> *in the sight of many nations, and they will know You are the LORD.*
> *LORD, magnify Yourself, sanctify Yourself, and make Yourself known*
> *in _____ and me. Let us never forget You are the LORD.*
> *In Your name, LORD Jesus~"*

Please read Ezekiel 39.

Meditate on verse 7.

*"My holy name I will make known in the midst of My people Israel,
and I will not let My holy name be profaned anymore.
And the nations will know that I am the
LORD, the Holy One in Israel."*

The story of the destruction of Gog and his army continues in this chapter. In the last days, God will so annihilate this enemy of Israel, it will take seven months to bury the bodies that weren't eaten by the birds and beasts (vs. 4, 12). A valley used for the burial ground will be so corpse-filled it will block passers-by (v. 11). God's salvation of Israel as He mercifully pours out His Spirit on them is incredible, especially in light of how treacherously they acted against Him (v. 23, 25, 29).

Your salvation story is equally incredible.

*He saved us, not on the basis of deeds which
we have done in righteousness,
but according to His mercy, by the washing
of regeneration and renewing
by the Holy Spirit, whom He poured out upon
us richly through Jesus Christ our Savior.*
—Titus 3:5-6

As a faithful, prayerful watchman (Isaiah 62:6-7), pray Ezekiel 39:24-26 and 29 over those who need an incredible salvation story.

*"LORD, You have dealt with _____ according to their uncleanness
and according to their transgressions, and You hid Your face
from them. Now restore them and have mercy on them for the
sake of Your holy name. Let them forget their disgrace and all
their treachery which they perpetrated against You. Let them live
securely with You with no one to make them afraid. Do not hide
Your face from them any longer; pour out Your Spirit on them.
For the sake of Your name, LORD Jesus-"*

Please read Ezekiel 40.

Meditate on verse 4.

> *The man said to me, "Son of man, see with your eyes, hear*
> *with your ears, and give attention to all that I am going to*
> *show you, for you have been brought here in order to show*
> *it to you. Declare to the house of Israel all that you see."*

Picture Ezekiel's situation. He had lived in Babylon as an exile for 25 years. By now, Jerusalem and the temple were totally destroyed. The last heartbreaking vision Ezekiel had of the temple was God's glory departing from it (Ezekiel 10:18). Now, 19 years later, God gives Ezekiel this glorious vision of His beautifully rebuilt temple. Can you imagine the hope this brought to the exiles in Babylon as Ezekiel described it to them in all the minute details you had the privilege of reading from this chapter?

Let God's Word bring you hope for heartbreaking situations over which you are praying. As you focus on Christ and His Word for the sake of those you love, ask God to show you minute details of what He will do in their lives. When the LORD gives you the vision, write it down and pray for God to bring it to fruition (Habakkuk 2:2-3).

Pray Ezekiel 40:4 over yourself to see clearly God's will for your family.

> *"LORD, please let me see with my eyes, hear with my ears,*
> *and give attention to all that You are going to show me, for*
> *You have brought me here in order to show it to me.*
> *Help me declare to _____ all that I see.*
> *For the sake of Your will, Jesus~"*

Please read Ezekiel 41.

Meditate on verse 22.

> *The altar was of wood, three cubits high and*
> *its length two cubits; its corners,*
> *its base and its sides were of wood. And he said to me,*
> *"This is the table that is before the LORD."*

The description of the LORD's temple is incredible. Here are some diagrams to help you picture what you have read.

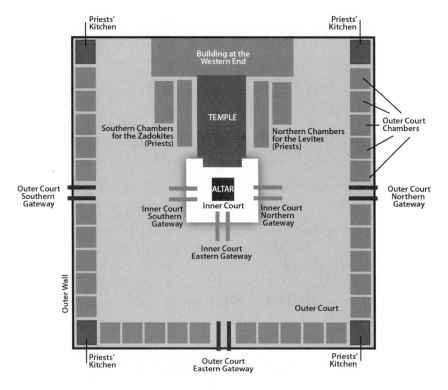

EZEKIEL'S TEMPLE
500 x 500 cubits = 750 x 750 ft.

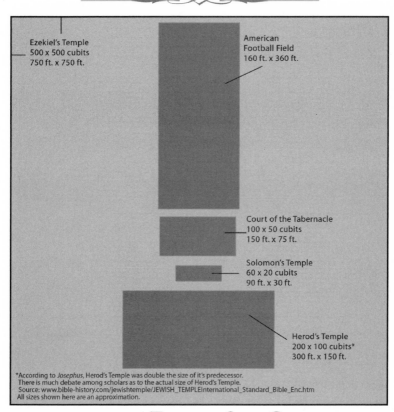

Ezekiel's Temple
500 x 500 cubits
750 ft. x 750 ft.

American
Football Field
160 ft. x 360 ft.

Court of the Tabernacle
100 x 50 cubits
150 ft. x 75 ft.

Solomon's Temple
60 x 20 cubits
90 ft. x 30 ft.

Herod's Temple
200 x 100 cubits*
300 ft. x 150 ft.

*According to *Josephus*, Herod's Temple was double the size of it's predecessor.
There is much debate among scholars as to the actual size of Herod's Temple.
Source: www.bible-history.com/jewishtemple/JEWISH_TEMPLEInternational_Standard_Bible_Enc.htm
All sizes shown here are an approximation.

TEMPLE SIZE COMPARISON
© 2018 by Wendy K. Walters. Used by permission.

The temple is grandiose in the vision God gave Ezekiel, yet inside this temple, there is only one piece of furniture mentioned, an altar described as "the table that is before the LORD" (v. 22). What a beautiful picture of coming into God's presence, laying everything on the altar through prayer and petition then sitting with the LORD at His table for nourishment and encouragement.

Hear God's invitation to come to His table for the grace and strength you need today. Thank Him, using the words from Ezekiel 41:22.

"LORD, thank You for Your altar where I can lay it all down.
Thank You for Your table where I can stay before You.
Because of You, LORD Jesus~"

APRIL 19

Please read Ezekiel 42.

Meditate on verse 20.

> *He measured it on the four sides; it had a wall*
> *all around, the length five hundred*
> *and the width five hundred, to divide*
> *between the holy and the profane.*

God is holy. He cannot be in the presence of the profane, so a massive wall, to keep the things that are sacred separate from the things that are not, surrounded His temple. As you picture this wall, thank Jesus for tearing down the wall that separated you from God, so you can run boldly into the holy place of God's presence.

> *But Jesus, on the other hand, because He continues forever,*
> *holds His priesthood permanently. Therefore, He is able also*
> *to save forever those who draw near to God through Him,*
> *since He always lives to make intercession for them.*
> —Hebrews 7:24-25

Because of the LORD Jesus Christ, you can draw near to God and partake of the most holy things (v. 13). What an amazing privilege you have!

Keeping in mind that as a Christian you are the temple of God and a priest to God (1 Corinthians 6:19-20; 1 Peter 2:5, 9), pray Ezekiel 42:13 over yourself and those for whom you stand guard as a faithful, prayerful watchman (Isaiah 62:6-7).

> *"LORD, let _____ and me always be those who are near to You.*
> *Let us eat the most holy things. Let us lay*
> *the most holy things before You.*
> *Let our offerings be holy, for the place is holy.*
> *Because of You, LORD Jesus~"*

Please read Ezekiel 43.

Meditate on verses 2-5.

> *Behold, the glory of the God of Israel was*
> *coming from the way of the east.*
> *And His voice was like the sound of many waters;*
> *and the earth shone with His glory.*
> *And it was like the appearance of the vision which I saw, like*
> *the vision which I saw when He came to destroy the city. And*
> *the visions were like the vision which I saw by the river Chebar,*
> *and I fell on my face. And the glory of the LORD came into*
> *the house by the way of the gate facing toward the east. And*
> *the Spirit lifted me up and brought me into the inner court;*
> *and behold, the glory of the LORD filled the house.*

What a joy and a relief this vision of God's glory returning to the temple must have been for Ezekiel! Nearly 20 years earlier he saw God's glory departing the temple and the city of Jerusalem (Ezekiel 10:18; 11:23). As Ezekiel beheld God's glory, his immediate response was to fall on his face, just as he had done years ago (Ezekiel 1:28; 3:23; 9:8; 11:13; 43:3).

What is your reaction to God's glory, to being in His presence? Falling to your knees or lying facedown on the floor are positions of humility and reverence. They are great prayer positions when bringing issues of concern to God Almighty.

If you are physically able, fall on your face before God, bringing your loved ones to Him. Start your prayers with Ezekiel 43:3-5.

> *"LORD, as I fall on my face before You, give me a vision for _____.*
> *LORD, let Your glory come into our house.*
> *Spirit, please lift us up and bring us into Your inner courts.*
> *LORD, let Your glory fill our house.*
> *For the sake of Your glorious name, Jesus~"*

Please read Ezekiel 44.

Meditate on verses 6 and 23.

> *"You shall say to the rebellious ones, to the house*
> *of Israel, 'Thus says the LORD God,*
> *"Enough of all your abominations, O house of Israel."'*
> *Moreover, they (the priests) shall teach My*
> *people the difference between the holy*
> *and the profane and cause them to discern*
> *between the unclean and the clean."*

The LORD does not take lightly the role of priest. In the past, many of the priests caused the Israelites to stumble in iniquity and idolatry (vs. 10, 12). The Babylonian exile and destruction of the temple and Jerusalem were God's punishment for nearly a millennium of rebellion against Him.

A time is coming when Israel's priests will minister before the LORD in proper holiness. As you wait to see the fulfillment of this final vision of Ezekiel, keep in mind that God already has a kingdom of priests ministering in His name. His priests are you and other Christians!

> *But you are a chosen race, a royal priesthood, a holy nation,*
> *a people for God's own possession, so that*
> *you may proclaim the excellencies*
> *of Him who has called you out of darkness into His marvelous light.*
> —1 Peter 2:9

Let that truth soak in and ask the LORD to make you His faithful priest. Start your prayers with the words from Ezekiel 44:23.

> *"LORD, as Your priest, help me teach Your people the*
> *difference between the holy and the profane, causing*
> *them to discern between the unclean and the clean.*
> *In Your name, Jesus~"*

Please read Ezekiel 45.

Meditate on verse 9.

> *Thus says the LORD GOD, "Enough, you*
> *princes of Israel; put away violence*
> *and destruction, and practice justice and righteousness.*
> *Stop your expropriations from My people," declares the LORD GOD.*

God not only takes the role of priest very seriously, He also holds the ministry of being a leader to His high standards. Recall from your readings in 1 and 2 Kings that most of Israel and Judah's rulers were described as evil in the sight of God. Their abominations didn't merely trickle down to the people; they cascaded, corrupting both people and land. As the land of Israel laid destitute and Ezekiel and the exiles sat in Babylon as punishment for those evil acts, God gave Ezekiel this vision of the land being used for His holy purposes and the princes of Israel no longer oppressing the people (vs. 1-4, 8). How encouraging that God can bring people up to His holy standards!

How would God describe you as a leader? Let this chapter both convict and reassure you. Ask God to remove areas of your life not in keeping with His holiness. Ask Him to fill you with His righteous ways. Ask Him to do the same in lives of leaders in your world. Use the words from Ezekiel 45:8-10 to pray over yourself and other leaders as a faithful, prayerful watchman (Isaiah 62:6-7).

> *"LORD, let _____ and me no longer oppress the people.*
> *Let us put away violence and destruction. Let*
> *us practice justice and righteousness.*
> *Do not let us expropriate anything from others. Give us just balances.*
> *In Your name, Jesus~"*

Please read Ezekiel 46.

Meditate on verse 18. The LORD is speaking.

> *"The prince shall not take from the people's inheritance,*
> *thrusting them out of their possession; he shall give*
> *his sons inheritance from his own possession*
> *so that My people will not be scattered, anyone from his possession."*

Recall how King Ahab took Naboth's vineyard by murdering him and seizing his property in 1 Kings 21. God told Ezekiel a day is coming when rulers will no longer take what does not belong to them. The inheritance of God's people will be secure; they will not be dispossessed.

As a child of God, you already live in the reality of that promise:

> *Blessed be the God and Father of our LORD Jesus*
> *Christ, who according to His great mercy*
> *has caused us to be born again to a living hope*
> *through the resurrection of Jesus Christ*
> *from the dead, to obtain an inheritance which*
> *is imperishable and undefiled*
> *and will not fade away, reserved in heaven*
> *for you, who are protected by*
> *the power of God through faith for a salvation*
> *ready to be revealed in the last time.*
> —1 Peter 1:3-5

Pray for the Jewish people to see the fulfillment of God's promises from the book of Ezekiel and thank the LORD for the assurance of these promises in your life.

Pray Ezekiel 46:18 in thanksgiving and supplication as a faithful, prayerful watchman (Isaiah 62:6-7).

> *"LORD, thank You that _____ and my*
> *inheritance in You cannot be taken from us;*
> *we cannot be thrust out of our possession.*
> *As Your people, we will not be scattered from*
> *our lasting possession in You.*
> *LORD, please make _____ one of Your people.*
> *In Your name, Jesus~"*

APRIL 24

Please read Ezekiel 47.

Meditate on verse 1a.

> *Then he brought me back to the door of the house,*
> *and behold, water was flowing from under the threshold of the house.*

Imagine this flow of water coming from the temple of the LORD. The farther it goes, the deeper it becomes, deep enough for swimming, bringing life and healing everywhere it flows. Doesn't this river's description make you want to dive in and experience its refreshment?

Hear Jesus' words to a hot and tired woman. As you listen to their conversation, hear Him speak these life-giving words to you.

> *Jesus answered and said to her, "If you knew the gift of God,*
> *and who it is who says to you, 'Give Me a drink,' you would*
> *have asked Him, and He would have given you living water."*
> *She said to Him, "Sir, You have nothing to*
> *draw with and the well is deep;*
> *where then do You get that living water?"*
> *Jesus answered and said to her, "Everyone who*
> *drinks of this water will thirst again,*
> *but whoever drinks of the water that I*
> *will give him shall never thirst,*
> *but the water that I will give him will become in him*
> *a well of water springing up to eternal life."*
> —John 4:10-11, 13-14

Jesus is the Living Water that flows through you by the power of the Holy Spirit. As you grow in Christ, the Living Water isn't merely a trickle (v. 2); it is a deep river bringing life to you and those in your realm of influence.

Pray for Ezekiel 47:9 to be a reality in your life and those you love.

> *"LORD, let _____ and me live in every*
> *place where Your river goes.*
> *Make us fresh in You. As Your river flows from our lives,*
> *let everything live wherever we go.*
> *Because of You, our Living Water, Jesus~"*

Please read Ezekiel 48.

Meditate on verse 35b.

And the name of the city from that day shall be, "The LORD is there."

As Ezekiel relayed the messages and visions from God to the exiles in Babylon, they must have been encouraged to learn a day was coming when Jerusalem and the temple will be rebuilt, and God's glory will return. Jerusalem's gates will be named for the 12 tribes of Israel (v. 31). Today, some of those gates are named: Herod Gate, Damascus Gate, and The Dung Gate—how exciting a name change will be! And, the best name change will be Jerusalem's new name: "The LORD Is There" (v. 35). God's glory will remain forever.

Name changes are a big deal, and if you are a Christian, you have been given some new names. Before Jesus, you were called: "son of disobedience" and "child of wrath" (Ephesians 2:2-3). In Christ, you are now known as: "child of God," "chosen of God," and "beloved" (1 John 3:1; Colossians 3:12). You can even be described as "The LORD is there" because His Spirit abides in you (John 14:17; 1 John 4:13).

Pray for the day to come when God fulfills His promises to Israel as recorded in Ezekiel. Pray for those you love to be described as "The LORD is there" by praying Ezekiel 48:35 as their faithful, prayerful watchman (Isaiah 62:6-7).

"LORD, I look forward to the day that Jerusalem
is named, 'The LORD Is There.'
Please come into the life of _____ so You are there, too.
In Your name, Jesus~"

Please read Romans 1.

Meditate on verses 7-8.

> *To all who are beloved of God in Rome, called as saints:*
> *Grace to you and peace from God our Father*
> *and the LORD Jesus Christ.*
> *First, I thank my God through Jesus Christ for you all*
> *because your faith is being proclaimed throughout the whole world.*

Paul was a great church planter. He saw the Holy Spirit move in people's lives and eternity change because of their faith. Paul wrote this letter to the Roman church because of news he heard about them from other global travelers. They were famous for their faith in God. Many churches, today, are famous for who their pastor is or how large they are. This church in Rome was famous for believing God is real and the Gospel is true.

Paul loved this church and prayed unceasingly for them (vs. 9-11). He desperately wanted them to be even more blessed, and he wanted to come and help them.

Add to your prayers for God to bless churches greatly and beg Him to let you be a blessing, so they may become more established in Him.

Pray Romans 1:7-8 over churches for whom you stand guard as a faithful, prayerful watchman (Isaiah 62:6-7).

> *"LORD, please bless all who are beloved of You in*
> *the church at _____ , called as saints.*
> *Give them grace and peace from You, our*
> *Father and the LORD Jesus Christ.*
> *I thank You, God, through Jesus Christ for all of them.*
> *Let their faith be proclaimed throughout the whole world.*
> *For the sake of Your name, Jesus~"*

Please read Romans 2.

Meditate on verse 7.

> *To those who by perseverance in doing good seek*
> *for glory and honor and immortality, eternal life.*

The meditation verse is interesting. It is placed between verses that describe the attitudes and actions of people who will experience God's wrath rather than His blessings. Many would say that seekers of glory, honor, and immortality are selfish people; however, God says that seeking those things will be rewarded with life eternal.

God is not saying to seek personal glory and honor, but rather His glory and honor. Glory is the essence of God's presence or nature revealed, and honor is due Him because He is God. Persevering in doing good for the glory and honor of God is the goal of every Christian—every attainer of immortality.

Let these words from Peter's letter bring additional insight into what God means by seeking glory and honor and immortality:

> *So that the proof of your faith, being more precious*
> *than gold … may be found to result in*
> *praise and glory and honor at the revelation of Jesus Christ.*
> —1 Peter 1:7

Prove your faith in the Giver of immortality by persevering in doing good for His praise and glory and honor.

Pray Romans 2:7-8 over yourself and those for whom you stand guard as a faithful, prayerful watchman (Isaiah 62:6-7).

> *"LORD, please let _____ and me persevere*
> *in doing good as we seek for Your*
> *glory and honor and immortality—eternal life.*
> *LORD, please help _____ and _____,*
> *who are selfishly ambitious*
> *and do not obey the truth, but obey unrighteousness;*
> *save them from wrath and indignation.*
> *For the sake of Your name, Jesus~"*

Please read Romans 3.

Meditate on verses 21-24.

> *But now apart from the Law, the righteousness*
> *of God has been manifested,*
> *being witnessed by the Law and the Prophets,*
> *even the righteousness of God through faith in*
> *Jesus Christ for all those who believe;*
> *for there is no distinction; for all have sinned*
> *and fall short of the glory of God,*
> *being justified as a gift by His grace through the*
> *redemption which is in Christ Jesus.*

Chapter 3 is a glorious chapter answering questions many were asking in the Roman church. It is assumed the founders of this church were Jews who had traveled to Jerusalem during the seasons of Passover and Pentecost, witnessing the crucifixion of Christ and the events following. They were some of the first believers who returned to the synagogues in Rome with news of Messiah's coming. Many of the Jews believed, as well as non-Jewish people who heard the Gospel. Paul is writing a church made up of Jewish and non-Jewish Christians, addressing questions that could be summed up as: What part of the Jewish traditions and Law are required to be a faithful Christian?

Paul answers by showing that The Law, the first testament of God, has been completed by Christ, and a new standard, the Law of Faith has been established. This New Testament, or Covenant, fulfills the requirements of righteousness through the death of Jesus for all mankind.

Pray Romans 3:21-24 in thanksgiving for what God in Christ accomplished.

> *"LORD, thank You that Your righteousness has been manifested*
> *apart from the Law. Thank You for Your righteousness for*
> *all those who believe through faith in Jesus Christ.*
> *Thank You that there is no distinction, for all of us*
> *have sinned and fallen short of Your glory. Thank*
> *You for justifying us as a gift of Your grace*
> *through the redemption which is in Christ Jesus.*
> *In Your name, Jesus~"*

Please read Romans 4.

Meditate on verses 2-3.

For if Abraham was justified by works, he has
something to boast about, but not before God.
For what does the Scripture say?
"Abraham believed God, and it was credited to him as righteousness."

It is important to know how to become righteous. Paul writes that salvation is not from works (vs. 2-8), religion (vs. 9-12), or the Law (vs. 13-15). Salvation by faith, as a result of God's grace, makes you righteous.

Abraham's faith is used as a model of this salvation. God promised 100-year-old Abraham that he would have a child with his 90-year-old wife, Sarah. Abraham doubted his or her body would be able to deliver, but he had faith that God would deliver on His promise.

In hope against hope he believed, so that he
might become a father of many nations
according to that which had been spoken,
"So shall your descendants be."
With respect to the promise of God, he did not
waver in unbelief but grew strong in faith,
giving glory to God, and being fully assured
that what God had promised,
He was able also to perform. Therefore, it was
also credited to him as righteousness.
—Romans 4:18, 20-22

Faith is how you know God's salvation and become a Christian.

Pray Romans 4:18 and 19-22 over yourself and those for whom you stand guard as a faithful, prayerful watchman (Isaiah 62:6-7).

"LORD, please give _____ and me hope against hope.
Let us not become weak in faith, nor waver in unbelief.
Help us be strong in faith, giving You glory, fully assured that
what You promised You are able to perform.
Let _____ be credited with righteousness by believing in You.
In Your name, Jesus-"

Please read Romans 5.

Meditate on verses 10-11.

> *For if while we were enemies we were reconciled*
> *to God through the death of His Son,*
> *much more, having been reconciled, we shall be saved by His life.*
> *And not only this, but we also exult in God*
> *through our LORD Jesus Christ,*
> *through whom we have now received the reconciliation.*

Paul was so excited about what God did through Jesus for all Christians that he reinforced these great acts of God with great responses to Him. Paul responded with "exultation." Exult comes from two Greek words meaning "to boast" and "to pray."[1] Exultation is a rich spiritual response to God while in His presence, a Holy Spirit generated reaction to a divine realization.

Paul exults in the hope of the glory of God (v. 2). "Wow, God! You have done so much and look at what You have promised!"

Paul also exults in his tribulations (v. 3). "God, we are going to get through this with You and grow as we go!"

Paul exults in God through the LORD Jesus Christ (v. 11). "God, You love me so much! I can talk to You and brag about You because You saved, justified, and reconciled me through the LORD Jesus Christ!"

Exultation results when you recognize God's hand in anything.

Pray Romans 5:2-4 and 11 in exultation to the LORD.

> *"God, I exult in the hope of Your glory!*
> *I exult in my tribulations, knowing they bring perseverance,*
> *then proven character, then hope! I exult in You, God!*
> *Through You, LORD Jesus Christ~"*

1. *Retrieved from www.blueletterbible.org/lang/lexicon/lexicon.cfm?Strongs=G2744&t=NASB*

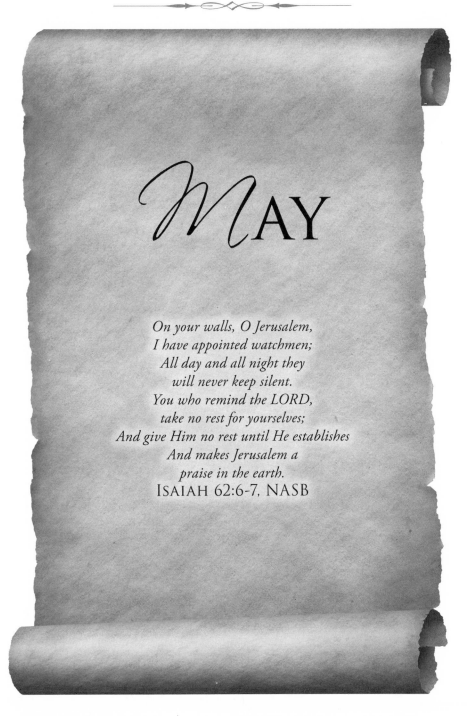

MAY

On your walls, O Jerusalem,
I have appointed watchmen;
All day and all night they
will never keep silent.
You who remind the LORD,
take no rest for yourselves;
And give Him no rest until He establishes
And makes Jerusalem a
praise in the earth.

ISAIAH 62:6-7, NASB

MAY 1

Please read Romans 6.

Meditate on verses 22-23.

But now having been freed from sin and enslaved
to God, you derive your benefit,
resulting in sanctification, and the outcome,
eternal life. For the wages of sin is death,
but the free gift of God is eternal life in Christ Jesus our LORD.

Spiritually resurrected people are alive in Christ and freed from the bondage of sin, the Law, and death. As a Christian, your old self is crucified, and you are raised with Christ. Sin, the Law, and death no longer master you. Now you are enslaved to God, righteousness, and grace (vs. 14, 18, 22). A word for being enslaved to God is "LORDSHIP." Jesus calls His followers to "LORDSHIP" when He says, "If anyone wishes to come after Me, he must deny himself and take up his cross daily and follow Me" (Luke 9:23).

Heed Christ's command to daily deny yourself and follow Him as LORD (Master). When you mess up and allow sin, the Law, and death to be your master, quickly ask God to forgive you and make Jesus LORD of your life again, walking wholeheartedly with Him.

Pray Romans 6:22-23 over yourself and those for whom you stand guard as a faithful, prayerful watchman (Isaiah 62:6-7).

"LORD, thank You that I have been freed
from sin and enslaved to You.
The benefit is sanctification (being made pure and
holy), and the outcome is eternal life.
LORD, please free _____ from the wages of sin,
which is death.
May they choose Your free gift of eternal
life in Christ Jesus our LORD.
In Your name, Jesus~"

Please read Romans 7.

Meditate on verse 4.

> *Therefore, my brethren, you also were made to die*
> *to the Law through the body of Christ,*
> *so that you might be joined to another, to*
> *Him who was raised from the dead,*
> *in order that we might bear fruit for God.*

Paul used a marriage illustration to explain salvation in Christ. A married woman is bound by law to her husband as long as he is alive, but if the husband dies, she is released from him (v. 2). If while the husband is living, the woman joins herself to another man, she is considered an adulteress (v. 3). When you become a Christian, you die to the Law and to your old self, and you are joined to Christ.

This is really great news! Christ makes you new. You live in and for Jesus. Having been released from the Law, you serve in newness of the Spirit (v. 6). Your life no longer bears fruit for death; now, you bear fruit for God (vs. 4-5).

Ponder these truths about who you are in Christ. Let the Spirit bear His fruit in you: love, joy, peace, patience, kindness, goodness, faithfulness, gentleness, and self-control (Galatians 5:22-23).

Pray Romans 7:4 and 6 over yourself and those for whom you stand guard as a faithful, prayerful watchman (Isaiah 62:6-7).

> *"LORD, thank You that I was made to die to the Law through*
> *the body of Christ, so I could be joined to You, Jesus, who was*
> *raised from the dead, in order to bear fruit for You, God.*
> *Please let _____ choose to die to the Law and be joined to You, too.*
> *Let us serve in newness of the Spirit.*
> *For the sake of Your name, Jesus~"*

Please read Romans 8.

Meditate on verses 14-16.

For all who are being led by the Spirit of God, these are sons of God.
For you have not received a spirit of slavery, leading to fear again,
but you have received a spirit of adoption as sons by which we cry out,
"Abba! Father!"
The Spirit Himself testifies with our spirit
that we are children of God.

One of the greatest gifts of being a Christian is becoming one of God's children. When Pentecost took place, the Holy Spirit started making Christians (Acts 1-2). They were a new type of creation (James 1:18). Their spiritual DNA changed, and they became new beings—children of God.

As God's child, you have access to Him. He wants you to draw near to Him. God doesn't want you to be nervous, but to come boldly to Him (Hebrews 10:19-22). What an incredible privilege you have! You can confidently be in the presence of God, calling Him "Daddy." Amazing!

Pray Romans 8:26-28, asking the LORD to intercede for you and those you love.

"Holy Spirit, help me in my weakness, for I do
not know how to pray as I should.
Thank You that You intercede for _____ and
me with groanings too deep for words.
LORD, You search hearts and know what the mind of the Spirit is.
Please intercede for the saints according to Your will, God.
We know You cause all things to work together for good
to those who love You, to those who are
called according to Your purpose.
Thank You, in Your name, Jesus~"

Please read Romans 9.

Meditate on verses 30-32a.

> *What shall we say then? That Gentiles, who did*
> *not pursue righteousness, attained righteousness,*
> *even the righteousness which is by faith;*
> *but Israel, pursuing a law of righteousness, did not arrive at that law.*
> *Why? Because they did not pursue it by faith,*
> *but as though it were by works.*

It is important for understanding the Bible to know this truth: God is moved by faith in Him rather than actions without faith. Many go through religious rituals, but if those rituals are not based on faith in Jesus, then they have no value, now or in eternity.

Paul knew that Jews who kept the Law, trying to achieve righteousness would be extremely disappointed (vs. 32-33). Their self-effort and religious actions did not lead them to recognize and follow by faith the One who completed the Law, Jesus Christ. Paul desperately wanted his fellow Jews to see the Law through faith, and by faith, recognize Jesus as the Messiah, just as the Gentiles were recognizing Jesus and being made righteous through faith in Him (vs. 3-5, 24, 30).

There are people in your life whom you desperately want to recognize Jesus the Messiah and believe in Him for righteousness and salvation. Pray Romans 9:30 and 32-33 over them as their faithful, prayerful watchman (Isaiah 62:6-7).

> *"LORD, please let _____ attain Your righteousness by faith.*
> *Do not let them pursue You by works and stumble over You.*
> *Let them believe in You, the Rock, so they will not be disappointed.*
> *In Your name, Jesus~"*

May 5

Please read Romans 10.

Meditate on verses 11-13.

> *For the Scripture says, "Whoever believes in*
> *Him will not be disappointed."*
> *For there is no distinction between Jew and Greek;*
> *for the same LORD is LORD of all, abounding*
> *in riches for all who call on Him;*
> *for "Whoever will call on the name of the LORD will be saved."*

Paul wanted no one, Jew or Greek, to stumble through life disappointed (Romans 9). Romans 10 provides the cure for disappointment and stumbling. It is believing Jesus is the Savior! Are there people on your prayer list that do not yet believe in Jesus? Pray confidently for them and for those the LORD will send to share the Gospel with them.

Pray Romans 10:8-10 and 14-17 over them now as their faithful, prayerful watchman (Isaiah 62:6-7).

> *"LORD, let Your Word be near _____, in*
> *their mouth and in their heart—*
> *the Word of Faith—which _____ and I are preaching.*
> *Help them confess with their mouth Jesus as LORD and*
> *believe in their heart that You raised Him from the dead.*
> *LORD, please save them! Help their heart to*
> *believe, resulting in righteousness,*
> *and their mouth to confess, resulting in salvation.*
> *Let them call on You and believe.*
> *Let them hear about Jesus so they can believe.*
> *LORD, send preachers so they can hear.*
> *Make beautiful the feet of those who bring*
> *Your good news of good things.*
> *Let _____ heed the good news and believe*
> *the report about You, Jesus.*
> *Let them hear the Word of Christ and have faith to believe it.*
> *For the glory of Your name, Jesus~"*

Please read Romans 11.

Meditate on verses 17-18a.

> *But if some of the branches were broken*
> *off, and you, being a wild olive,*
> *were grafted in among them and became partaker*
> *with them of the rich root of the olive tree,*
> *do not be arrogant toward the branches.*

The first eleven chapters of Romans describe the great things God has done for salvation to work. Chapter 12 will begin with how Christians should live as a result of all God's work. Chapter 11 finishes the discussion on God's heart for the Jewish people and the wonderful opportunity Gentiles have to be grafted into the olive tree. Therefore, those of us who are Christians and not from a Jewish heritage should be both proud of our new roots and humbled by God's choice to allow us into the family.

The chapter ends with this powerful confession of God's greatness and trust in Him (vs. 33-36). Pray it with praise to your all-powerful God!

> *"Oh, the depth of the riches both of the wisdom*
> *and knowledge of You, God!*
> *How unsearchable are Your judgments and unfathomable Your ways!*
> *For who has known Your mind, LORD,*
> *or who became Your counselor?*
> *Or who has first given to You that it might be paid back to You again?*
> *For from You and through You and to You are all things.*
> *To You be the glory forever. Amen."*

Please read Romans 12.

Meditate on verses 1-2.

> *Therefore, I urge you, brethren, by the mercies of God, to*
> *present your bodies a living and holy sacrifice, acceptable*
> *to God, which is your spiritual service of worship. And do*
> *not be conformed to this world, but be transformed by the*
> *renewing of your mind, so that you may prove what the will*
> *of God is, that which is good and acceptable and perfect.*

Romans 12:1-2 is the pivot point from the first eleven chapters which teach the truths of God to the last five chapters which teach how Christians are to function as a result of those truths. Based upon what God has done for you, offer yourself as a living sacrifice, which means giving Jesus LORDSHIP of your life, letting Him transform you, proving God saved you, and is changing you from the inside out.

The rest of chapter 12 makes an amazing prayer for your transformation, asking God's help every step of the way.

Pray Romans 12:3-21 over yourself and those for whom you stand guard as a faithful, prayerful watchman (Isaiah 62:6-7).

> *"LORD, help _____ and me not to think more highly*
> *of ourselves than we ought to think but to think so as to*
> *have sound judgment. Help us be one body in Christ, and*
> *individually members one of another. Help us exercise our*
> *gifts appropriately. Help our love be without hypocrisy.*
> *Help us abhor what is evil and cling to what is good.*
> *Help us be devoted to one another in brotherly love,*
> *giving preference to one another in honor.*
> *Help us not lag behind in diligence but make us*
> *fervent in spirit, serving You, LORD.*
> *Help us rejoice in hope, persevere in tribulation,*
> *and be devoted to prayer.*

Help us contribute to the needs
of the saints and practice hospitality.
Help us bless those who persecute us;
help us bless and not curse.
Help us rejoice with those who rejoice
and weep with those who weep.
Help us be of the same mind toward one another,
not haughty, associating with the lowly.
Help us not be wise in our own estimation.
Help us never pay back evil for evil to anyone.
Help us respect what is right in the sight of all men,
being at peace with all men.
Help us never take your own revenge
but leave room for Your wrath.
Help us not be overcome by evil
but overcome evil with good.
For the sake of Your name, Jesus–"

MAY 8

Please read Romans 13.

Meditate on verses 5-7.

> *Therefore, it is necessary to be in subjection, not only because of wrath,*
> *but also for conscience' sake. For because of this you also pay taxes,*
> *for rulers are servants of God, devoting themselves to this very thing.*
> *Render to all what is due them: tax to whom tax is due;*
> *custom to whom custom; fear to whom fear; honor to whom honor.*

A friend of ours was told by a high-level official in a large secular country that the Christians are the best citizens in their land. They pay their taxes, contribute to the betterment of their communities, and are very law-abiding. However, the government is officially opposed to Christianity. The believers in this country are loyal to their government. They submit to authority and only appeal to a Higher Authority when they have to based on God's standards. These Christians are ministering with their integrity by obeying the principles laid out in Romans 13.

Most of you are living in countries, provinces, states, and cities with varying levels of good governance. Some of you are in desperate situations, living in ungoverned territory or fleeing for your life. Pray for God's governance, being a good witness and trusting Him with your circumstances.

Pray Romans 13:5 and 7-8 over yourself and those for whom you stand guard as a faithful, prayerful watchman (Isaiah 62:6-7).

> *"LORD, help _____ and me be in subjection to our government,*
> *paying our taxes, customs, respect, and honor.*
> *Help us owe nothing to anyone except to love one another,*
> *for in loving our neighbors, we have fulfilled the law.*
> *For the sake of Your name, Jesus~"*

Please read Romans 14.

Meditate on verse 8.

For if we live, we live for the LORD, or if
we die, we die for the LORD;
therefore, whether we live or die, we are the LORD's.

Paul addressed issues dividing the body of Christ in this chapter. Arguments about foods to eat or not eat, beverages to drink or not drink, and which day is best for worshiping God tear down the church rather than build it up. Paul drew the line with this principle: "So then, we pursue the things which make for peace and the building up of one another. Do not tear down the work of God for the sake of food" (vs. 19-20).

Is something dividing your faith community that is really not that important? If people are upset with each other about a non-essential thing, then they are not paying attention to God and building up His people.

Here is the antidote for division within the body of Christ: As a believer, your life is now and forever intertwined with the LORD Jesus Christ. You no longer live for yourself; you live for Him; therefore, live in such a way that you do not hurt the faith of a fellow Christian for whom Christ died (v. 15).

Pray Romans 14:7-9 and 15 over yourself and those for whom you stand guard as a faithful, prayerful watchman (Isaiah 62:6-7).

"LORD, please help _____ and me not live
for ourselves, and not die for ourselves,
for if we live, we live for You, or if we die, we die for You;
therefore, whether we live or die, we are Yours, LORD.
You died and lived again, so You are LORD
of the dead and of the living.
Help us walk in love and not destroy those for whom You died.
For the sake of Your name, Jesus~"

MAY 10

Please read Romans 15.

Meditate on verses 29-30. Paul is speaking.

> *"I know that when I come to you, I will come*
> *in the fullness of the blessing of Christ.*
> *Now I urge you, brethren, by our LORD Jesus*
> *Christ and by the love of the Spirit,*
> *to strive together with me in your prayers to God for me."*

After visiting Jerusalem, Paul hoped to go to Spain and see the Romans on the way (v. 24). He asked the church in Rome to pray for God's blessings for his journey. His prayer requests were quite remarkable—consider praying them for your life's journeys.

Paul wanted to come to the Roman church in the fullness of Christ's blessing (v. 29). Can you imagine how different your time spent with family and friends would be if you encountered each other in "the fullness of the blessing of Christ" (v. 29)? Ask God to make that happen for you and your loved ones.

Paul desired to be rescued from the disobedient and for his service to prove acceptable to the saints (v. 31). Pray for God to do the same for your family.

Paul wanted his journeys joyful and in God's will (v. 32). He hoped for refreshing rest in the company of those he loved (v. 32). Pray for time spent with family and friends to be joyful, refreshing, and restful rather than stressful.

Pray Romans 15:29 and 31-33 over visits with your loved ones as a faithful, prayerful watchman (Isaiah 62:6-7).

> *"LORD, please let _____ and me visit _____ in*
> *the fullness of the blessing of You, Christ.*
> *Rescue us from those who are disobedient and let*
> *our service prove acceptable to the saints.*
> *Let us come to _____ in joy by Your will, God,*
> *and find refreshing rest in their company.*
> *God of peace be with us. Amen."*

MAY 11

Please read Romans 16.

Meditate on verses 25-27.

> *Now to Him who is able to establish you according to my Gospel*
> *and the preaching of Jesus Christ, according*
> *to the revelation of the mystery*
> *which has been kept secret for long ages past, but now is manifested,*
> *and by the Scriptures of the prophets, according*
> *to the commandment of the eternal God,*
> *has been made known to all the nations, leading to obedience of faith;*
> *to the only wise God, through Jesus Christ,*
> *be the glory forever. Amen.*

God inspired Paul to close this letter with these three verses, a single sentence, praising God, summarizing the letter, and catapulting believers to a greater relationship with Him. The sentence opens and closes, acknowledging God as the reason for Christianity and worthy of all praise:

> *Now to Him...the only wise God, through*
> *Jesus Christ, be the glory forever.*

Paul fills in the sentence with truths about God:

- God is able. "Able," the Greek word dynamai, means power.[1]
- God's power establishes you in the Gospel. Romans begins with the same word:

> *For I am not ashamed of the Gospel, for it*
> *is the power of God for salvation.*
> —Romans 1:16a

- ❧ God establishes the Gospel through the preaching of Jesus Christ.
- ❧ At God's command, His mystery, Jesus Christ, is made apparent and visible.
- ❧ God wills all nations to know these truths, believing and following Him.

Pray Romans 16:25-27, praising Almighty God.

> *"Now to You, Father, who is able to establish*
> *_____ and me according to Your Gospel*
> *and the preaching of Jesus Christ,*
> *according to the revelation of the mystery*
> *which has been kept secret for long ages past,*
> *but now is manifested,*
> *and by the Scriptures of the prophets,*
> *according to Your commandment,*
> *Eternal God, has been made known to all the nations,*
> *leading to obedience of faith; to the only wise God,*
> *through Jesus Christ, be the glory forever. Amen."*

1. Retrieved from www.blueletterbible.org/lang/lexicon/lexicon.cfm?Strongs=G1410&t=NASB

Please read Hosea 1.

Meditate on verse 2.

> *When the LORD first spoke through Hosea, the LORD said to Hosea,*
> *"Go, take to yourself a wife of harlotry and have children of harlotry,*
> *for the land commits flagrant harlotry, forsaking the LORD."*

Can you imagine the LORD telling a young preacher to start doing ministry by marrying a prostitute? Well, that is exactly what God told the prophet Hosea to do. Hosea would be God's walking sermon illustration with his wife Gomer and three young children in tow.

The names of the five individuals in this family are important for God's sermon points:

- Hosea means "salvation"[1]
- Gomer means "complete"[2]
- Jezreel means "God sows"[3]
- Lo-ruhamah means "no mercy"[4]
- Lo-ammi means "not my people"[5]

Keep their names and meanings in mind as you continue to read this story of God sowing into the lives of people who do not deserve His mercy for the purpose of bringing salvation and completeness, making them His people.

Pray Hosea 1:7 over a situation where you need the LORD to bring deliverance.

> *"LORD, please have compassion on the house*
> *of _____ and deliver them,*
> *not by bow, sword, battle, horses, or horsemen,*
> *but by You, LORD our God.*
> *For the glory of Your name, Jesus~"*

1. Retrieved from www.blueletterbible.org/lang/lexicon/lexicon.cfm?Strongs=H1954&t=NASB
2. Retrieved from www.blueletterbible.org/lang/lexicon/lexicon.cfm?Strongs=H1586&t=NASB
3. Retrieved from www.blueletterbible.org/lang/lexicon/lexicon.cfm?Strongs=H3157&t=NASB
4. Retrieved from www.blueletterbible.org/lang/lexicon/lexicon.cfm?Strongs=H3819&t=NASB
5. Retrieved from www.blueletterbible.org/lang/lexicon/lexicon.cfm?Strongs=H3818&t=NASB

Please read Hosea 2.

Meditate on verse 1.

> *Say to your brothers, "Ammi," and to your sisters, "Ruhamah."*

Ah, a name change! Ammi means "my people,"[1] and Ruhamah means "to be shown compassion."[2] God removed the Lo, which means "not or no,"[3] from their names— "Not my people," "No compassion" (Hosea 1:6, 9). He miraculously changed the names of these children of a harlot.

And, He miraculously does the same for you. Before becoming a Christian, some of your names were: "Child of wrath" and "Child of the devil" (Ephesians 2:3; 1 John 3:10). Because of God's merciful salvation, some of your new names are: "Child of God," "Child of Promise," and "Child of Light" (John 1:12; Galatians 4:28; Ephesians 5:8).

As a faithful, prayerful watchman (Isaiah 62:6-7), pray Hosea 2:19-20 over those who need the merciful salvation of God in order to receive a name change.

> *"LORD, please betroth _____ to You forever; betroth them to You*
> *in righteousness and justice, in lovingkindness and compassion.*
> *Betroth them to You in faithfulness, so they will know You, LORD.*
> *Thank You for betrothing me to Yourself.*
> *For the sake of Your name, Jesus~"*

---

1. Retrieved from www.blueletterbible.org/lang/lexicon/lexicon.cfm?Strongs=H5971&t=NASB

2. Retrieved from www.blueletterbible.org/lang/lexicon/lexicon.cfm?Strongs=H7355&t=NASB

3. Retrieved from www.blueletterbible.org/lang/lexicon/lexicon.cfm?strongs=H3808&t=NASB

MAY 14

Please read Hosea 3.

Meditate on verse 1.

> *Then the LORD said to me, "Go again; love a*
> *woman who is loved by her husband,*
> *yet an adulteress, even as the LORD loves the sons of Israel,*
> *though they turn to other gods and love raisin cakes."*

God's living sermon illustration took another twist when He commanded Hosea to buy back Gomer after she ran off to continue in adultery and ended up in slavery. Not only did God want Hosea to ransom her from her pathetic situation; He commanded Hosea to love her again. Unbelievable!

Yet, here is God's story of salvation perfectly illustrated by an enslaved harlot and a man willing to pay all he had to save her.

Think about it. Before Christ, you were enslaved to sin, loving the world and its ways more than the God who created you. Jesus gave everything for you, dying to pay the price of redemption for an enslaved prostitute. Not only does Jesus buy you out of that slavery, He loves you more than His own life and wants to intimately and eternally walk with you. Amazing!

Pray Hosea 3:5 in thankful commitment to the LORD as His faithful, prayerful watchman (Isaiah 62:6-7).

> *"LORD my God, Jesus my King, I return and seek You.*
> *I come trembling to You and Your goodness.*
> *May _____ do the same before the last days.*
> *Because of Your name, Jesus~"*

MAY 15

Please read Hosea 4.

Meditate on verses 1-2.

> *Listen to the Word of the LORD, O sons of Israel, for the LORD*
> *has a case against the inhabitants of the land because there is*
> *no faithfulness or kindness or knowledge of God in the land.*
> *There is swearing, deception, murder, stealing, and adultery.*
> *They employ violence, so that bloodshed follows bloodshed.*

God's people did not behave like His people—their actions and attributes were opposite of His, and they were perishing (vs. 1-2, 6). God held the priests accountable for the grievous situation because they did not give the people the knowledge of His Word (v. 6).

Just as God took up His case against Israel and the priests nearly 2800 years ago, He examines His people today—no knowledge of God in the land, swearing, deception, murder, stealing, adultery, violence, and bloodshed. Would He condemn today's priests, preachers, teachers, professors, leaders, and parents?

Take God's Word to heart, giving heed to the LORD (v. 10):

- God and His Word do not change; commit to know what He says.
- Be taught by those who know the Bible is inerrant, teaching every Word.
- Be the parent, friend, teacher, leader, preacher, Christian—who unashamedly shares the knowledge of God, so others are not destroyed.

Pray to be the opposite of Hosea 4:6 over yourself and those for whom you stand guard as a faithful, prayerful watchman (Isaiah 62:6-7).

> *"LORD, let Your people no longer be destroyed for lack of knowledge.*
> *Do not let _____ and me reject Your knowledge.*
> *Make us Your faithful priests who remember Your law and teach it.*
> *LORD, do not forget our children.*
> *In Your name, Jesus~"*

MAY 16

Please read Hosea 5.

Meditate on verse 1a.

> *Hear this, O priests! Give heed, O house of Israel!*
> *Listen, O house of the king! For the judgment applies to you.*

The LORD held everyone accountable for their deeds and refusal to know Him (vs. 1-2, 4). God's judgment was no respecter of one's rank or position—clergy, kings, and common people came under the scrutiny of God and His Word.

Let God examine your life with His Words from Hosea 5. Ask Him to reveal areas of unconfessed sin and seek His forgiveness as His faithful, prayerful watchman (Isaiah 62:6-7).

> *"LORD, please do not withdraw from me! Search me, O LORD.*

- ๑ Am I a snare to others (v. 1)?
- ๑ Am I a revolter deep in depravity (v. 2)?
- ๑ Do I play the harlot and defile myself (v. 3)?
- ๑ Do my deeds keep me from returning to You (v. 4)?
- ๑ Is there a spirit of harlotry within me that keeps me from knowing You (v. 4)?
- ๑ Does my pride testify against me (v. 5)?
- ๑ Am I stumbling in iniquity and causing others to stumble with me (v. 5)?
- ๑ Am I seeking You, LORD, but not finding You (v. 6)?
- ๑ Have I dealt treacherously against You (v. 7)?
- ๑ Have I borne illegitimate children—those not truly followers of Christ because of watered-down teaching (v. 7)?
- ๑ Am I following man's command instead of Your command, God (v. 11)?

> *I acknowledge my guilt and seek Your face.*
> *Please forgive me in Your name, Jesus~"*

MAY 17

Please read Hosea 6.

Meditate on verse 1.

Come, let us return to the LORD. For He
has torn us, but He will heal us;
He has wounded us, but He will bandage us.

Oh, the joy that comes with restoration! God's goal is always restoration. He gave His life for the purpose of restoring your relationship with Him. Do not let the liar and father of lies (John 8:44) deceive you into believing you have sinned so badly and are so far from God there is no hope for you. Hosea is all about God loving and restoring the hopeless. Just look at the words He uses in the first three verses of this chapter:

- heal
- bandage
- revive
- raise up
- live

- press on
- going forth
- come to
- spring rain watering

Only God could offer such hope to those of us who have transgressed and dealt treacherously against Him (v. 7).

Pray Hosea 6:1-3 over yourself and those for whom you stand guard as a faithful, prayerful watchman (Isaiah 62:6-7).

"LORD, _____ and I come and return to You.
You have torn us, but You will heal us.
You have wounded us, but You will bandage us.
You will revive us after two days; You will
raise us up on the third day,
that we may live before You. Let us press on to know You, LORD.
Your going forth is as certain as the dawn, and
You will come to us like the rain,
like the spring rain watering the earth.
Water us in Your name, Jesus~"

Please read Hosea 7.

Meditate on verse 12.

> *When they go, I will spread My net over them;*
> *I will bring them down like the birds of the sky.*
> *I will chastise them in accordance with the*
> *proclamation to their assembly.*

Observe God's intimate involvement with Israel. He never takes His eyes off of her. He knows all her evil, wicked deeds, yet He desires to heal her (v. 1). In disobedience, the people seek help from Egypt, Assyria—anyone—except the One who can actually bring deliverance (vs. 10-11). God wants to redeem; they continue to rebel. God's persevering pursuit of Israel is incredibly amazing.

Miraculously, He pursues you and your loved ones with the same dogged determination. Take that truth to heart as you pray for those running from the LORD. Hosea 7 gives you lots of Scripture to pray over them as their faithful, prayerful watchman (Isaiah 62:6-7). Prayers formed from Hosea 7:10-16 are printed below.

> *"LORD, the pride of _____ testifies against them,*
> *yet they have not returned to You, nor have they sought You.*
> *They are like a silly dove without sense. Spread Your net over them;*
> *bring them down like the birds of the sky.*
> *Chastise them in order to save them!*
> *They have strayed from You; destruction is theirs,*
> *for they have rebelled against You.*
> *Redeem them, LORD! Let them stop speaking lies against You!*
> *Make them cry to You from their heart when they wail on their beds.*
> *Make them stop turning away from You! Please*
> *train and strengthen their arms;*
> *do not let them devise evil against You. May they turn upward;*
> *do not let them be deceitful. Remove from them an insolent tongue.*
> *For the sake of Your name, Jesus~"*

Please read Hosea 8.

Meditate on verse 7.

> *For they sow the wind, and they reap the whirlwind.*
> *The standing grain has no heads; it yields no grain.*
> *Should it yield, strangers would swallow it up.*

Notice how deceived Israel is. They cry out to God claiming to know Him, yet they do not know God at all. They choose their own kings, appoint their own princes, make their own idols, and completely forget their Maker (vs. 2, 4, 14). Blatant rebellion against God results in being swallowed by their enemies (v. 8).

Examine your life. Do you profess to know God, crying out to Him from time to time, yet you make your own plans, do your own thing, and live your own life without really giving much thought to your Maker? That kind of lifestyle results in reaping a whirlwind instead of a bountiful crop of life-giving grain (v. 7).

Confess areas of pride and self-sufficiency and pray Hosea 8:7-8 and 11-14 over yourself and those for whom you stand guard as a faithful, prayerful watchman (Isaiah 62:6-7).

> *"LORD, _____ and I have sown the*
> *wind and reaped the whirlwind.*
> *Please forgive us. Please let us yield grain, and*
> *do not let strangers swallow it up.*
> *LORD, do not let us be swallowed up! Do*
> *not let us multiply altars for sin.*
> *You have written ten thousand precepts of Your law for*
> *us; may we not regard them as a strange thing. Please*
> *forgive our sins and do not remember our iniquity.*
> *Though we deserve it, please do not punish us for our sins.*
> *Let us never forget You, our Maker. Please do not consume us.*
> *In Your name, Jesus~"*

Please read Hosea 9.

Meditate on verse 9.

> *They have gone deep in depravity as in the days of Gibeah;*
> *He will remember their iniquity; He will punish their sins.*

What a sad chapter in God's Word! Ephraim (one of the twelve tribes of Israel and a name for the northern kingdom of Israel in Hosea[1]) had been a watchman and a prophet with the LORD (v. 8). Tragically, the people got full of themselves and full of sin; the results were devastating—the death of their children, hated by God, and wandering among the nations (vs. 10-17).

As you ponder these difficult truths from Hosea 9, thank God for the salvation He gives you through Jesus Christ. Do not take lightly His everlasting love for you. Purpose in your heart to hate sin like God does because trivializing and toying with it results in devastation.

Pray to be the opposite of Hosea 9:8-9 and 17 over yourself and those for whom you stand guard as a faithful, prayerful watchman (Isaiah 62:6-7).

> *"LORD, keep _____ and me with You as*
> *Your faithful watchmen and prophets.*
> *Keep us from the snare of a bird catcher. Remove*
> *hostility from Your house, God.*
> *Keep us from deep depravity. Forgive our*
> *iniquity and do not remember it.*
> *Keep us from sin and its punishment. Do not cast us away.*
> *Make us listen to You. Keep us from wandering.*
> *In Your name, Jesus~"*

---

1. Retrieved from www.blueletterbible.org/lang/lexicon/lexicon.cfm?Strongs=H669&t=NASB

Please read Hosea 10.

Meditate on verses 12-13.

> *Sow with a view to righteousness, reap in accordance with kindness;*
> *break up your fallow ground, for it is time to seek the LORD*
> *until He comes to rain righteousness on you.*
> *You have plowed wickedness; you have reaped injustice;*
> *You have eaten the fruit of lies.*
> *Because you have trusted in your way, in your numerous warriors.*

Israel used God's fertile blessings to produce fruit for herself rather than fruit for God (v. 1). As she continued to selfishly plow and harvest, she became more and more wicked, eating the fruit of the lies of self-sufficiency and self-made success (v. 13). God said, "Enough!" But rather than destroy her completely, He harnessed her with His yoke and gave her the opportunity to harvest righteousness rather than injustice (vs. 12-13).

> *"Take My yoke upon you and learn from Me,*
> *for I am gentle and humble in heart,*
> *and you will find rest for your souls."*
> —Matthew 11:29

Ask God to show you areas where you are plowing with a view of yourself, rather than a view of God's Kingdom and His righteousness. Get in the yoke with God and pray Hosea 10:11-12 over yourself and those for whom you stand guard as a faithful, prayerful watchman (Isaiah 62:6-7).

> *"LORD, harness _____ and me with Your yoke. Let us*
> *sow with a view to righteousness and reap in accordance*
> *with kindness. Break up our fallow ground,*
> *for it is time to seek You, LORD! Come and rain righteousness on us!*
> *For the glory of Your name, Jesus~"*

MAY 22

Please read Hosea 11.

Meditate on verses 8-9.

> *How can I give you up, O Ephraim? How*
> *can I surrender you, O Israel?*
> *How can I make you like Admah? How can I treat you like Zeboiim?*
> *My heart is turned over within Me; all My compassions are kindled.*
> *I will not execute My fierce anger; I will not destroy Ephraim again.*
> *For I am God and not man, the Holy One in your midst,*
> *and I will not come in wrath.*

Oh, the steadfast love of God! Oh, the incomprehensible compassion of the Almighty! Oh, His forgiveness and mercy! Oh, His unquenchable desire for His people to know Him!

Perhaps God's unending pursuit of His rebellious children leaves you shaking your head. Yet, it is His determination to not give-up on Israel—and you—and me—that drives Him to the cross to pay the price for mankind's sinful rebellion. Incredible!

Come humbly and gratefully to the LORD, thanking Him for all He has done and is doing for you and those you love by praying the words from Hosea 11:3-4 and 9-10 as a faithful, prayerful watchman (Isaiah 62:6-7).

> *"LORD, thank You for teaching _____ and*
> *me how to walk with You.*
> *Thank You for taking us in Your arms and for healing us.*
> *Thank You for leading us with the bonds of Your love.*
> *Thank You for lifting the yoke from our jaws*
> *and for bending down to feed us.*
> *Thank You for not executing Your fierce*
> *anger and for not destroying us.*
> *You are God, the Holy One in our midst, and*
> *You will not come against us in wrath.*
> *We will walk after You, LORD, and You will*
> *roar like a lion. Indeed, You will roar.*
> *And we will come trembling before You—*
> *In Your name, Jesus~"*

Please read Hosea 12.

Meditate on verses 1a and 8.

> *Ephraim feeds on wind, and pursues the east wind continually;*
> *he multiplies lies and violence.*
> *And Ephraim said, "Surely I have become rich;*
> *I have found wealth for myself.*
> *In all my labors, they will find in me no*
> *iniquity, which would be sin."*

Ephraim (Israel) was so delusional in their sin they convinced themselves they weren't sinning (v. 8). God said they were feeding on wind, and as their pride and wealth increased, God condemned them for multiplying their violence and lies (vs. 1, 8, 14).

On what are you feeding? Satan and the world want you to feed on a continual diet of wind, leaving you unfulfilled and longing for more because what you are devouring is actually nothingness. God wants to fill you with His divine power, which gives you everything you need for life and Godliness (2 Peter 1:3). Stop eating the wind by devouring Christ and His Word.

> *Man shall not live on bread alone, but on EVERY Word*
> *that proceeds out of the mouth of God.*
> *—Deuteronomy 8:3; Matthew 4:4*

Pray God's Word from Hosea 12:1 and 6 over yourself and those for whom you stand guard as a faithful, prayerful watchman (Isaiah 62:6-7).

> *"LORD, do not let _____ and me feed on wind*
> *and pursue the east wind any longer.*
> *Please stop our multiplication of lies and violence.*
> *Our covenant is with You, LORD! We return to You, our God.*
> *Help us observe kindness and justice and wait for You continually.*
> *In Your name, Jesus~"*

MAY 24

Please read Hosea 13, taking to heart the LORD's condemnation of Israel and purposing to live wholeheartedly for Him so He does not have to say these words to you.

Meditate on verse 9.

> *It is your destruction, O Israel, that you are*
> *against Me, against your help.*

Thankfully, God recorded the events from the past, so we do not have to make the same mistakes. Hear and heed God's warning and exhortation from 1 Corinthians 10:11-12, for He does not want you to take His Word lightly, treating it merely as a history book:

> *Now these things happened to them as an example,*
> *and they were written for our instruction, upon whom*
> *the ends of the ages have come. Therefore, let him who*
> *thinks he stands take heed that he does not fall.*

Pray the words from Hosea 13:1-6, 9, and 12, asking God to keep you and those you love from sinning.

> *"LORD, do not let _____ and me exalt ourselves.*
> *We do not want to die because we have done wrong.*
> *Stop us from sinning more and more, becoming like the morning cloud*
> *and dew which soon disappears. Do not let us be like chaff,*
> *which is blown away from the threshing floor*
> *and like smoke from a chimney.*
> *LORD, You are our God! We know no other god except You!*
> *There is no savior besides You!*
> *You have cared for us in the wilderness, in the land of drought.*
> *Do not let us become satisfied and proud in the pasture You provide.*
> *Let us never forget You! Let us never be against You!*
> *LORD, You are our Help! Help us, LORD!*
> *Free us from the iniquity bound up in us! Do not let us store up sin!*
> *Because of Your name, Jesus~"*

Please read Hosea 14.

Meditate on verses 1 and 4. The LORD is speaking.

> *"Return, O Israel, to the LORD your God, for you*
> *have stumbled because of your iniquity.*
> *I will heal their apostasy; I will love them freely,*
> *for My anger has turned away from them."*

God's steadfast love and unending mercy undergird His gracious invitation to return to Him. Hear the LORD as He extends the invitation to you, filling the blank with your name (vs. 1-2):

> *Return, O _____, to the LORD your God,*
> *for you have stumbled because of your iniquity.*
> *Take words with you and return to the LORD.*
> *Say to Him, "Take away all iniquity and receive me graciously,*
> *that I may present the fruit of my lips."*

Pray Hosea 14 in acceptance of God's gracious invitation.

> *"LORD, I have stumbled because of my iniquity.*
> *I am returning to You. Take away all iniquity and receive me*
> *graciously. Please receive these words as fruit from my lips.*
> *No one can save me but You, LORD. Never again will I say,*
> *'My god,' to the work of my hands, for in You, I find mercy.*
> *LORD, heal my apostasy. Thank You for loving me freely and*
> *turning Your anger away from me. Be like the dew to me. Let*
> *me blossom like the lily and take root like the cedars of Lebanon.*
> *Let my shoots sprout and my beauty be like the olive tree*
> *and my fragrance like the cedars of Lebanon. Let those whom I*
> *love again raise grain and blossom like the vine. Let our renown*
> *be like the wine of Lebanon. Let us have nothing more to do with*
> *idols. It is You who answers and looks after us. You are like a*
> *luxuriant cypress; from You comes our fruit. Make us wise, so we*
> *understand these things; make us discerning, so we know them, for*
> *Your ways are right, LORD, and the righteous will walk in them.*
> *Make us Your righteous ones. Keep us from*
> *transgressors who stumble in Your ways.*
> *In Your name, Jesus~"*

MAY 26

Please read Galatians 1.

Meditate on verse 10.

> *For am I now seeking the favor of men, or of*
> *God? Or am I striving to please men?*
> *If I were still trying to please men, I would*
> *not be a bond-servant of Christ.*

After God used Paul to start the church in Galatia, Paul wrote to encourage them in their faith. This church was doing well until they started listening to false teachings that added additional requirements for being a Christian (v. 6).

Paul's frustration with them is found throughout the letter because he realizes the stakes are high for his beloved Galatians. When salvation is involved, and people miss it because of false teaching, it is truly a tragedy. So, Paul wrote boldly, hoping they would turn back to the truth.

Paul taught that pleasing men over pleasing God prevents believers from becoming bond-servants of the LORD Jesus Christ, willingly surrendering to serve and please Him.

In order to be a true disciple of Jesus, you have to make Him LORD (Master) of your life. Are you in a situation where pleasing someone else is preventing you or others from being in a right relationship with God and doing His will?

Pray Galatians 1:10 over yourself and those for whom you stand guard as a faithful, prayerful watchman (Isaiah 62:6-7).

> *"LORD, show _____ and me where we are seeking*
> *the favor of men or striving to please men.*
> *Help us to seek Your favor, God, and be*
> *Your bond-servants, LORD Jesus.*
> *In Your name, Jesus~"*

MAY 27

Please read Galatians 2.

Meditate on verses 4-5.

> *But it was because of the false brethren secretly brought in,*
> *who had sneaked in to spy out our liberty*
> *which we have in Christ Jesus,*
> *in order to bring us into bondage. But we did not*
> *yield in subjection to them for even an hour, so that*
> *the truth of the Gospel would remain with you.*

Paul's frustrations continue in this chapter. Working to integrate Christians of Jewish and non-Jewish backgrounds, he traveled to Jerusalem to learn what was required to be a believer. In addition, he received a blessing to continue ministering to the non-Jewish people. Some desired all Christians to follow all of the Jewish standards found in the Law, or the Old Testament. Paul was caught in a type of trap that ended up with Titus refusing to go through a Jewish ritual not necessary for salvation or good standing in the Body of Christ (v. 3).

You may be in a situation where you are challenged by lost people at school, home, work, or even church to compromise your beliefs to fit in with their group. When rules, power, and teachings have the effect of preventing the Gospel from going to others, then you need to pray for God to work in your life to have courage and wisdom to intercede in the situation, so others can know the truth.

Pray Galatians 2:4-5 over yourself and those for whom you stand guard as a faithful, prayerful watchman (Isaiah 62:6-7).

> *"LORD, expose false brethren.*
> *Thank You for the liberty that _____ and*
> *I have in You, Christ Jesus.*
> *Do not let false brethren bring us into bondage.*
> *Help us not to yield in subjection to them for even an hour.*
> *Let the truth of the Gospel remain with the believers.*
> *In Your name, Jesus~"*

Please read Galatians 3.

Meditate verses 26-28.

For you are all sons of God through faith in Christ Jesus.
For all of you who were baptized into Christ
have clothed yourselves with Christ.
There is neither Jew nor Greek; there is neither slave nor free man;
there is neither male nor female, for you are all one in Christ Jesus.

Paul continued to help the Galatians see the difference between seeking God with the Law and seeking Him with the Spirit. Salvation comes as a result of the Spirit in a new covenant that frees believers from the Law; salvation is not perfected by works of the Law.

Jesus very specifically creates a new system of righteousness. His redemption on the cross allows both Jews and Gentiles to receive the promise of the Spirit (vs. 13-14). The Spirit of God perfects believers in His holiness, convicting and teaching Christians how to live in Christ (John 16:7-15).

In verses 2 and 5, Paul uses a phrase "hearing with faith" to describe how people become Christians. You hear the Gospel and believe it. Hearing with faith is the faith that creates Christians and sets them apart from those who are not believers. And once you have received Jesus by faith and become sons of God through faith in Jesus Christ, your status changes in how you are viewed by God (vs. 26, 28).

Pray Galatians 3:5 and 28 over yourself and those for whom you stand guard as a faithful, prayerful watchman (Isaiah 62:6-7).

"LORD, help _____ and me to hear by faith.
Thank You for providing Your Spirit,
LORD, work miracles among us.
Help us be one in You, Christ Jesus.
In Your name, Jesus~"

MAY 29

Please read Galatians 4.

Meditate on verse 6.

> *Because you are sons, God has sent forth the*
> *Spirit of His Son into our hearts,*
> *crying, "Abba! Father!"*

Yesterday, in Galatians 3:26, you learned that salvation is provided by Jesus, and you become "sons of God through faith in Jesus Christ." In Chapter 4, Paul defines that relationship even more.

> *But when the fullness of time came, God sent*
> *forth His Son, born of a woman,*
> *born under the Law, so that He might redeem*
> *those who were under the Law,*
> *that we might receive the adoption as sons. Because you are sons,*
> *God has sent forth the Spirit of His Son into*
> *our hearts, crying, "Abba! Father!"*
> *Therefore, you are no longer a slave, but a son;*
> *and if a son, then an heir through God.*
> —Galatians 4:4-7

It is amazing how much God loves you! Look at all of the things He did so you can be His child who calls Him, "Abba, Father" (v. 6). (Abba means "Daddy.") None of us have perfect fathers to emulate when we think about God. You may not have had a father in your life. You may have had a horrible one. A woman came to us with tears of joy after hearing a sermon about how much God wants to be our Abba Father, Daddy. She said, "My earthly father never wanted me. I am so happy that God wants me! For the first time in my life, I have a dad!"

Pray Galatians 4:4-7 over yourself and those for whom you stand guard as a faithful, prayerful watchman (Isaiah 62:6-7).

> *"LORD, thank You for working in the fullness of time.*
> *Thank You for sending Your Son.*
> *Thank You for redeeming _____ and me as adopted sons.*
> *Thank You for Your Spirit by which we cry out, 'Abba! Father!'*
> *Please redeem _____ and make them Your child and heir.*
> *In Your name, Jesus~"*

Please read Galatians 5.

Meditate on verses 16 and 25.

> *But I say, walk by the Spirit, and you will not*
> *carry out of the desire of the flesh.*
> *If we live by the Spirit, let us also walk by the Spirit.*

The Galatian church was learning not to seek righteousness in the Law. Verse 7 is sad. Paul asked them why they were no longer running well with the LORD. They had been hindered, but this was not from the God who called them. God deeply desired the Galatians to journey with Him. He wanted them free from the things negatively affecting their walks.

Is there something in your life that hinders your walk or run with the LORD? Is there a teaching you heard that made you doubt or believe less? Is there a persuasive teacher you listen to drawing your attention away from the LORD? Do they have rules you have to follow? Do they talk about themselves more than the LORD?

God wants you to walk with Him by being in step with the Spirit and bearing the fruit of the Spirit (vs. 22-23).

Pray Galatians 5:16 and 25 over yourself and those for whom you stand guard as a faithful, prayerful watchman (Isaiah 62:6-7).

> *"LORD, help _____ and me walk by the Spirit.*
> *Do not let us carry out of the desires of the flesh.*
> *Help us live by the Spirit.*
> *Let us walk with You by walking with the Spirit.*
> *In Your name, Jesus~"*

Please read Galatians 6.

Meditate on verses 7-9.

> *Do not be deceived, God is not mocked;*
> *for whatever a man sows, this he will also reap.*
> *For the one who sows to his own flesh will*
> *from the flesh reap corruption,*
> *but the one who sows to the Spirit will*
> *from the Spirit reap eternal life.*
> *Let us not lose heart in doing good,*
> *for in due time we will reap if we do not grow weary.*

Paul concluded this letter to the church of Galatia, wanting them to be on the right track and living as a church that understood the Christian life does not find its righteousness in the Law. He wanted them to stop investing time and faith into things that do not honor Jesus.

Paul used a farming illustration of sowing to make a simple truth. If you plant wheat, then wheat will grow. If you plant rice, then rice will grow. If you plant things of the flesh, you will reap corruption. If you plant things of the Spirit, you will reap eternal life.

Are you thinking and doing things in your mind and body not of God? Stop planting those things and start planting things of God into your life.

Be encouraged to keep running the race of faith Jesus has called you to run. He wants you to keep going with Him and finish strong!

Pray Galatians 6:8-9 over yourself and those for whom you stand guard as a faithful, prayerful watchman (Isaiah 62:6-7).

> *"LORD, help _____ and me not sow to*
> *our own flesh and reap corruption.*
> *Help us sow to the Spirit, and from the Spirit, reap eternal life.*
> *Let us not lose heart in doing good, for You*
> *promised in due time, we will reap.*
> *Help us not grow weary.*
> *In Your name, Jesus~"*

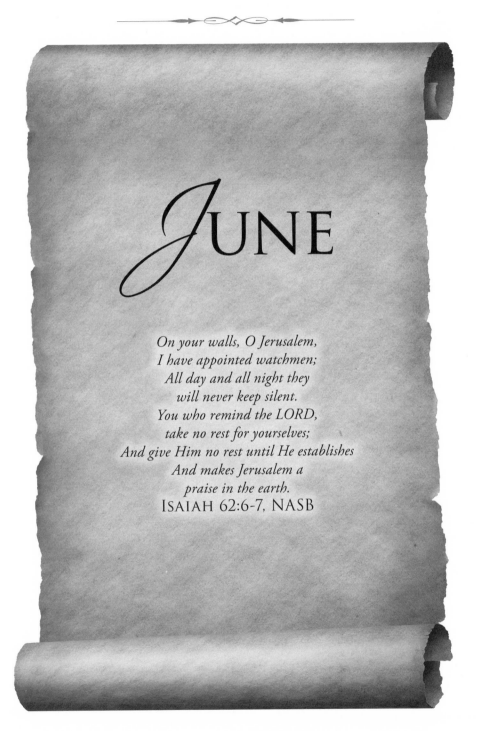

JUNE

On your walls, O Jerusalem,
I have appointed watchmen;
All day and all night they
will never keep silent.
You who remind the LORD,
take no rest for yourselves;
And give Him no rest until He establishes
And makes Jerusalem a
praise in the earth.
ISAIAH 62:6-7, NASB

JUNE 1

Please read Nehemiah 1.

Meditate on verse 11.

> *"O LORD, I beseech You, may Your ear be*
> *attentive to the prayer of Your servant*
> *and the prayer of Your servants who delight to revere Your name,*
> *and make Your servant successful today and*
> *grant him compassion before this man."*

Nearly 100 years had passed since the Israelites began returning to their homeland after 70 years of exile in Babylon, and the walls of Jerusalem were still torn down. When Nehemiah heard the report that the people and the city were a wreck, he prayed fervently (vs. 3-4). Nehemiah knew there was only One who could fix this hopeless situation.

What is your first response when you receive distressful news? Learn from Nehemiah: Stop what you are doing and cry out to God; fast, confess, and pray as a faithful, prayerful watchman (Isaiah 62:6-7).

Start your prayer with the words from Nehemiah 1:5-7 and 10-11.

> *"I beseech You, O LORD God of heaven, the great and*
> *awesome God, who preserves the covenant and lovingkindness*
> *for those who love You and keep Your commandments;*
> *let Your ear now be attentive and Your eyes*
> *open to hear the prayer of Your servant*
> *which I am praying before You now, day and night,*
> *on behalf of _____ and me,*
> *confessing our sins which we have sinned against You; I and*
> *my father's house have sinned. We have acted very corruptly*
> *against You and have not kept the commandments,*
> *nor the statutes, nor the ordinances which You commanded us.*
> *We are Your servants and Your people whom*
> *You redeemed by Your great power*
> *and by Your strong hand. O LORD, I beseech You, may*
> *Your ear be attentive to the prayer of Your servant and the*
> *prayer of Your servants who delight to revere Your name,*
> *and make Your servants successful today and*
> *grant us compassion before You and man.*
> *In Your name, Jesus~"*

JUNE 2

Please read Nehemiah 2.

Meditate on verse 4.

> *Then the king said to me, "What would you request?"*
> *So I prayed to the God of heaven.*

Can you imagine a king, president, boss, or other official saying to you, "I perceive you have a need; tell me everything you request." Those were the words Nehemiah heard from his boss, the king of Persia, after fasting and praying for God to grant him success and compassion before the man (Nehemiah 1:11). As God answered his prayer, Nehemiah did not stop praying; he continued talking to the LORD to know exactly what he should ask of the king. God told him what to say, and King Artaxerxes granted Nehemiah's requests because the good hand of God was on him (v. 8).

How would you respond to someone who wanted to give you everything you needed? Learn from Nehemiah who first talked to the Giver of all things, seeking His desires.

> *Every good thing given and every perfect gift is from*
> *above, coming down from the Father of lights, with*
> *whom there is no variation or shifting shadow.*
> *—James 1:17*

As a faithful, prayerful watchman (Isaiah 62:6-7), pray Nehemiah 2:4, 8, 17-18, and 20 over situations where you and those you love have needs.

> *"LORD, I am praying to You, the God of heaven.*
> *Please grant _____ and me these*
> *requests; let Your good hand be upon us.*
> *You see the bad situation we are in, that _____ is desolate.*
> *LORD, help us to rebuild so we will no longer be a reproach.*
> *Let Your hand be favorable to us. Let us arise and build;*
> *let us put our hands to the good work. God*
> *of heaven, please give us success.*
> *Cause us, Your servants, to arise and build.*
> *For the sake of Your name, Jesus~"*

Please read Nehemiah 3.

Meditate on verse 12.

> *Next to him, Shallum the son of Hallohesh,*
> *the official of half the district of Jerusalem,*
> *made repairs, he and his daughters.*

Repair is a repeated word in this chapter. It is the Hebrew word *chazaq*, which means "to repair and strengthen, sustain, encourage, make bold and firm, to support"[1] So many people were involved in repairing the walls and gates of Jerusalem. How encouraging this must have been to Nehemiah! And it was certainly a big deal to God because He recorded their names for eternity.

As you think about this chapter, let the Holy Spirit convict you of areas in your life and the lives of those you love that need repair. Let God encourage and sustain you to complete the task. Let Him give you the words and actions to embolden others to repair and rebuild, so they can be firm in Christ and His will. Making repairs is a big deal to God with eternal consequences.

Don't procrastinate in making the repairs God tells you to make. Mend relationships; build your prayer life; strengthen your walk with Christ by faithfully being with His church and in His Word. Be firm in your commitment to follow Him.

Pray Nehemiah 3:20 over yourself and those for whom you stand guard as a faithful, prayerful watchman (Isaiah 62:6-7).

> *"LORD, help _____ and me zealously*
> *repair another section of our lives.*
> *In Your name, Jesus~"*

---

1. *Retrieved from www.blueletterbible.org/lang/lexicon/lexicon.cfm?Strongs=H2388&t=NASB*

JUNE 4

Please read Nehemiah 4.

Meditate on verse 15.

> *When our enemies heard that it was known to us,*
> *and that God had frustrated their plan,*
> *then all of us returned to the wall, each one to his work.*

What an encouraging chapter for discouraging times! The antagonists, Sanballat and Tobiah, angry that the walls of Jerusalem were being rebuilt, insulted and belittled the Jews (vs. 1-3). Rather than respond to their demeaning comments, Nehemiah talked to the LORD about the frustrating situation, giving God his enemies. Then, Nehemiah armed his builders; some stood guard as others built; some laid brick with one hand while holding a weapon in the other. Naysayers would not stop the work of the LORD!

Be aware of "Sanballats" and "Tobiahs" in your life. They are those who mock what God is doing and try to demoralize you by saying things like: "That will never work; it costs too much; you will never get enough people to help; it's impossible!" Give your Sanballat and Tobiah to God; do not be afraid of them—they are often bullies who are simply jealous of what God is doing in your life. Arm yourself with the Word of God, praying over the situation and obediently doing everything God tells you.

Pray Nehemiah 4:10, 14-15, and 20 over difficult situations as a faithful, prayerful watchman (Isaiah 62:6-7).

> *"LORD, the strength of _____ and*
> *me is failing, yet there is much rubbish,*
> *and we ourselves are unable to rebuild....*
> *Do not let us be afraid of _____ LORD,*
> *You are great and awesome;*
> *help us fight for our brothers, our sons, our*
> *daughters, our wives, and our homes.*
> *God, frustrate the plan of our enemies, and let us return to our work.*
> *Rally us, LORD! God, You will fight for us!*
> *In Your name, Jesus~"*

Please read Nehemiah 5.

Meditate on verse 15.

> *But the former governors who were before*
> *me laid burdens on the people*
> *and took from them bread and wine besides forty shekels of silver;*
> *even their servants domineered the people.*
> *But I did not do so because of the fear of God.*

Rebuilding the wall took a financial toll on many of the people because time spent rebuilding did not leave time for providing for the needs of their families. Fields and homes were mortgaged to buy food and pay taxes. Children were sold into slavery. Moneylenders charged exorbitant interest rates. The situation was dire, and Nehemiah intervened as an excellent leader. He persuaded the nobles and rulers to stop exacting usury from their fellow Israelites (v. 7). The fields, vineyards, olive groves, houses, money, grain, wine, and oil were returned to their original owners (vs. 11-12). Nehemiah led by example, not eating from the governor's food allowance or laying heavy burdens on the people (vs. 14-15). He worked on the wall himself, and his servants' time was spent building the wall instead of waiting on Nehemiah (v. 16). Nehemiah even shared his dinner table with over 150 guests each day at his own expense (v. 18). Incredible! What was his motivation for being so above reproach? Nehemiah feared God (v. 15).

Thankfully you have the book of Nehemiah to help you become a great, God-fearing leader. Ask God to make you selfless, hard-working, and above reproach. Ask Him to make you His servant who fears Him for the sake of others.

Pray Nehemiah 5:19 over yourself as a faithful, prayerful watchman (Isaiah 62:6-7).

> *"Remember me, O my God, for good,*
> *according to all that I have done for this people.*
> *In Your name, Jesus~"*

JUNE 6

Please read Nehemiah 6.

Meditate on verse 9.

> *For all of them were trying to frighten us, thinking,*
> *"They will become discouraged with the*
> *work, and it will not be done."*
> *But now, O God, strengthen my hands.*

What an excellent and discerning leader Nehemiah was! Sanballat's threatening and slanderous letters did not dissuade Nehemiah from finishing Jerusalem's wall. He simply replied with: "Such things as you are saying have not been done, but you are inventing them in your own mind" (v. 8).

When Shemaiah tried to lure him into the temple to seek protection, Nehemiah discerned God had not sent him; he was only saying what Tobiah and Sanballat paid him to say (v. 12). Rather than worry about his enemies, Nehemiah focused on the goal of completing the wall, asking God to strengthen his hands (v. 9). Miraculously, the wall was finished in 52 days and the enemies defeated because of Almighty God (vs. 16-17).

What task has God given you? Is someone discouraging you from completing it? Ask the LORD to strengthen your hands. Ask Him for discernment to perceive the motives of others and how to respond. Ask Him to make you above reproach in every area of your life. Let Him accomplish His work in you.

Pray Nehemiah 6:9 and 16 over yourself and those for whom you stand guard as a faithful, prayerful watchman (Isaiah 62:6-7).

> *"LORD, let no one frighten _____ and*
> *me. Do not let us become discouraged*
> *with Your work, and it not be done. Now,*
> *O God, strengthen our hands.*
> *Let all our enemies hear and see what You are doing.*
> *Let them lose their confidence when they recognize that this work*
> *has been accomplished with Your help, God.*
> *In Your name, Jesus~"*

JUNE 7

Please read Nehemiah 7.

Meditate on verse 2.

> *Then I put Hanani, my brother, and Hananiah, the*
> *commander of the fortress, in charge of Jerusalem, for he*
> *was a faithful man and feared God more than many.*

Nehemiah chose Hananiah to be in charge of Jerusalem because he was a faithful, God-fearing man. Wow, what an admirable description of a person! Hananiah was faithful. This means he was "stable, trustworthy, and established."[1] He also feared God, meaning he "stood in awe of, reverenced, honored, respected, and was astonished with"[2] the LORD.

Do "faithful" and "God-fearing" describe you and those you love? Pray for the LORD to establish those characteristics in you and those for whom you stand guard as a faithful, prayerful watchman (Isaiah 62:6-7) by praying Nehemiah 7:2 and 5a.

> *"LORD, make _____ and me faithful,*
> *stable, trustworthy, and established in You.*
> *Let us fear You more than many. May we always stand in awe of,*
> *reverence, honor, respect, and be astonished with You, LORD.*
> *Let us be obedient to do everything You put into our hearts to do.*
> *For the glory of Your name, Jesus~"*

1. Retrieved from www.blueletterbible.org/lang/lexicon/lexicon.cfm?Strongs=H571&t=NASB
2. Retrieved from www.blueletterbible.org/lang/lexicon/lexicon.cfm?Strongs=H3372&t=NASB

Please read Nehemiah 8.

Meditate on verse 2.

> *Then Ezra the priest brought the law before the*
> *assembly of men, women, and all who could listen with*
> *understanding, on the first day of the seventh month.*

What a beautiful chapter for how to appropriately respond to God's Word! Ponder these truths:

- The people asked for God's Word, attentively listening to it with understanding (vs. 1-3).
- When God's Word was opened, all the people stood up (v. 5).
- Ezra, the priest and reader of the Word, blessed the LORD the great God. The people raised their hands and said, "Amen, Amen!" Then, they bowed low and worshiped (v. 6).
- The people stayed in their place while the Word of God was explained to them (vs. 7-8).
- The people wept when they heard God's Word (v. 9).
- The leaders wanted to gain even more insight into God's Word (v. 13).
- Reading and understanding God's Word was reason to rejoice (v. 17).
- God's Word was read daily to the people (v. 18).

Bless the LORD, the great God, for giving you His Word, desiring to read it daily. As you read, ask the Holy Spirit to give you understanding and greater insight, so it makes sense. Don't be afraid to engage God's Word on an emotional level, weeping at times and rejoicing at other times.

Pray Nehemiah 8:3 and 10 over yourself and those for whom you stand guard as a faithful, prayerful watchman (Isaiah 62:6-7).

> *"LORD, make _____ and me people*
> *who understand and are attentive*
> *when Your Word is read. This day is holy to You, LORD.*
> *Do not let us grieve, for Your joy, LORD, is our strength.*
> *Thank You, LORD Jesus~"*

Please read Nehemiah 9.

Meditate on verse 5b.

> *Arise, bless the LORD your God forever and ever!*

The Israelites stood listening to God's Word for six hours; they were so greatly impacted, they spent another six hours confessing their sins and worshiping God. Thankfully, Nehemiah recorded some of their words, so you can use them for confession and worship.

Pray Nehemiah 9:5-6, 17, 20, and 31-33 over yourself and those for whom you stand guard as a faithful, prayerful watchman (Isaiah 62:6-7).

> *"Bless You, LORD our God, forever and ever! O may Your glorious name be blessed and exalted above all blessing and praise! You alone are the LORD. You have made the heavens, the heaven of heavens with all their host, the earth and all that is on it, the seas and all that is in them. You give life to all of them, and the heavenly host bows down before You. Forgive _____ and me when we refuse to listen and do not remember Your wondrous deeds which You have performed among us. Forgive us when we become stubborn. You are a God of forgiveness, gracious and compassionate, slow to anger and abounding in lovingkindness; You do not forsake us. You give Your good Spirit to instruct us. In Your great compassion, You do not make an end of us or forsake us, for You are a great and compassionate God. Now therefore, our God, the great, the mighty, and the awesome God, who keeps covenant and lovingkindness, do not let all the hardship seem insignificant before You, which has come upon us. However, You are just in all that has come upon us, for You have dealt faithfully, but we have acted wickedly. Please forgive us in Your name, Jesus~"*

Please read Nehemiah 10.

Meditate on verses 28-29.

> *Now the rest of the people, the priests, the*
> *Levites, the gatekeepers, the singers,*
> *the temple servants, and all those who had separated themselves*
> *from the peoples of the lands to the law of God,*
> *their wives, their sons, and their daughters,*
> *all those who had knowledge and understanding,*
> *are joining with their kinsmen,*
> *their nobles, and are taking on themselves a*
> *curse and an oath to walk in God's law,*
> *which was given through Moses, God's*
> *servant, and to keep and to observe*
> *all the commandments of God our LORD,*
> *and His ordinances and His statutes.*

God's Word not only caused the people to confess and worship, it caused them to desire holiness. They committed to walk in God's ways and keep His commandments. The people wanted to change their lifestyle based on what the Word of God said.

How does the Bible affect you? As you read and hear it, let it cut out everything that displeases God, and let it mold and shape you into Christlikeness (Hebrews 4:12).

Pray Nehemiah 10:28-29 over yourself and those for whom you stand guard as a faithful, prayerful watchman (Isaiah 62:6-7).

> *"LORD, let _____ and me separate ourselves*
> *from the ways of the peoples of the lands*
> *to Your Law. Give us knowledge and understanding*
> *to commit to walk in Your Law,*
> *and to keep and to observe all Your commandments, God our LORD,*
> *and Your ordinances and Your statutes.*
> *For the sake of Your name, Jesus~"*

Please read Nehemiah 11.

Meditate on verses 2 and 6.

And the people blessed all the men who
volunteered to live in Jerusalem.
All the sons of Perez who lived in Jerusalem were 468 able men.

Jerusalem and the temple needed special care, and those who volunteered for the task could not be weak and faint-hearted. The Hebrew word translated as "able" in the meditation verses also means "strong, virtuous, powerful, efficient, wealthy, mighty, and especially warlike."[1] These volunteers were strong in the LORD and had the wherewithal to leave their homes in other parts of Israel to serve God in Jerusalem.

We hope these verses stir your heart to pray for your family to serve God well in the places He calls you to live, willing to go anywhere for the sake of His Kingdom. Use the words from Nehemiah 11:6, 12, 16-17, 19, and 21-22 to pray over yourself and those for whom you stand guard as a faithful, prayerful watchman (Isaiah 62:6-7).

"LORD, make _____ and me able
to do everything You want us to do.
Let us perform the work of Your temple. Give
us the ability to be in charge of
the outside work of Your house, God. Make us leaders
in beginning the thanksgiving at prayer. Help us keep
watch at the gates. Make us Your temple servants.
Let us sing for the service of Your house, O God.
For the sake of Your name, Jesus~"

---

1. *Retrieved from www.blueletterbible.org/lang/lexicon/lexicon.cfm?Strongs=H2428&t=NASB*

JUNE 12

Please read Nehemiah 12.

Meditate on verse 43.

> *And on that day, they offered great sacrifices and rejoiced*
> *because God had given them great joy, even*
> *the women and children rejoiced,*
> *so that the joy of Jerusalem was heard from afar.*

Imagine the joyful dedication of Jerusalem's wall. The Levites gathered to lead all the people in songs of praise and thanksgiving (vs. 24, 27). They cleansed themselves and the people before the worship began, so they could truly praise the LORD with pure hearts (v. 30). Two enormous choirs lined the wall—men, women, and children singing with all their hearts as they marched to the temple where they continued to glorify God, their songs being heard far beyond Jerusalem's gates (vs. 31-43).

What a powerful picture of authentic worship! Nehemiah 12 can help you obey Christ's command in John 4:23-24:

> *"But an hour is coming, and now is, when the*
> *true worshipers will worship the Father*
> *in spirit and truth; for such people the*
> *Father seeks to be His worshipers.*
> *God is spirit, and those who worship Him*
> *must worship in spirit and truth."*

Worship the LORD with a purified heart by confessing sin and walking wholeheartedly with Him. Spiritual worship is all about God, communicating with and honoring Him. When you live to worship God, your praise will be heard far beyond what you can imagine, impacting others who need a joy-filled relationship with their Creator.

Pray Nehemiah 12:24, 27, 30, and 43 over yourself and those for whom you stand guard as a faithful, prayerful watchman (Isaiah 62:6-7).

"LORD, let _____ and me praise and give
thanks to You. As we dedicate ourselves to You,
let us celebrate the dedication with gladness, with
hymns of thanksgiving, and with songs.
Purify us, LORD! Keep us pure! We offer You great sacrifices,
and we rejoice because You have given us great joy.
Let our joy be heard from afar.
Because of You, Jesus~"

Please read Nehemiah 13.

Meditate on verse 14.

> *Remember me for this, O my God, and do not blot out my loyal deeds*
> *which I have performed for the house of my God and its services.*

As God's Word was read, the people recognized sin that was being casually ignored and blatantly tolerated. Tobiah, an Ammonite and enemy of the Jews (Nehemiah 2:10; 6:1), was even given a room in the temple by Eliashib the priest (vs. 4-5). Unbelievable! Upon learning about such atrocities in the house of God, Nehemiah unapologetically threw out all of Tobiah's stuff and had the room cleansed of the impurity caused by allowing a heathen to live there (v. 8).

You live in a day when Nehemiah's bold actions for the sake of God's holiness would be decried as intolerant. Some places of worship are so seeker-friendly it is difficult to distinguish between the church (those who believe in Christ as the only source of eternal salvation) and those who are actually enemies of Christ, yet have slipped into the pews, not for the purpose of obtaining eternal life, but to revile the things of God (Jude 1:4-23).

Pray for the courage of Nehemiah to stand firm on God's Word and take action according to God's holiness. Pray Nehemiah 13:14, 22, and 31 over yourself and those for whom you stand guard as a faithful, prayerful watchman (Isaiah 62:6-7).

> *"Remember _____ and me for this, O my*
> *God, and do not blot out our loyal deeds*
> *which we have performed for Your house and its services.*
> *Help us teach others to purify themselves*
> *according to Your commands.*
> *For this also remember us, O my God, and have compassion on us*
> *according to the greatness of Your lovingkindness.*
> *Remember us, O my God, for good.*
> *In Your name, Jesus-"*

Please read Philippians 1.

Meditate on verse 12.

> *Now I want you to know, brethren, that my circumstances*
> *have turned out for the greater progress of the Gospel.*

The Philippian church was very special to Paul. It was started on his missionary journey to Macedonia, now part of northern Greece. Read Acts 16 to see the miracles that took place, including a jailhouse earthquake that changed a family's life for eternity.

Interestingly, Paul wrote this letter to the Philippians from a different jail. This imprisonment was the "my circumstances" God was using to further the Gospel (v. 12). Can you imagine the excitement in the Philippian church as they gathered to hear Paul's letter read? Can you picture the Philippian jailer, his family, and friends nodding their heads with glory-filled smiles and giving Macedonian high-fives as Paul wrote of the good happening from his imprisonment (vs. 12-14)?

One of the greatest aspects of being a Christian is realizing that God is always working in you and through your circumstances. Be confident that the Holy Spirit and the prayers of others will see you through your next adventure with the ability to be faithful and bold (vs. 19-20). God turns even negative circumstances into something that glorifies Him.

Pray Philippians 1:12 and 19-22 over yourself and those for whom you stand guard as a faithful, prayerful watchman (Isaiah 62:6-7).

> *"LORD, may _____ and my circumstances turn*
> *out for the greater progress of the Gospel. Thank You for Your*
> *deliverance and the provision of the Spirit of Jesus Christ. Let*
> *us not be put to shame in anything, but with all boldness,*
> *let Christ always be exalted in our bodies, whether by life*
> *or by death. For to live is Christ and to die is gain.*
> *LORD, if we live on in the flesh, let our lives*
> *mean fruitful labor for the sake of others.*
> *Because of Your name, Jesus."*

JUNE 15

Please read Philippians 2.

Meditate on verses 1-2.

> *Therefore, if there is any encouragement in*
> *Christ, if there is any consolation of love,*
> *if there is any fellowship of the Spirit, if any affection and*
> *compassion, make my joy complete by being of the same mind,*
> *maintaining the same love, united in spirit, intent on one purpose.*

These verses serve as a bridge between Paul's suffering and the great passage about Jesus pouring Himself out to become a human and die for us (vs. 5-8). Paul's willingness to suffer for the sake of the Gospel and Jesus' willingness to die so there would even be a Gospel, bring sobriety to the readers of this letter. Suddenly, life is no longer about pleasing self, but pleasing the One who saves and living for the sake of others.

As you read this letter called Philippians, let it help you get your spiritual bearing. Because of what Jesus did for you, your attitudes and behaviors ought to line up with His expectations. The life of Jesus and the presence of the Holy Spirit among you should produce supernatural, God-glorifying effects in you and your church.

Take some time to go slowly through the qualities listed in Philippians 2:1-2, meditating on them with God. Pray for God to help you and your loved ones live these qualities as a Godly community of faith.

Pray Philippians 2:1-2 over yourself and those for whom you stand guard as a faithful, prayerful watchman (Isaiah 62:6-7).

> *"LORD Jesus, encourage _____ and*
> *me and console us with Your love.*
> *Spirit, fellowship with us and our church.*
> *LORD, make us affectionate and compassionate.*
> *Make our joy complete by making us of the same mind,*
> *maintaining the same love, united in spirit,*
> *and intent on one purpose—*
> *Your purpose, LORD Jesus~"*

JUNE 16

Please read Philippians 3.

Meditate on verses 7-8a.

But whatever things were gain to me,
those things I have counted as loss for the sake of Christ.
More than that, I count all things to be loss
in view of the surpassing value of knowing Christ Jesus my LORD.

Paul's brilliant resume would have launched him into senior leadership in his company, "Pharisees-R-Us." He had the attitude, academics, and mentor, leading him to be the project officer for destroying a new faction known as 'The Way." Paul left Jerusalem to persecute the church in other cities, and God intersected his life (Acts 22:3-21). His learning, sponsorship, and religious fervor did not earn him favor with God. Paul realized nothing a person does or owns achieves bragging rights in God's Kingdom, and nothing in the universe compares to the value and worth of knowing and following Jesus.

The surpassing greatness of knowing Jesus is like being carried away by a tsunami. Completely commit yourself to Him by praying Philippians 3:7-11 as a faithful, prayerful watchman (Isaiah 62:6-7).

"LORD, whatever things were gain to me,
those things I count as loss for the sake of You, Christ.
More than that, I count all things to be loss
in view of the surpassing value of knowing
You, Christ Jesus my LORD.
For You, I'm willing to suffer the loss of all things
and count them but rubbish so that I may
gain You and may be found in You,
not having a righteousness of my own derived from the Law,
but that which is through faith in You, Christ,
the righteousness which comes from God on the basis of faith,
that I may know You and the power of Your resurrection
and the fellowship of Your sufferings, being conformed to Your death;
in order that I may attain to the resurrection from the dead.
For the sake of Your name, Jesus-"

JUNE 17

Please read Philippians 4.

Meditate on verses 6-7.

Be anxious for nothing, but in everything by prayer and supplication,
with thanksgiving, let your requests be made known to God.
And the peace of God, which surpasses all comprehension,
will guard your hearts and your minds in Christ Jesus.

Prayer warriors, look at these verses. If you have not memorized them yet, please do it today. Look at all the things God wants to etch upon your heart and mind.

1. Be anxious for nothing – do not worry about anything
2. But, in everything, let your requests be made known to God by:
   a. Prayer
   b. Supplication - prayers for specific requests or needs
   c. Thanksgiving - faith that God is going to answer your prayers
3. Then the peace of God
   a. That surpasses all comprehension
   b. Will guard your hearts and minds in Christ Jesus

When you joyfully trust the LORD with your prayers, then you have God's peace guarding your heart and mind in Christ Jesus! God does not want you to be a worrier about anything. Come to Him with everything.

Pray Philippians 4:4-7 over yourself and those for whom you stand guard as a faithful, prayerful watchman (Isaiah 62:6-7).

"LORD, let _____ and me rejoice in You always!
Let our gentle spirit be known to all men.
LORD, You are near.
Make us anxious for nothing, but in everything,
by prayer and supplication, with thanksgiving,
let us make our requests known to You, God.
May Your peace, which surpasses all comprehension,
guard our hearts and our minds
In You, Christ Jesus~"

Please read Esther 1.

Meditate on verses 3a and 4-5a.

> *In the third year of his (King Ahasuerus') reign, he gave a banquet.*
> *And he displayed the riches of his royal glory and the splendor*
> *of his great majesty for many days, 180 days. When these days*
> *were completed, the king gave a banquet lasting seven days.*

Imagine a 187-day party! King Ahasuerus threw a grand party to show-off a lot of stuff to a lot of people. The last "thing" he wanted to boast about was his beautiful wife, Queen Vashti. On day 187, when he was drunk, he called her away from her girls' party to be ogled at by the guys at his party (vs. 7-11). Vashti refused. Ahasuerus' grand gala ended with a royal thud.

Vashti's refusal to submit to her husband's drunken command probably came from her desire to protect her dignity, even if it meant losing her royal position and probably her life. Her decision is an illustration for Colossians 3:18:

> *Wives, be subject to your husbands, as is fitting in the LORD.*

Wives are to submit to their husbands so long as what they ask is not contrary to what God says. God's call to submission is actually a protective gift to women and brings Godly order to families. Even Christ was submissive to the Father, and wives are to follow His example (1 Peter 2:21-3:1-2).

Pray for husbands not to be drunken, arrogant Ahasueruses, and pray for women to give honor to their husbands using the words from Esther 1:4 and 20.

> *"LORD, please make _____ a Godly, humble*
> *husband who does not desire to display the riches of his*
> *royal glory and the splendor of his great majesty.*
> *Help all women give honor to their husbands.*
> *In Your name, Jesus~"*

Please read Esther 2.

Meditate on verse 15b.

And Esther found favor in the eyes of all who saw her.

As you continue reading Esther, carefully observe the Godly, humble woman for whom the book was named, for she is one to be emulated.

King Ahasuerus began his search for a woman to replace Vashti as his queen. A beautiful, submissive lady named Esther was the obvious choice. This Jewish orphan conducted herself brilliantly among servants and royalty alike. And despite her quick rise to royal position, she did not think more highly of herself than she ought, deferring to and paying homage to her cousin Mordecai, who had raised her as his own daughter (v. 7; Romans 12:3). God honored her behavior, giving her favor and compassion with the king and others in the royal court (vs. 15, 17).

Is there someone in your life to whom God wants you to defer, yet your pride keeps you from obedience? Is there someone in your life to whom you have not given proper credit, perhaps even stealing the limelight for yourself, when the recognition does not really belong to you? Ask God to give you a humble heart like Esther. Give your need for recognition to Him and use the words from Esther 2:14-15 and 17 to pray for God's favor over yourself and those you love as a faithful, prayerful watchman (Isaiah 62:6-7).

> *"LORD, You know _____ and my situation.*
> *Please let _____ delight in us and summon us by name.*
> *Let us find favor in the eyes of all who see us.*
> *Let us be loved by and find favor and*
> *kindness with _____ .*
> *For the sake of Your Name and Kingdom, Jesus~"*

Please read Esther 3.

Meditate on verse 1.

> *After these events, King Ahasuerus promoted Haman,*
> *the son of Hammedatha the Agagite, and advanced him*
> *and established his authority over all the princes who were with him.*

Haman, an archenemy of the Jews, was a descendant of the Amalekite King Agag, whom the LORD commanded King Saul to utterly destroy (1 Samuel 15). The Amalekites had been enemies of Israel since the time of Moses (Exodus 17:8-16).

> *Then the LORD said to Moses, "Write this in a book as a*
> *memorial and recite it to Joshua, that I will utterly blot*
> *out the memory of Amalek from under heaven."*
> —Exodus 17:14

> *"Now go and strike Amalek and utterly destroy*
> *all that he has, and do not spare him."*
> *But Saul and the people spared Agag.*
> —1 Samuel 15:3a, 9a

Saul did not obey, and approximately 575 years later, Haman, the Agagite, issued the decree to totally annihilate all the Jews in a single day (v. 13). Do not take disobedience to God lightly; the ramifications can last for centuries, impacting innumerable people.

Notice Mordecai's refusal to bow to Haman (vs. 2, 5). Not even a king's command and letters carrying a death sentence persuaded him to bend the knee to this hater of God and His people.

Ask God to give you and those you love the courage of Mordecai to stand firm by praying Esther 3:2 as a faithful, prayerful watchman (Isaiah 62:6-7).

> *"LORD, even when others bow down and*
> *pay homage to Your enemies,*
> *do not let _____ and me bow down or pay homage.*
> *We bow only to You, King Jesus~"*

Please read Esther 4.

Meditate on verse 14. Mordecai is speaking.

> *"For if you remain completely silent at this*
> *time, relief and deliverance will arise*
> *for the Jews from another place, but you and*
> *your father's house will perish.*
> *Yet who knows whether you have come to the*
> *kingdom for such a time as this?" (NKJV)*

The situation was unbelievably horrible—every Jew, in every province, in the entire kingdom of Persia was to be killed in a single day! Imagine you and your loved ones in that situation and the heart-pounding, knee-buckling fear it would invoke. The Jews responded with fasting, weeping, and wailing, crying for deliverance. They needed a miracle!

As Mordecai writhed in anguish, he had the presence of mind to see that perhaps God had already arranged for that miracle when He put a young, orphaned Jewish girl on the throne of Persia. Perhaps God wanted Esther to make a bold move for the sake of His people and His Kingdom.

What about you? If you are a Christian, you have come to the Kingdom of God for such a time as this. God has a purpose and a calling for your life, and if you choose to act in courageous obedience, the result will be eternal consequences for good.

Commit to fasting and praying for the sake of those God wants to deliver from the annihilation caused by sin. Be willing to do whatever God tells you to do "for such a time as this" (v. 14).

Pray Esther 4:14 over yourself and those for whom you stand guard as a faithful, prayerful watchman (Isaiah 62:6-7).

> *"LORD, do not let _____ and*
> *me remain silent at this time.*
> *Use us to bring relief and deliverance*
> *for _____. Do not let my family perish.*
> *LORD, You have brought us to Your Kingdom for such a time as this.*
> *Use us in Your name, Jesus~"*

Please read Esther 5.

Meditate on verses 7-8.

> *So Esther replied, "My petition and my request is: if I*
> *have found favor in the sight of the king, and if it pleases*
> *the king to grant my petition and do what I request,*
> *may the king and Haman come to the banquet*
> *which I will prepare for them,*
> *and tomorrow I will do as the king says."*

As you continue to observe Queen Esther, notice her deferential tone as she speaks to the king. Her attitude and words so softened his heart that King Ahasuerus extended his scepter and promised to give her whatever she requested, up to half of his kingdom. Perhaps you could use some of her words as you speak to people who have authority over your life. Her words could even be said as you pray to the King of the universe.

Use the words from Esther 5:2, 4, and 8 as you begin your prayer time today as a faithful, prayerful watchman (Isaiah 62:6-7).

> *"LORD, please grant me favor in Your sight.*
> *As You extend Your scepter to me, I come near to You.*
> *If it pleases You, my King, may _____ .*
> *If I have found favor in Your sight, my King,*
> *and if it please You, my King,*
> *to grant my petition and do what I request,*
> *please _____ .*
> *In Your name, King Jesus~"*

Please read Esther 6.

Meditate on verse 3.

> *The king said, "What honor or dignity has*
> *been bestowed on Mordecai for this?"*
> *Then the king's servants who attended him said,*
> *"Nothing has been done for him."*

This chapter has several themes, such as: "God's Timing is Perfect," "Do Not Think Too Highly of Yourself," and "Pride Comes Before a Fall."

Notice the stark contrast between Mordecai and Haman. God's Word does not indicate Mordecai ever entertained the idea he should be recognized for saving the king's life. The thought of being honored probably did not cross the mind of this humble man of God. Haman, on the other hand, presumed that if someone was being honored, it must be him. How arrogant! And God, in His perfect timing, quickly raised-up humble Mordecai while promptly putting prideful Haman in such a lowly place, he would never rise to the top again.

Approach this passage of Scripture with humility, asking the LORD to reveal "Hamanish" attitudes lurking inside you. Ask Him to give you a Mordecai heart that does not seek honor for yourself, even if it is due, but instead helps others rise to royal position, like Mordecai did for his beloved Esther (Esther 2:11).

Pray for Haman's words from Esther 6:6 never to cross your mind or come out of your mouth.

> *"My LORD and King,*
> *when You desire to honor someone,*
> *do not let me presume it is I.*
> *Let these words NEVER enter my mind or be on my lips:*
> *'Whom would the king desire to honor more than me?'*
> *Keep me humble for the sake of Your name, King Jesus~"*

Please read Esther 7.

Meditate on verse 6.

> *Esther said, "A foe and an enemy is this wicked Haman!"*
> *Then Haman became terrified before the king and queen.*

Haman is a picture of Satan, the wicked foe and enemy of God's people. "He (the devil) was a murderer from the beginning and does not stand in the truth because there is no truth in him. He is a liar and the father of lies" (John 8:44).

Take heart; you have an all-powerful King who promises to protect you from Satan.

> *Finally, brethren, pray for us that the Word of the LORD*
> *will spread rapidly and be glorified, just as it did also with you;*
> *and that we will be rescued from perverse*
> *and evil men; for not all have faith.*
> *But the LORD is faithful, and He will strengthen*
> *and protect you from the evil one.*
> *—2 Thessalonians 3:1-3*

Appeal to your LORD the King with Esther 7:3-4 and 6 as a faithful, prayerful watchman (Isaiah 62:6-7).

> *"If I have found favor in Your sight, O King,*
> *and if it pleases You, my King,*
> *let my life be given me as my petition, and my people as my request,*
> *for Satan would love to sell us to be destroyed,*
> *to be killed, and to be annihilated.*
> *A foe and an enemy is this wicked Satan!*
> *Terrify him before You and us.*
> *In Your name, King Jesus~"*

Please read Esther 8.

Meditate on verses 1b and 3.

> *Mordecai came before the king, for Esther*
> *had disclosed what he was to her.*
> *Then Esther spoke again to the king, fell at his feet, wept and*
> *implored him to avert the evil scheme of Haman the Agagite*
> *and his plot which he had devised against the Jews.*

Is there someone for whom you are praying that you really want God to answer your prayers? Esther 8 gives you a powerful way to pray for those you love.

In verse one, Esther disclosed what Mordecai was to her. She probably not only told Ahasuerus he was her Jewish cousin but how important Mordecai was to her and how much she loved and cared for him. As you pray for your loved ones, tell God everything about them and what they mean to you.

In verse three, Esther unashamedly fell at the king's feet, crying and begging him to save Mordecai and all the Jews. Have you ever prayed that way, literally falling at the feet of King Jesus, weeping and crying for those you love, telling Jesus everything you need Him to do for them? This kind of prayer draws you into deeper intimacy with God and brings the miraculous into the lives of those you love (James 5:16).

Pray Esther 8:1, 3, and 16 for those you love as their faithful, prayerful watchman (Isaiah 62:6-7).

> *"O LORD my King, I am bringing _____ before*
> *You and disclosing what they are to me.*
> *I fall at Your feet, weeping and imploring You*
> *to avert the evil scheme of the devil*
> *and his plot devised against them. (Continue*
> *to cry out to God on their behalf.)*
> *LORD, as You answer my prayers, let this be a time of*
> *light and gladness and joy and honor for them.*
> *In Your name, King Jesus~"*

JUNE 26

Please read Esther 9.

Meditate on verse 28.

> *So these days were to be remembered and celebrated throughout*
> *every generation, every family, every province and every city;*
> *and these days of Purim were not to fail from among the Jews,*
> *or their memory fade from their descendants.*

God miraculously cared for His people, and on the day that all the Jews were to be annihilated, they instead struck their enemies, killing and destroying those who hated them (v. 5). The king even granted the Jews an additional day to rid themselves of their enemies as requested by Queen Esther (vs. 13-16). After the great Jewish victory, Mordecai sent letters to all the provinces telling the people to celebrate the magnificent triumph with two days of joyful feasting (vs. 20-21). And as commanded in your meditation verse, the Feast of Purim* is still celebrated every year, with the two days usually falling in March on the Gregorian calendar, the 14th and 15th of Adar on the Hebrew calendar.

Let the story of Esther, Mordecai, and the Jewish people encourage you to trust God with your impossible situations. Pray Esther 9:1 as a faithful, prayerful watchman (Isaiah 62:6-7).

> *"LORD, _____ and my enemies hope to gain mastery over us.*
> *Please turn it to the contrary so that we gain*
> *the mastery over those who hate us.*
> *For the sake of Your Name and Kingdom, Jesus~"*

*This website gives additional information on the Feast of Purim and tells about two modern-day Jewish miracles where the LORD spared his people from those who hated them. Both miracles happened on the Feast of Purim. Incredible! Check it out: www.chabad.org/holidays/purim/article_cdo/aid/645309/jewish/What-Is-Purim.htm

Please read Esther 10.

Meditate on verse 3.

> *For Mordecai the Jew was second only to King*
> *Ahasuerus, and great among the Jews*
> *and in favor with his many kinsmen, one*
> *who sought the good of his people*
> *and one who spoke for the welfare of his whole nation.*

Esther is such an amazing book! Although God's name is not written in the book, His sovereign hand orchestrated every word of the story. Here are just a few of the things the LORD did for His people:

- ৯ God arranged for an unknown Jewish orphan to enter a competition to become queen of Persia (Esther 2:7-8).
- ৯ God caused Esther to be outstanding among all the women in the competition (Esther 2:9-15).
- ৯ God orchestrated the decreed timing for killing the Jews, so Mordecai and Esther had time to appeal to God and King Ahasuerus for a change of plans (Esther 3:12-5:3).
- ৯ God did not allow Haman to kill Mordecai immediately (Esther 5:10).
- ৯ God arranged the timing of Esther's banquets to give King Ahasuerus a sleepless night and a bedtime story about Mordecai (Esther 5:8-6:2).
- ৯ God timed the delayed recognition of Mordecai to line-up perfectly with His salvation for the Jews (Esther 6:3-7:10).

Only God could weave together such an incredible story! Be encouraged that He is weaving an incredible story for you and your loved ones.

As a faithful, prayerful watchman (Isaiah 62:6-7), pray for God's favor using Esther 10:3.

> *"LORD, let _____ and me be great among Your*
> *people and in favor with them for the purpose of seeking*
> *the good of Your people and speaking for their welfare.*
> *For the sake of Your Kingdom, LORD Jesus~"*

Please read Titus 1.

Meditate on verse 16.

> *They profess to know God, but by their deeds, they deny Him,*
> *being detestable and disobedient and worthless for any good deed.*

Paul gave Titus the important task of appointing elders in the church at Crete. They had to be Godly men with the 18 characteristics listed in verses 6-9. The job called for such stringent qualifications because there were rebellious people in the church, upsetting entire families with their deceptive teaching (vs. 10-11). The elders were to severely reprove these ungodly people, so they might be sound in the faith (v. 13).

Our churches today need Godly elders leading in Christlikeness and ensuring the rebellious and non-believers are not allowed to teach. Pray for your church to obey the sound doctrine of God's Word and put people into leadership who conform to Godliness.

As their faithful, prayerful watchman (Isaiah 62:6-7), pray for the people of your church not to be those described in Titus 1:10-16.

> *"LORD, do not let the people of my church be*
> *rebellious, empty talkers, and deceivers*
> *who must be silenced. Do not let our teachers upset*
> *whole families by teaching things they should not for the*
> *sake of sordid gain. Remove all false-prophets.*
> *Let no one prejudicially call a people-group*
> *'liars, evil beasts, and lazy gluttons.'*
> *Give our elders the courage to reprove severely*
> *when needed so we may all be sound*
> *in the faith. Do not let us pay attention to*
> *myths and commandments of men*
> *who turn us away from the truth. Make*
> *us pure; do not let us be defiled*
> *and unbelieving. Keep our minds and consciences from being defiled.*
> *We profess to know You, God; may our deeds never deny You.*
> *Do not let us be detestable, disobedient,*
> *and worthless for any good deed.*
> *For the sake of Your church and Your name, Jesus~"*

Please read Titus 2.

Meditate on verse 1.

> *But as for you, speak the things which are fitting for sound doctrine.*

Titus 2 contains over 30 Godly characteristics for believers and is a powerful chapter to pray over yourself and those you love. Consider memorizing and praying it every day.

Pray it now as a faithful, prayerful watchman (Isaiah 62:6-7).

> *"LORD, as for _____ and me, let us speak things fitting for sound doctrine. Make us temperate, dignified, sensible, sound in faith, sound in love, sound in perseverance. Let us be reverent in our behavior, not malicious gossips, not enslaved to much wine; let us teach what is good. Help us encourage young women to love their husbands, to love their children, to be sensible, pure, stayers-at-home, kind, subject to their own husbands, so Your Word will not be dishonored. LORD, make us sensible. In all things, let us show ourselves to be an example of good deeds with purity in doctrine, dignified, sound in speech, which is beyond reproach, so the opponent will be put to shame and have nothing bad to say about us.*
> *Master, as Your bondslaves, make us subject to You in everything. Make us well-pleasing, not argumentative, not pilfering, but showing all good faith so we will adorn Your doctrine, God our Savior, in every respect. For Your grace has appeared to all people, bringing salvation, instructing us to deny ungodliness and worldly desires and to live sensibly, righteously, and Godly in the present age, looking for the blessed hope and the appearing of Your glory, our great God and Savior, Christ Jesus. You gave Yourself for us to redeem us from every lawless deed and to purify for Yourself a people for Your own possession, zealous for good deeds. Let us speak these things and exhort and reprove with all authority. Let no one disregard us.*
> *For the sake of Your name, Jesus~"*

JUNE 30

Please read Titus 3.

Meditate on verse 8a.

> *This is a trustworthy statement, and concerning these things,*
> *I want you to speak confidently.*

The trustworthy statement Titus is to confidently speak is found in verses 4-7, and it says:

> *But when the kindness of God our Savior and*
> *His love for mankind appeared,*
> *He saved us, not on the basis of deeds which*
> *we have done in righteousness,*
> *but according to His mercy, by the washing of regeneration*
> *and renewing by the Holy Spirit, whom He poured out upon us richly*
> *through Jesus Christ our Savior, so that being justified by His grace*
> *we would be made heirs according to the hope of eternal life.*

This is an extraordinary statement because God chose to pour out His kindness, love, and mercy on foolish, disobedient, and hateful people. God saved us and made us His heirs, not based on anything we did, but based solely on the power of the Holy Spirit through the Savior, Jesus Christ (vs. 3-7).

Titus 3:3-8 is your story! Pray it and meditate on it so you can confidently speak it to others.

> *"LORD, I was once foolish, disobedient, deceived, enslaved to various*
> *lusts and pleasures, spending my life in malice and envy, hateful*
> *and hating others. But, God my Savior, when Your kindness and*
> *love for me appeared, You saved me not on the basis of deeds*
> *which I have done in righteousness, but according to Your*
> *mercy, by the washing of regeneration and renewing by the*
> *Holy Spirit, whom You poured out upon me richly*
> *through Jesus Christ my Savior, so that being justified by His*
> *grace, I would be made Your heir according to the hope of*
> *eternal life. LORD, help me speak these things confidently,*
> *so others may believe and be careful to engage in good deeds.*
> *These things are good and profitable for all people.*
> *For the sake of Your Kingdom, Jesus~"*

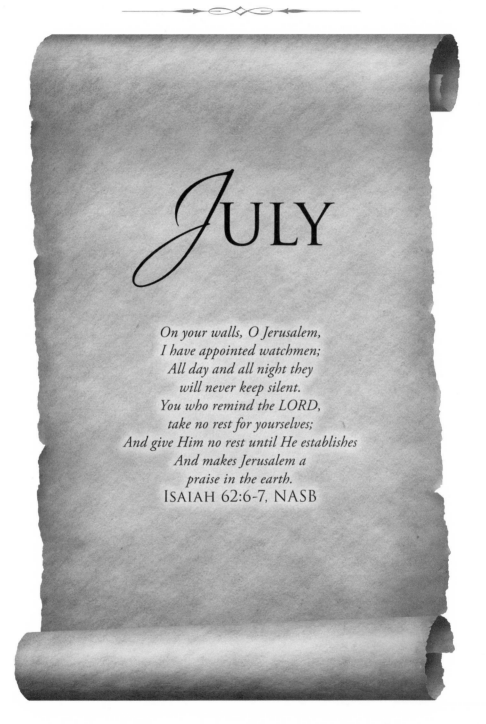

JULY

On your walls, O Jerusalem,
I have appointed watchmen;
All day and all night they
will never keep silent.
You who remind the LORD,
take no rest for yourselves;
And give Him no rest until He establishes
And makes Jerusalem a
praise in the earth.
ISAIAH 62:6-7, NASB

A NOTE AS YOU BEGIN THE JULY DEVOTIONAL

In *The Watchman on the Wall, Vol. 1,* devotionals were written for the book of *Proverbs* with insights into each chapter and a few of the verses formed into prayers. *Proverbs* is so rich with verses to pray for your loved ones that we wanted to include the book in *The Watchman on the Wall, Vol. 3.* This time, a verse will be highlighted for you to think about; then the entire chapter will be used for the prayer. We hope you love praying the *Proverbs*, and you see God do the miraculous in your life and the lives of those you love.

JULY 1

Please read Proverbs 1.

Meditate on verse 7a.

> *The fear of the LORD is the beginning of knowledge.*

Pray Proverbs 1 over yourself and those for whom you stand guard as a faithful, prayerful watchman (Isaiah 62:6-7).

> *"LORD, as I spend the next 31 days praying the*
> *Proverbs, may Your Words cause me:*

- *to know wisdom and instruction*
- *to discern the sayings of understanding*
- *to receive instruction in wise behavior, righteousness, justice, and equity*
- *to give prudence to the naïve*
- *to give the youth knowledge and discretion.*

> *LORD, make _____ and me wise, so we*
> *will hear and increase in learning.*
> *Make us people of understanding who acquire wise counsel.*
> *Help us understand a proverb and a figure,*
> *the words of the wise and their riddles.*
> *The fear of You, LORD, is the beginning of knowledge.*
> *Do not let us be fools who despise wisdom and instruction.*
> *May we hear our fathers' instruction and not forsake*
> *our mothers' teaching, for they are a graceful wreath*
> *to our head and ornaments about our neck.*
> *If sinners entice us, do not let us consent.*
> *Do not let us walk in the way with sinners;*
> *keep our feet from their path.*
> *Make us listen to Your wisdom, LORD.*
> *Do not let us be naïve, simple-minded scoffers*
> *and fools who hate knowledge!*

Pour out Your Spirit of wisdom on us and
make Your Words known to us.
We will not refuse them; we will pay attention
to Your counsel and reproof.
As we do, please keep us from calamity, dread, distress, and anguish.
Answer us when we call; let us find Your
wisdom when we diligently seek it.
Let us love Your knowledge and choose the fear of You, LORD.
Do not let us eat the fruit of our own way
and be satiated with our own devices,
for the waywardness of the naïve will kill them,
and the complacency of fools will destroy them.
Let us listen to Your wisdom, LORD, so we shall live
securely and be at ease from the dread of evil.
In Your name, Jesus~"

Please read Proverbs 2.

Meditate on verse 2.

*Make your ear attentive to wisdom; incline
your heart to understanding.*

Pray Proverbs 2 over yourself and those for whom you stand guard as a faithful, prayerful watchman (Isaiah 62:6-7).

*"LORD, let _____ and me receive Your Words
and treasure Your commandments within us.
Make our ears attentive to wisdom; incline our
hearts to understanding. May we cry for discernment
and lift our voices for understanding;
let us seek her as silver and search for her as for hidden treasures,
so we will discern the fear of You, LORD,
and discover Your nowledge, God.
For LORD, You give wisdom; from Your mouth
come knowledge and understanding.
You store up sound wisdom for the upright;
You are a shield to those who walk in integrity.
You guard the paths of justice, and You
preserve the way of Your Godly ones.
Make us Your Godly ones!
Let us discern righteousness and justice and
equity and every good course.
Let wisdom enter our hearts and knowledge be pleasant to our souls.
Let discretion guard us and understanding watch over us.
LORD, deliver us from the way of evil, from the man
who speaks perverse things, from those who leave the
paths of uprightness to walk in the ways of darkness.
Deliver us from those who delight in doing evil,
who rejoice in the perversity of evil.
Deliver us from those whose paths are crooked
and who are devious in their ways.*

*Deliver us from strange women, from the
adulteress who flatters with her words,
who leaves the companion of her youth and
forgets the covenant of her God.
LORD, may we always remember Your covenant, so our homes will
not sink down to death, and our tracks will not lead to the dead.
We want to reach the paths of life!
Let us walk in the way of good men and
keep to the paths of the righteous,
for the upright will live in the land, and
the blameless will remain in it.
LORD, cut off the wicked from the land
and uproot the treacherous.
For the sake of Your name, Jesus~"*

Please read Proverbs 3.

Meditate on verse 7.

> *Do not be wise in your own eyes; fear the*
> *LORD and turn away from evil.*

Pray Proverbs 3 over yourself and those for whom you stand guard as a faithful, prayerful watchman (Isaiah 62:6-7).

> *"LORD, do not let _____ and me forget Your teaching;*
> *may our hearts keep Your commandments, for length of*
> *days, years of life, and peace they will add to us.*
> *Do not let kindness and truth leave us; bind them around our*
> *necks and write them on the tablets of our hearts, so we will*
> *find favor and good repute in the sight of You and man.*
> *Help us trust You, LORD, with all our hearts; do*
> *not let us lean on our own understanding.*
> *In all our ways, let us acknowledge You, so*
> *You will make our paths straight.*
> *Do not let us be wise in our own eyes; let us*
> *fear You and turn away from evil.*
> *Let the fear of You, LORD, bring healing to our*
> *bodies and refreshment to our bones.*
> *Let us honor You from our wealth and from the first*
> *of all our produce, so our barns will be filled with*
> *plenty and our vats overflow with new wine.*
> *Do not let us reject Your discipline, LORD, or loathe*
> *Your reproof, for You reprove those You love, even as*
> *a father corrects the son in whom he delights.*
> *LORD, bless us as we find wisdom and gain understanding.*
> *May we profit from her more than from silver, gold, and jewels.*
> *May we desire nothing more than Your*
> *wisdom and understanding, God.*
> *In Your wisdom are: long life, riches, honor,*
> *pleasant ways, and paths of peace.*

Let Your wisdom be a tree of life to us as we take hold
of her; let us be happy as we hold her fast.
LORD, by wisdom, You founded the earth; by
understanding, You established the heavens.
By Your knowledge, the deeps were broken up, and the
skies drip with dew. LORD, let us keep sound wisdom and
discretion; do not let them vanish from our sight.
Let them be life to our souls and adornment to our necks.
Let us walk in our way securely; do not let our feet stumble.
When we lie down, do not let us be afraid; let our sleep be sweet.
Do not let us be afraid of sudden fear nor of the
onslaught of the wicked when it comes.
LORD, You will be our confidence;
You will keep our feet from being caught.
Let us not withhold good when it is in our power to do it.
Do not let us devise harm against our neighbor.
Let us not contend with others without cause,
if they have done us no harm.
Do not let us envy a violent man or choose any of his ways.
The devious are an abomination to You, LORD,
but You are intimate with the upright.
LORD, make us righteous!
You bless the dwelling of the righteous.
Please give us Your grace when we are afflicted and make us wise,
so we can inherit honor rather than display dishonor.
Because of Your name, Jesus~"

Please read Proverbs 4.

Meditate on verse 24.

> *Put away from you a deceitful mouth and*
> *put devious speech far from you.*

Pray Proverbs 4 over yourself and those for whom you stand guard as a faithful, prayerful watchman (Isaiah 62:6-7).

> *"LORD, let _____ hear the instruction of a father*
> *and give attention to gain understanding.*
> *Help _____ and me give the children in our lives sound teaching.*
> *Do not let them abandon our instruction.*
> *Let their hearts hold fast to our words; let them*
> *keep our commandments and live.*
> *LORD, help them acquire wisdom and understanding!*
> *Do not let them forget nor turn away from the words of our mouths.*
> *Let us not forsake Your wisdom, God, for she will guard us.*
> *Let us love her, and she will watch over us.*
> *The beginning of wisdom is to acquire wisdom.*
> *As we acquire wisdom, help us get understanding.*
> *When we prize Your wisdom, God, she will exalt us.*
> *She will honor us if we embrace her.*
> *She will place on our heads a garland of grace.*
> *She will present us with a crown of beauty.*
> *Let our children hear and accept what we say,*
> *so the years of their lives may be many.*
> *Let us direct them in the way of wisdom.*
> *Let us lead them in upright paths.*
> *When they walk, let their steps not be impeded,*
> *and if they run, do not let them stumble.*
> *Let them take hold of Your instruction and not let go.*
> *Let them guard Your instruction, for she is their life.*
> *Do not let them enter the path of the wicked*
> *nor proceed in the way of evil men.*

LORD, make them avoid it; do not let them pass by
it; make them turn away from evil and pass on.
Keep us on the path of the righteous!
It is like the light of dawn, that shines brighter
and brighter until the full day.
Oh, LORD, let our children give attention to our
words and incline their ears to our sayings.
Do not let them depart from their sight; keep
them in the midst of their hearts.
Let what we say be only Your Words, LORD, for Your Words
are life to those who find them and health to our body.
Let us watch over our heart with all diligence,
for from it flows the springs of life.
Put away from us a deceitful mouth and
put devious speech far from us.
Let our eyes look directly ahead, and let our
gaze be fixed straight in front of us.
Let us watch the path of our feet,
so all our ways will be established.
Do not let us turn to the right nor to the left;
turn our feet from evil.
In Your name, Jesus~"

July 5

Please read Proverbs 5.

Meditate on verse 7.

> *Now then, my sons, listen to me and do not*
> *depart from the words of my mouth.*

Pray Proverbs 5 over yourself and those for whom you stand guard as a faithful, prayerful watchman (Isaiah 62:6-7).

> *"LORD, let _____ and me give attention to Your wisdom*
> *and incline our ears to Your understanding; that we may*
> *observe discretion and our lips reserve knowledge.*
> *Do not let us listen to the lips of an adulteress which drip*
> *honey, whose speech is smoother than oil; but in the end, she*
> *is bitter as wormwood, sharp as a two-edged sword.*
> *Keep us away from her because her feet go down*
> *to death; her steps take hold of Sheol.*
> *She does not ponder the path of life; her ways*
> *are unstable; she does not know it.*
> *Let us listen to You, LORD, and not depart*
> *from the Words of Your mouth.*
> *Keep our way far from the adulteress; do not let us go near her house.*
> *Do not let us give our vigor to others and our years to the cruel one.*
> *Do not let strangers be filled with our strength or our hard-*
> *earned good go to the house of an alien, so we groan at our*
> *final end, when our flesh and body are consumed.*
> *Do not let us hate instruction and our hearts spurn reproof!*
> *Let us listen to the voice of our teachers and*
> *incline our ears to our instructors!*
> *Keep us from utter ruin in the midst of the assembly and congregation.*
> *Let us drink water from our own cistern and*
> *fresh water from our own well.*
> *Do not let our springs be dispersed abroad or*
> *our streams of water be in the streets.*
> *Let them be ours alone and not for strangers.*

Let our fountain be blessed and let our men
rejoice in the wife of their youth.
As a loving hind and a graceful doe, let her
breasts satisfy her husband at all times.
Let her husband be exhilarated always with her love.
Do not let us be exhilarated with an adulteress
and embrace the bosom of a foreigner.
For our ways are before Your eyes, LORD,
and You watch all our paths.
Do not let us be the wicked, captured by our own
iniquities and held with the cords of our sin.
Do not let us die for lack of instruction;
do not let us go astray in the greatness of our folly.
In Your name, Jesus~"

Please read Proverbs 6.

Meditate on verse 20.

> *My son, observe the commandment of your father*
> *and do not forsake the teaching of your mother.*

Pray Proverbs 6 over yourself and those for whom you stand guard as a faithful, prayerful watchman (Isaiah 62:6-7).

> *"LORD, do not _____ and me become surety for*
> *a neighbor, nor give a pledge for a stranger.*
> *Do not let us be snared and caught with the words of our mouth.*
> *As we humble ourselves, deliver us, LORD.*
> *Do not let us be sluggards. Make us wise. Keep us from*
> *the worthless, wicked person who walks with a perverse*
> *mouth, winks with his eyes, signals with his feet,*
> *and points with his fingers.*
> *Keep us from one with perversity in his heart who continually*
> *devises evil and spreads strife because his calamity will come*
> *suddenly; instantly he will be broken, and there will be no*
> *healing. LORD, keep us from the six things which You hate;*
> *yes, from the seven which are an abomination to You:*
> *haughty eyes, a lying tongue, hands that shed innocent blood,*
> *a heart that devises wicked plans, feet that run rapidly to evil,*
> *a false witness who utters lies, and one who*
> *spreads strife among brothers.*
> *LORD, let us and our children observe the commandments of*
> *our fathers and not forsake the teaching of our mothers.*
> *Let us bind them continually on our hearts*
> *and tie them around our necks.*
> *When we walk about, let them guide us;*
> *when we sleep, let them watch over us;*
> *when we awake, let them talk to us.*
> *For the commandment is a lamp, and the teaching is light;*

and reproofs for discipline are the way of life
to keep us from the evil woman,
from the smooth tongue of the adulteress.
Do not let us desire her beauty in our hearts,
nor let her capture us with her eyelids.
For on account of a harlot, one is reduced to a loaf of
bread, and an adulteress hunts for the precious life.
Do not let us take fire in our bosom
and our clothes be burned.
Do not let us walk on hot coals and our feet be scorched.
Do not let us go in to our neighbor's wife;
we do not want to be punished.
Do not let us be thieves.
Do not let us lack sense and destroy
ourselves by committing adultery;
we do not want such wounds, disgrace, and
reproach that will not be blotted out.
In Your name, Jesus~"

Please read Proverbs 7.

Meditate on verse 2.

> *Keep my commandments and live, and my*
> *teaching as the apple of your eye.*

Pray Proverbs 7 over yourself and those for whom you stand guard as a faithful, prayerful watchman (Isaiah 62:6-7).

> *"LORD, help _____ and me keep Your Words*
> *and treasure Your commandments within us.*
> *Let us keep Your commandments and live;*
> *let us keep Your teaching as the apple of our eye.*
> *Let us bind them on our fingers and write*
> *them on the tablet of our hearts.*
> *Make Your wisdom our sister and understanding our*
> *intimate friend, that they may keep us from an adulteress,*
> *from the foreigner who flatters with her words.*
> *LORD, do not let us be naïve and lack sense!*
> *Do not let us be seized by the boisterous and rebellious!*
> *Protect us from seduction!*
> *Do not let us follow a harlot as an ox goes to the slaughter,*
> *or as one in fetters goes to the discipline of a fool.*
> *Do not let our choices become an arrow that pierces our livers.*
> *Do not let us be like a bird hastening to the snare.*
> *Keep us from choosing things and people that will cost us our lives!*
> *LORD, let us listen to You and pay attention*
> *to the Words of Your mouth.*
> *Do not let our hearts turn aside to the ways of the*
> *adulteress; do not let us stray into her paths.*
> *For many are the victims she has cast down,*
> *and numerous are all her slain.*
> *Her house is the way to Sheol, descending to the chambers of death.*
> *LORD, let our house be filled with Your Life,*
> *leading others to You.*
> *For the sake of Your name, Jesus~"*

JULY 8

Please read Proverbs 8.

Meditate on verse 13.

> *The fear of the LORD is to hate evil; pride and arrogance*
> *and the evil way and the perverted mouth, I hate.*

Pray Proverbs 8 over yourself and those for whom you stand guard as a faithful, prayerful watchman (Isaiah 62:6-7).

> *"LORD, let _____ and me possess Your wisdom.*
> *Let us speak noble things; let the opening*
> *of our lips reveal right things.*
> *Let our mouths utter truth, and let wickedness*
> *be an abomination to our lips.*
> *Let all the utterances of our mouth be in righteousness;*
> *let there be nothing crooked or perverted in them.*
> *LORD, Your wisdom is straightforward to us who*
> *understand and right to us who find knowledge.*
> *May we choose Your instruction and not silver; may*
> *we choose knowledge rather than choicest gold.*
> *For Your wisdom is better than jewels, and all*
> *desirable things cannot compare with her.*
> *LORD, let us dwell in wisdom, prudence,*
> *knowledge, discretion, and the fear of You.*
> *Let us hate evil, pride, arrogance, and the perverted mouth.*
> *LORD, give us Your counsel, sound wisdom,*
> *understanding, and power.*
> *Let us love Your wisdom and diligently seek her, for in her*
> *are riches, honor, enduring wealth, and righteousness.*
> *Her fruit is better than pure gold, and her*
> *yield is better than choicest silver.*
> *In Your wisdom, is the way of righteousness and the paths of justice.*
> *Endow us with wealth as we love Your wisdom.*
> *Let her fill our treasuries.*

LORD, let us listen to Your wisdom, for
blessed are those who keep her ways.
Let us heed instruction and be wise; do not let us neglect it.
Bless us as we listen to Your wisdom.
Let us watch daily at her gates and wait at her doorposts.
For those who find her, find life and obtain favor from
You, but those who sin against Your wisdom injure
themselves; those who hate her love death.
LORD, we want Your life and favor!
Give us Your wisdom!
In Your name, Jesus~"

Please read Proverbs 9.

Meditate on verse 10.

> *The fear of the LORD is the beginning of wisdom,*
> *and the knowledge of the Holy One is understanding.*

Pray Proverbs 9 over yourself and those for whom you stand guard as a faithful, prayerful watchman (Isaiah 62:6-7).

> *"LORD, let _____ and me live in the house of Your wisdom.*
> *Do not let us be naïve, lacking understanding.*
> *Let us eat and drink Your wisdom.*
> *Let us forsake our folly and live; let us proceed*
> *in the way of understanding.*
> *Do not let us correct a scoffer, who will bring us dishonor.*
> *Do not let us reprove the wicked who insult us.*
> *Do not let us reprove a scoffer who hates us.*
> *Let us reprove a wise man who will love us.*
> *Make us the wise man who accepts instruction to be still wiser.*
> *Make us righteous. Make us teachable and increase our learning.*
> *Let us fear You, LORD, for that is the beginning of wisdom.*
> *Let us know You, Holy One, for that is understanding.*
> *Let Your wisdom and understanding multiply*
> *our days, adding years of life.*
> *Keep us from a boisterous woman of folly*
> *who is naïve and knows nothing.*
> *Do not let us turn aside to her; keep our paths straight.*
> *Do not let us be naïve, lacking understanding.*
> *Do not let us go into her house of the dead,*
> *into the depths of Sheol. LORD, we want to*
> *remain in Your house of wisdom and life.*
> *In Your name, Jesus~"*

Please read Proverbs 10.

Meditate on verse 9.

> *He who walks in integrity walks securely,*
> *but he who perverts his ways will be found out.*

Pray Proverbs 10 over yourself and those for whom you stand guard as a faithful, prayerful watchman (Isaiah 62:6-7).

> *"LORD, may _____ and I be wise,*
> *making You glad rather than bringing You grief.*
> *Make us righteous, so that:*

- *we are delivered from death, and You do not allow us to hunger*
- *our hands are diligent, making us rich*
- *we wisely gather in the summer, not shamefully sleeping during the harvest*
- *blessings are on our heads, and our memories are blessed*
- *our wise hearts receive commands, and we walk securely in integrity*
- *our mouths are a fountain of life; wisdom is found on our discerning lips*
- *we are wise, storing up knowledge; our wages are life*
- *we stay on the path of life, heeding instruction*
- *we are wise, restraining our lips*
- *our tongues are choice silver; our lips feed many*
- *Your blessing makes us rich, and You add no sorrow to it*
- *we are people of understanding who do wisdom*
- *our righteous desires are granted, and we have an everlasting foundation*
- *our lives are prolonged because we fear You; gladness is our hope*
- *Your way, LORD, is our stronghold; we will never be shaken*
- *our mouths flow with wisdom, and our lips bring forth what is acceptable*

> *Because You are our righteousness, Jesus~"*

Please read Proverbs 11.

Meditate on verse 25.

> *The generous man will be prosperous,*
> *and he who waters will himself be watered.*

Pray Proverbs 11 over yourself and those for whom you stand guard as a faithful, prayerful watchman (Isaiah 62:6-7).

> *"LORD, keep _____ and me from being an abomination*
> *to You. May we be Your delight and do what is just.*
> *Keep us from pride; let us be humble and have Your*
> *wisdom. Make us upright; let integrity guide us. LORD,*
> *let Your righteousness deliver us from death. Make us*
> *blameless in Your righteousness and smooth our way.*
> *Make us upright in Your righteousness and deliver us; deliver us from*
> *trouble. Deliver us through Your knowledge. Let our city rejoice when*
> *it goes well with the righteous; exalt our city by blessing the upright.*
> *LORD, make us trustworthy people of understanding*
> *who know when to conceal a matter and keep silent.*
> *Let us not be talebearers. Make us wise counselors, bringing*
> *victory. Make us gracious, merciful people who attain honor*
> *and do good. Let us sow righteousness and get a true reward.*
> *Make us steadfast in righteousness, attaining life. May*
> *we be blameless in our walk and be Your delight.*
> *Keep us in Your righteousness and deliver our descendants. As Your*
> *righteous people, our desire is only good. As we scatter Your blessings,*
> *let us increase all the more. As we are generous, make us prosperous.*
> *As we water, let ourselves be watered.*
> *As we do not withhold our grain, let blessings be*
> *on our heads. As we diligently seek good,*
> *we seek Your favor. Make us the righteous*
> *who flourish like the green leaf;*
> *let our fruit be a tree of life.*
> *Make us wise and let us win souls.*
> *Because Your righteousness is our reward, Jesus~"*

Please read Proverbs 12.

Meditate on verse 28.

> *In the way of righteousness is life,*
> *and in its pathway, there is no death.*

Pray Proverbs 12 over yourself and those for whom you stand guard as a faithful, prayerful watchman (Isaiah 62:6-7).

"LORD, make _____ and me love discipline
and knowledge. Do not let us be stupid,
hating reproof. Make us good people who obtain Your favor.
Give us a righteous root that will not be moved.
Make _____ an excellent wife, the crown of her husband.
Make us righteous; let our thoughts be just.
Give us upright mouths that deliver us.
Make us righteous; let our house stand.
Let us be praised according to Your insight.
Make us righteous; let us regard the life of our animal.
As we till the land, give us plenty of bread; let our root of
righteousness yield fruit. Make us righteous; let us escape trouble.
Let us be satisfied with good by the fruit of our
words and let the deeds of our hands
return to us. Make us wise, listening to counsel.
Make us prudent, concealing dishonor.
Let us speak truth and tell what is right.
Give us wise tongues that bring healing.
Let our truthful lips be established forever.
Make us joyful counselors of peace. LORD, please
make us righteous and let no harm befall us.
May we deal faithfully and be Your delight.
Give us diligent hands that are able to rule. Let us speak good
words, making hearts glad. May we be righteous, guiding
our neighbors. Let diligence be our precious possession.
In the way of righteousness is life, and in
its pathway, there is no death.
Keep us in the righteous way.
Because of Your righteousness, Jesus~"

Please read Proverbs 13.

Meditate on verse 14.

> *The teaching of the wise is a fountain of life,*
> *to turn aside from the snares of death.*

Pray Proverbs 13 over yourself and those for whom you stand guard as a faithful, prayerful watchman (Isaiah 62:6-7).

> *"LORD, make _____ and me wise, accepting discipline.*
> *Do not let us be scoffers who will not listen to rebuke. Let us*
> *enjoy good from the fruit of our mouths. Help us guard our*
> *mouths, so we preserve our lives, for the one who opens wide his*
> *lips comes to ruin. Make us diligent souls. Keep us righteous;*
> *may we hate falsehood. Do not let us be wicked people, acting*
> *disgustingly and shamefully. Let Your righteousness guard our*
> *way, making it blameless. Let us rejoice in righteousness.*
> *Make us wise and willing to receive counsel. Increase our wealth*
> *as we labor. Please fulfill our righteous desires. Let us never despise*
> *Your Word; rather let us fear Your commandments and receive Your*
> *reward. Make us wise; let our teaching be a fountain of life, turning*
> *others aside from the snares of death. Give us good understanding*
> *that produces favor; keep us from the hard way of the treacherous.*
> *Make us prudent, acting with knowledge; do not let us be fools*
> *displaying folly. Make us faithful envoys who bring healing.*
> *Poverty and shame come to those who neglect discipline; may*
> *we be honored as we regard reproof. Let our desire realized*
> *be sweet to our souls. May we walk with wise people who*
> *make us wise. Adversity pursues sinners, so please keep us*
> *righteous and reward us with prosperity. Make us good and*
> *let us leave an inheritance to our children's children.*
> *Let us love our children and discipline them diligently.*
> *LORD, make us righteous and satisfy our appetite.*
> *With Your righteousness, Jesus~"*

Please read Proverbs 14.

Meditate on verse 26.

> *In the fear of the LORD, there is strong confidence,*
> *and his children will have refuge.*

Pray Proverbs 14 over yourself and those for whom you stand guard as a faithful, prayerful watchman (Isaiah 62:6-7).

"LORD, make _____ a wise woman who builds her house; do not let her be foolish, tearing it down with her own hands. Help _____ and me to walk in uprightness, fearing You, LORD. Let our wise lips protect us. Make us trustworthy witnesses who do not lie. Give us understanding; make it easy for us to obtain knowledge. Keep us from the presence of fools so we will discern words of knowledge. Make us sensible; give us wisdom to understand our way. Let us never be fools, mocking at sin. Keep us among the upright where there is good will. The house of the wicked will be destroyed; keep our tent upright; let it flourish! Make us sensible people who consider our steps. Make us wise and cautious, turning away from evil. Do not let us be arrogant, careless, and quick-tempered fools. LORD, let us be sensible and crown us with knowledge. Help us be gracious to the poor. Give us Your kindness and truth; help us devise good. Make us truthful witnesses, saving lives; do not let us utter treacherous lies. Give us strong confidence as we fear You, LORD. Give our children refuge. The fear of You is a fountain of life. May we always fear You and avoid the snares of death. Give us great understanding to be slow to anger; do not let us be quick-tempered. Give us tranquil hearts, bringing life to our bodies. Do not let us taunt You, our Maker, by oppressing the poor. Help us to honor You by being gracious to the needy. Keep us righteous, so we will have a refuge when we die. Let Your wisdom rest in our hearts; give us Your understanding. Let Your righteousness exalt our nation. Make us Your servants who act wisely. In Your name, King Jesus-"

Please read Proverbs 15.

Meditate on verse 9.

> *The way of the wicked is an abomination to the LORD,*
> *but He loves one who pursues righteousness.*

Pray Proverbs 15 over yourself and those for whom you stand guard as a faithful, prayerful watchman (Isaiah 62:6-7).

> *"LORD, help _____ and me give gentle answers that turn*
> *away wrath, instead of harsh words that stir up anger.*
> *Give us wise tongues that make knowledge acceptable.*
> *Your eyes are in every place, watching the evil and the good.*
> *Give us soothing tongues that are a tree of life; let there be*
> *no perversion in our tongues which crush the spirit.*
> *Do not let _____ be a fool who rejects his father's discipline;*
> *make him sensible; let him regard reproof. Let there be great wealth*
> *in our righteous house. Give us wise lips that spread knowledge;*
> *do not let us have hearts of fools.*
> *Make us upright and let our prayers be Your delight.*
> *LORD, You love those who pursue righteousness;*
> *may we always pursue Your righteousness.*
> *Give us joyful hearts that make our faces cheerful.*
> *Give us intelligent minds that seek knowledge.*
> *Give us cheerful hearts with a continual feast.*
> *Better is a little with the fear of You, LORD,*
> *than great treasure and turmoil with it.*
> *Better is a dish of vegetables where love is than*
> *a fattened ox served with hatred.*
> *Do not let us be hot-tempered, stirring up strife;*
> *let us be slow to anger, calming a dispute.*
> *The path of the upright is a highway; keep us on that path!*
> *Make _____ a wise son, who makes his father glad;*
> *do not let him be foolish, despising his mother.*
> *Make us people of understanding who walk straight.*

Send us the counselors we need to make our plans succeed.
Give us joy in an apt answer and let us delight in a
timely word. Keep us on the path of life, leading upward
for the wise; let it keep us from Sheol below.
LORD, You will tear down the house of the proud;
do not let us be proud! Establish the boundary for the widow,
LORD, please protect her. Evil plans are an abomination to
You; let our plans be made with pure, pleasant words.
Let us hate bribes. Give us righteous hearts which
ponder how to answer; remove all wickedness from
our mouths which pours out evil things.
LORD, You are far from the wicked;
make us righteous, so You will hear our prayers.
Give us ears to listen to a life-giving reproof,
so we can dwell among the wise.
Let us listen to reproof and gain understanding.
The fear of You is the instruction for wisdom,
and before honor comes humility.
Keep us humbly fearing You.
In Your name, Jesus~"

Please read Proverbs 16.

Meditate on verse 9.

The mind of man plans his way, but the LORD directs his steps.

Pray Proverbs 16 over yourself and those for whom you stand guard as a faithful, prayerful watchman (Isaiah 62:6-7).

"LORD, as _____ and I make plans in our hearts,
we know the answer of the tongue is from You.
Weigh our motives and make our way clean in Your sight.
As we commit our works to You, LORD, please establish our plans.
LORD, use us for Your purposes. Do not let us be proud in heart,
for that is an abomination to You and will be punished.
By lovingkindness and truth, iniquity is atoned for;
let us always fear You, LORD; keep us away from evil.
Make our ways pleasing to You; make even
our enemies be at peace with us.
Keep us content with a little with righteousness, so
we will not desire great income with injustice.
As we plan our way, direct all of our steps, LORD.
Let divine decisions be on our leaders' lips;
do not let them err in judgment.
Do not let them commit wicked acts; establish them
in righteousness; keep them from abomination.
Give our leaders righteous lips; may they be
loved as they speak what is right.
Give us the favor of our leaders and not their
fury; let us be wise with them.
LORD, to get Your wisdom is better than gold!
And Your understanding is to be chosen above silver.
The highway of the upright is to depart from evil;
let us watch our way and preserve our lives.
LORD, free us from pride and a haughty spirit;
keep us from destruction and stumbling.

Let us be humble in spirit with the lowly, rather
than divide the spoil with the proud.
Let us give attention to Your Word and find
good; bless us as we trust in You!
Make us wise in heart; give us understanding;
let our speech be sweet and increase our persuasiveness.
Let understanding be a fountain of life to us.
Give us wise hearts that instruct our mouths
and add persuasiveness to our lips.
Let us speak pleasant words that are sweet to the
soul and bring healing to the bones.
LORD, do not let us be worthless, perverse, slanderous, violent people!
Let us grow gray with the crown of glory
on Your way of righteousness.
Let us be slow to anger and help us rule our spirits.
Let us accept every decision that comes from You, LORD.
In Your name, Jesus~"

Please read Proverbs 17.

Meditate on verse 27.

> *He who restrains his words has knowledge,*
> *and he who has a cool spirit is a man of understanding.*

Pray Proverbs 17 over yourself and those for whom you stand guard as a faithful, prayerful watchman (Isaiah 62:6-7).

"LORD, let _____ and my house be filled with quietness
rather than strife. Make us Your servants who act wisely;
help us rule over our children if they act shamefully.
LORD, please keep them from shameful behavior!
LORD, test our hearts. Do not let us be
evildoers who listen to wicked lips.
Do not let us be liars who pay attention to a destructive tongue.
Do not let us taunt You, our Maker, by mocking
the poor; do not let us rejoice at calamity.
Let our grandchildren be our crown and our children
be our glory. May we have excellent speech;
let us not have lying lips.
Do not let us separate intimate friends by telling
about the transgressions of others.
Make us people of understanding;
may rebukes have a deep impact on us.
Do not let us be rebellious seekers of evil.
Keep us from fools in their folly.
Do not let us return evil for good.
Help us to abandon a quarrel before it breaks out.
Do not let us be an abomination to You by justifying
the wicked and condemning the righteous.
Let us be friends who love at all times and
are there for others in adversity.
Give us good sense not to make pledges and become a guarantor.

*Do not let us love transgression and strife. Straighten
out our crooked minds and keep our language from
perversion; we do not want to fall into evil.
LORD, do not let our children be fools!
Please let them bring us joy and not sorrow.
Give us joyful hearts that are good medicine.
Make us people of wisdom and understanding.
Do not let our children be foolish, bringing us grief and bitterness.
Do not let us be fined for being righteous and keep us
from being struck for being noble and upright.
Make us knowledgeable, restraining our words;
give us understanding and a cool spirit.
Make us wise and prudent in the closing of our lips.
Let us know when to keep silent.
For the sake of Your name, Jesus-"*

Please read Proverbs 18.

Meditate on verse 10.

> *The name of the LORD is a strong tower; the*
> *righteous runs into it and is safe.*

Pray Proverbs 18 over yourself and those for whom you stand guard as a faithful, prayerful watchman (Isaiah 62:6-7).

> *"LORD, do not let _____ and me seek our own*
> *desires and separate ourselves from others.*
> *Do not let us quarrel against sound wisdom.*
> *Do not let us be fools who do not delight in understanding, but*
> *only in revealing our own minds. Let our mouths be a fountain*
> *of wisdom, a bubbling brook. Let us not show partiality to the*
> *wicked, nor thrust aside the righteous in judgment. Let us not have*
> *fool's lips that bring strife; do not let our mouths call for blows.*
> *Do not let our mouths be our ruin and our lips the*
> *snare of our souls. Let us not be slack in our work.*
> *LORD, Your name is a strong tower; make us righteous;*
> *we will run into You and be safe. Do not let our hearts be*
> *haughty; keep us from destruction. Keep us humble, for*
> *humility goes before honor. Help us to listen before we give*
> *an answer, so our answer is not folly and shame to us.*
> *Do not let our spirits be broken. Give us prudent minds that*
> *acquire knowledge and make us wise with ears that seek*
> *knowledge. LORD, gift us for going where and to whom*
> *You desire to send us. Let Your decisions put an end to strife.*
> *LORD, keep us from offending our brother; free us from*
> *contentions. Let the fruit of our mouths be satisfying.*
> *Death and life are in the power of the lips—may our lips speak life!*
> *Let _____ find a good wife and obtain favor from*
> *You, LORD. If You allow us to be rich,*
> *do not let us answer others roughly.*
> *Give us a friend who sticks closer than a brother.*
> *In Your name, Jesus~"*

Please read Proverbs 19.

Meditate on verse 21.

> *Many plans are in a man's heart, but the*
> *counsel of the LORD will stand.*

Pray Proverbs 19 over yourself and those for whom you stand guard as a faithful, prayerful watchman (Isaiah 62:6-7).

> *"LORD, let _____ and me walk in integrity; let us not*
> *be fools with perverse speech. Give us Your knowledge.*
> *Do not let us err because of hurrying footsteps.*
> *A man's foolishness ruins his way.*
> *LORD, please let us never be that person; let*
> *our hearts never rage against You!*
> *Make us truthful witnesses; help us not tell lies.*
> *LORD, give us Your wisdom and let us keep*
> *understanding, so we can find good.*
> *Let us never be a false witness; keep us from*
> *telling lies, so we will not perish.*
> *Give us discretion to be slow to anger; may it be*
> *our glory to overlook a transgression.*
> *Keep us from the wrath of those who rule over us;*
> *let their favor be on us like dew on the grass.*
> *Do not let our children be foolish, bringing us destruction.*
> *Do not let _____ be a contentious wife who is like a constant*
> *dripping; make her a prudent wife, a gift from You, LORD.*
> *Do not let laziness cast us into a deep sleep; do not let us be*
> *idle. Let us keep Your commandments and keep our souls.*
> *Do not let us be careless in conduct; do not let*
> *us die because of careless conduct.*
> *Help us to be gracious to a poor man, for that is lending to*
> *You, LORD, and You will repay us for our good deed.*

*Help us to discipline our children while there is hope for we do
not desire their deaths. Do not let us be people of great anger.
Let us listen to counsel and accept discipline, so
we may be wise the rest of our days.
LORD, we have many plans in our hearts; thank You that
Your counsel will stand. Let Your kindness be evident in us.
Let us fear You, LORD, for it will lead to life, and we will
sleep satisfied, untouched by evil. Do not let us be sluggards.
Make us people of understanding, gaining knowledge when reproved.
Keep our children from being shameful and disgraceful;
let them never assault us nor drive us away!
Let them never cease listening to discipline; let them
never stray from the words of knowledge.
Do not let us be rascally witnesses who make a mockery of justice.
Do not let us have wicked mouths that spread iniquity.
Do not let us be scoffers and fools.
Because of Your name, Jesus~"*

Please read Proverbs 20.

Meditate on verse 7.

A righteous man who walks in his integrity—
how blessed are his sons after him!

Pray Proverbs 20 over yourself and those for whom you stand guard as a faithful, prayerful watchman (Isaiah 62:6-7).

"LORD, make _____ and me wise.
Do not let us be intoxicated with wine and strong drink;
we do not want to be mockers and brawlers.
Do not let us provoke our leaders to anger.
Keep us away from strife; do not let us be quarreling
fools. Do not let us be sluggards.
Make us people of understanding who can help others
draw out the plans You put in their hearts.
Make us trustworthy.
Make us righteous people who walk in integrity;
may our children be blessed.
Make our leaders just, able to disperse all
evil with just the look in their eyes.
Jesus, only You can cleanse our hearts and purify us from sin!
Do not let us be abominable to You by using
differing weights and measures.
Let our children distinguish themselves by their deeds;
keep their conduct pure and right.
LORD, You made our hearing ears and seeing eyes; open
our eyes and let us be satisfied with Your provision.
Give us lips of knowledge that are more precious
than gold and jewels. Do not let us obtain bread by
falsehood, for it will fill our mouths with gravel.
Help us to prepare plans by consultation
and make war by wise guidance.
Do not let us be secret revealing slanderers;
do not let us associate with gossips.

Do not let us curse our father or mother; we do not
want our lamp to go out in times of darkness.
Do not let us repay evil; we will wait for You,
LORD; You will save us. LORD, ordain our steps;
help us to understand the way You have for us.
Keep us from rash vows; keep us from rashly calling
something or someone holy when they are not.
Make our leaders wise; may they winnow the wicked.
May our spirits be Your lamp, LORD; search
the innermost parts of our being.
May loyalty and truth preserve our leaders;
may they uphold their positions by righteousness.
Let the glory of our young men be their strength in You,
and as we grow old, let our gray hair bring us honor.
Scour away evil from our innermost parts.
For the sake of Your name, Jesus~"

Please read Proverbs 21.

Meditate on verse 23.

> *He who guards his mouth and his tongue*
> *guards his soul from troubles.*

Pray Proverbs 21 over yourself and those for whom you stand guard as a faithful, prayerful watchman (Isaiah 62:6-7).

> *"LORD, the king's heart is like channels of water in Your*
> *hand; turn it wherever You wish. LORD, weigh the heart*
> *of _____ and me; may our ways be right in Your eyes.*
> *Help us do righteousness and justice, for You*
> *desire that more than sacrifice.*
> *Keep us from haughty eyes and a proud heart,*
> *the lamp of the wicked, for it is sin.*
> *Make us diligent; let our plans lead surely to advantage.*
> *Do not let us be hasty, coming surely to poverty.*
> *Let us acquire no treasures by a lying tongue for*
> *that is a fleeting vapor, the pursuit of death.*
> *The violence of the wicked will drag them away; the way of a guilty*
> *man is crooked, so make us pure; let our conduct be upright.*
> *Do not let _____ be a contentious woman; let*
> *it not be better for her husband to live in a corner*
> *of a roof than inside the house with her.*
> *Keep our souls from being wicked and desiring evil.*
> *Give us favor with our neighbors. Make us wise;*
> *instruct us and let us receive Your knowledge.*
> *Make us righteous; do not let our house be*
> *ruined because of wickedness.*
> *Do not let us shut our ears to the cry of the poor.*
> *Let justice be exercised, bringing joy to the righteous.*
> *Do not let us wander from the way of understanding.*
> *Do not let us love pleasure, wine, and oil*
> *because that will not make us rich.*

Do not let _____ be a contentious and vexing woman.
Let our home be known as the dwelling of the
wise, filled with precious treasure and oil.
As we pursue righteousness and loyalty, let us find life,
righteousness, and honor. Make us wise with the ability
to scale the city of the mighty and bring down
the stronghold in which they trust.
Let us guard our mouth and tongue, guarding our soul from troubles.
Do not let us act with insolent pride; we do not want
our names to be: 'Proud,' 'Haughty,' and 'Scoffer.'
Let our hands desire and be able to work.
Keep us from the desires of a sluggard, for they put him to death.
Make us the righteous who give and do not hold back. Make
us people who listen to the truth and who speak forever.
Keep us upright and make our way sure.
LORD, no wisdom, no understanding, and
no counsel can stand up against You.
Help us prepare for the day of battle.
Because the victory belongs to You, LORD Jesus~"

JULY 22

Please read Proverbs 22.

Meditate on verse 4.

> *The reward of humility and the fear of the
> LORD are riches, honor, and life.*

Pray Proverbs 22 over yourself and those for whom you stand guard as a faithful, prayerful watchman (Isaiah 62:6-7).

"LORD, _____ and I desire a good name more than great wealth;
Your favor is better than silver and gold.
LORD, You are the Maker of the rich and the
poor; therefore, we have a common bond.
Make us prudent; let us hide ourselves from evil.
Let us be humble and fear You, LORD; let us be rewarded
with riches, honor, and life. Let us guard ourselves and keep us
far from the thorns and snares of the way of the perverse.
Help us train our children in the way they should go; when
they are old, do not let them depart from that way.
Do not let us sow iniquity and reap vanity.
Make us generous; bless us; let us give some of our food to the poor.
As we drive out the scoffer, make contention go
out; make strife and dishonor cease.
May the king be our friend as we love purity
of heart and have gracious speech.
LORD, Your eyes preserve knowledge;
overthrow the words of the treacherous man.
Do not let us be sluggards and keep us from the pit of the
adulteress; we do not want to be cursed by You, LORD.
Do not let foolishness be bound up in the hearts of our children;
may the rod of discipline remove foolishness far from them.
Do not let us oppress the poor to make more for ourselves.
Let us incline our ears and hear the words of the wise;
let us apply our minds to Your knowledge, for it will be pleasant if
we keep Your Words within us that they may be ready on our lips.

*Our trust is in You, LORD! Help us teach others; help
us write excellent things of counsels and knowledge,
to make people know the certainty of the Word of Truth,
that they may give correct answers. Keep us from robbing the
poor and crushing the afflicted, for You will plead their
case and take the life of those who rob them.
Do not let us associate with a man given to anger
or go with a hot-tempered man; we do not want to
learn his ways and find a snare for ourselves.
Do not let us be among those who give pledges
and become guarantors for debts.
If we have nothing with which to pay, do not
let our bed be taken from under us.
Do not let us move the ancient boundary set by our fathers.
Make us skilled in our work; let us stand before kings.
For the sake of Your Kingdom, King Jesus~"*

Please read Proverbs 23.

Meditate on verse 17.

> *Do not let your heart envy sinners but live*
> *in the fear of the LORD always.*

Pray Proverbs 23 over yourself and those for whom you stand guard as a faithful, prayerful watchman (Isaiah 62:6-7).

> *"LORD, when You give _____ and me the opportunity*
> *to dine with a ruler, let us consider carefully what is before*
> *us; remove our appetite for deceptive delicacies.*
> *Do not let us weary ourselves to gain wealth; let us cease*
> *consideration of it, for when we set our eyes on wealth, it*
> *is gone like an eagle that flies toward the heavens.*
> *Do not let us eat the bread of a selfish man or desire his*
> *delicacies, for as he thinks within himself, so he is.*
> *He says, 'Eat and drink!' but his heart is not with*
> *us; we will vomit the morsel we have eaten.*
> *Do not let us waste our compliments on that selfish*
> *person. Do not let us speak in the hearing of a fool,*
> *for he will despise the wisdom of our words.*
> *Do not let us move the ancient boundary or go into*
> *the fields of the fatherless, for their Redeemer is strong;*
> *we do want You to plead their case against us.*
> *Make us apply our hearts to discipline and*
> *our ears to words of knowledge.*
> *Do not let us hold back discipline from our children; if*
> *we need to strike them with the rod, they will not die,*
> *and it will rescue their souls from Sheol (hell).*
> *Give our children wise hearts, so our own hearts will be glad.*
> *Our innermost being will rejoice when their lips speak*
> *what is right. Do not let their hearts envy sinners; let*
> *them always live in the fear of You, LORD.*

May they remember that surely there is a
future; do not let their hope be cut off.
Let our children listen and be wise; direct their hearts in Your Way.
Do not let them be with heavy drinkers of wine or with gluttonous
eaters of meat, for the heavy drinker and the glutton will
come to poverty, and drowsiness will clothe one with rags.
May our children listen to us and not despise us when
we are old. Let them buy truth and not sell it; let them
get wisdom and instruction and understanding.
Make us parents of the righteous; let us greatly rejoice!
Let us sire wise children and be glad in them.
Make us glad in our children; let us rejoice in them!
May our children give us their hearts; let
their eyes delight in our ways.
Keep them from the deep pit of the harlot and the
narrow well of the adulterous woman.
Do not let her rob our family and increase faithlessness among men!
Do not let our family linger over wine, for it brings woe, sorrow,
contentions, complaining, wounds, and redness of eyes.
Do not let us look on the red wine that sparkles in
the cup and goes down smoothly because it ends up
biting like a serpent and stinging like a viper.
We do not want our eyes to see strange things and our minds
to utter perverse things or be like one who lies down in the
middle of the sea or like one who lies down on top of a mast.
Do not let us wake up seeking another drink.
For the sake of Your name, Jesus~"

Please read Proverbs 24.

Meditate on verses 3-4.

*By wisdom, a house is built, and by understanding, it is established;
and by knowledge, the rooms are filled with
all precious and pleasant riches.*

Pray Proverbs 24 over yourself and those for whom you stand guard as a faithful, prayerful watchman (Isaiah 62:6-7).

*"LORD, do not let _____ and me be envious of
evil men nor desire to be with them, for their minds
devise violence and their lips talk of trouble.
Let our house be built by Your wisdom, and by
Your understanding, let it be established.
By Your knowledge, let the rooms be filled with all
precious and pleasant riches. Make us wise and strong;
make us people of knowledge who increase in power.
Let us wage war with Your wise guidance and give us
victory through an abundance of counselors.
Do not let fools open their mouths in the gates.
Do not let us scheme evil plans or devise folly, which is sin.
Keep us from scoffers who are an abomination to men.
Do not let us be slack in the day of distress
so that our strength is limited.
LORD, deliver those who are being taken away to death and those
who are staggering to slaughter; oh, hold back those who destroy!
LORD, do not let us say, 'See, we did not know this,' for
You consider what we say and weigh our hearts.
You know what we say and keep our souls.
You will render to each man according to his works.
Let our children eat good honey from the comb that is sweet to
the taste and is wisdom for their souls; let them find Your wisdom
so they will have a future and their hope will not be cut off.*

Keep us righteous and do not let a wicked man lie in wait
against our dwelling nor destroy our resting place. Keep
us righteous, so even if we fall seven times, we will rise
again, for the wicked stumble in time of calamity.
Do not let us rejoice when our enemy falls, and do not
let our heart be glad when he stumbles, or You, LORD,
will see it and be displeased and turn Your
anger away from him.
Do not let us fret because of evildoers or be envious
of the wicked, for there is no future for the evil man;
the lamp of the wicked will be put out.
Let our children fear You and the king; do not let
them associate with those who are given to change;
keep them from sudden calamity and ruin.
Do not let us show partiality in judgment. Do not
let us call the wicked, 'righteous,' because people
will curse him; nations will abhor him.
Help us rebuke the wicked; let delight and good
blessing come upon us when we do.
Let our right answer be a kiss on the lips.
Let us build our house after we prepare our work outside and
make it ready in the field. Do not let us be a witness against our
neighbor without cause, and do not let us deceive with our lips.
Do not let us say, 'Thus I shall do to him as he has done to
me; I will render to the man according to his work.'
Do not let us be sluggards and people lacking sense; do not
let our fields and vineyards be completely overgrown with
thistles, covered with nettles, and our walls broken down.
When we see the field of a sluggard, let us reflect upon it;
let us look and receive instruction, for a little sleep, a little slumber,
a little folding of the hands to rest, then poverty will come as
a robber and want like an armed man. Keep us diligent.
For the sake of Your name, Jesus~"

Please read Proverbs 25.

Meditate on verse 25.

Like cold water to a weary soul,
so is good news from a distant land.

Pray Proverbs 25 over yourself and those for whom you stand guard as a faithful, prayerful watchman (Isaiah 62:6-7).

"LORD, it is to Your glory to conceal a matter, but
the glory of kings is to search out a matter.
May our rulers seek You to reveal what matters.
May our rulers allow You to search their hearts.
LORD, take away the dross from the silver;
make _____ and me a vessel for You.
Take away the wicked before the king so his throne
will be established in righteousness.
Do not let us claim honor in the presence of the king
and do not let us stand in the place of great men.
If it is Your will, LORD, let it be said to us, 'Come up here.'
Do not let us be placed lower in the presence of the prince
because we placed ourselves too high in our own eyes.
Do not let us go out hastily to argue our case so
that our neighbor humiliates us in the end.
Give us wisdom how to argue our case with our neighbor
and do not let us reveal the secrets of others.
We do not want to be reproached by the one who hears it; do not
let there be an evil report about us that will not pass away.
Let our words be spoken in right circumstances
like apples of gold in settings of silver.
Make us wise reprovers to listening ears, like an
earring of gold and an ornament of fine gold.
Make us faithful messengers to those who send us; let us refresh the
soul of our masters like the cold of snow in the time of harvest.

Do not let us be like clouds and wind without
rain by boasting about our gifts falsely.
Give us forbearance to persuade a ruler; give us soft tongues
to break the bone. When we find honey, let us only eat what
we need so we do not have it in excess and vomit it.
Let our foot rarely be in our neighbor's house so he
does not become weary of us and hate us.
Do not let us bear false witness against our neighbor and
become like a club and a sword and a sharp arrow.
Let others have confidence in us to be faithful in time of
trouble. Give us wisdom for what to do for a troubled
heart; do not let us sing songs to them for that is like taking
off a garment on a cold day or like vinegar on soda.
If our enemy is hungry, let us give him food to eat;
if he is thirsty, let us give him water to drink, for
we will heap burning coals on his head.
LORD, please reward us. Do not let us have a backbiting
tongue that brings an angry countenance.
Do not let _____ be a contentious woman whose
family would rather live in a corner of a roof than share
a house with her. Please bring good news from a distant
land; it will be like cold water to our weary souls.
Keep the righteous from giving way before the wicked, for
that is like a trampled spring and a polluted well.
There is no glory in searching out our own glory;
let us not be tempted to seek it.
Help us control our spirits so we are not like a
city that is broken into without walls.
For the sake of Your name, Jesus~"

Please read Proverbs 26.

Meditate on verse 4.

> *Do not answer a fool according to his folly,*
> *or you will also be like him.*

Pray Proverbs 26 over yourself and those for whom you stand guard as a faithful, prayerful watchman (Isaiah 62:6-7).

> *"LORD, do not let _____ and me be fools.*
> *Make us fit for honor. Do not let a curse without cause alight on us.*
> *Do not let us be fools who need a rod to the back.*
> *Do not let us answer a fool according to his folly and be like him.*
> *Help us answer him as his folly deserves so*
> *he is not wise in his own eyes.*
> *Do not let us cut off our own feet and drink violence*
> *by sending a message by the hand of a fool.*
> *Do not let us pay attention to useless proverbs in the mouth of fools.*
> *Do not let us give honor to a fool or hire a fool, for fools*
> *repeat their folly like a dog returns to its vomit.*
> *Do not let us be wise in our own eyes.*
> *Do not let us be sluggards that talk about there being a*
> *lion in the road but refuse to do anything about it.*
> *Do not let us be sluggards who turn in our*
> *beds like a door on its hinges.*
> *Do not let us be sluggards that bury our hand in the dish*
> *and are too weary to bring the dish to our mouth.*
> *Do not let us be sluggards that are wise in our own eyes.*
> *Keep us from meddling with strife that does not belong to us.*
> *Do not let us deceive our neighbor and say we were just joking.*
> *May we quiet contention by not whispering it.*
> *Do not let us be contentious kindlers of strife.*
> *Do not let us be whisperers of dainty morsels of gossip*
> *that go into the innermost parts of the body.*
> *Do not let us have burning lips and a wicked heart.*

Do not let us use our lips to disguise hate, and
do not let us lay-up deceit in our hearts.
Do not let us believe one who speaks graciously but has seven
abominations in his heart, for though his hatred covers itself with
deceit, his wickedness will be revealed before the assembly.
Keep us from digging a pit that we will fall into and
from rolling a stone that will come back on us.
Keep us from a lying tongue that hates
those it crushes and from a flattering mouth that works ruin.
In Your name, Jesus~"

July 27

Please read Proverbs 27.

Meditate on verse 2.

> *Let another praise you and not your own mouth,*
> *a stranger and not your own lips.*

Pray Proverbs 27 over yourself and those for whom you stand guard as a faithful, prayerful watchman (Isaiah 62:6-7).

> *"LORD, do not let _____ and me boast about tomorrow,*
> *for we do not know what a day may bring forth.*
> *Let another praise us and not our own mouth, a stranger*
> *and not our own lips. Keep us from the provocation*
> *of a fool; do not let us be fools who provoke.*
> *Keep us from jealousy, anger, and wrath.*
> *Help us accept and learn from an open rebuke.*
> *Do not let us conceal love. Help us learn from*
> *the faithful wounds of a friend.*
> *Do not let us be fooled by the deceitful kisses of*
> *an enemy. Let us give to the famished.*
> *Do not let _____ wander from his home.*
> *Make our counsel sweet to our friends.*
> *Do not let us forsake our friends. Give us wisdom*
> *where to turn in the day of calamity.*
> *Let our children be wise and make our hearts glad.*
> *Let us be above reproach.*
> *Let us be prudent and hide ourselves when we see evil.*
> *Do not let us naively proceed into evil and pay the penalty.*
> *Do not let us become surety for a stranger or*
> *give a pledge to an adulteress woman.*
> *Do not let us bless others with a loud voice early in the*
> *morning; do not let our voices become a curse to others.*
> *Do not let _____ be a constantly dripping,*
> *contentious woman. Restrain her, LORD.*
> *Let us sharpen each other as iron sharpens iron.*

Let us tend the fig tree, so we can eat its fruit.
Let us be honored as we care for our master.
Our hearts reflect who we are; make us like You, Jesus.
Let our eyes be satisfied with what You give us.
The crucible is for silver and the furnace for gold;
let us test the praise given to us.
Pound the foolishness out of us! Let us know well the
condition of our flocks and pay attention to our herds.
Let us always remember riches are not forever,
nor does a crown endure to all generations.
LORD, thank You for Your provision, for when
the grass disappears, the new growth is seen, and
the herbs of the mountains are gathered in.
The lambs will be for our clothing, and the
goats will bring the price of a field.
Let there be goats' milk enough for our food and the food
of our household and sustenance for our maidens.
Because of You, Jesus~"

Please read Proverbs 28.

Meditate on verse 20.

A faithful man will abound with blessings,
but he who makes haste to be rich will not go unpunished.

Pray Proverbs 28 over yourself and those for whom you stand guard as a faithful, prayerful watchman (Isaiah 62:6-7).

"LORD, please make _____ and me righteous and bold as a lion.
Do not let us be the wicked who flee when no one is pursuing.
Let our land be led by a man of understanding
and knowledge so it will endure.
Do not let us oppress the lowly.
Help us keep the law and not praise the wicked.
Make us people who seek You, LORD;
help us to understand all things.
May we walk in integrity; do not let us
strive to be rich by being crooked.
Let our children be discerning keepers of the law; do not let
them humiliate us by being a companion of gluttons.
Do not let us increase our wealth by interest and usury;
let us be gracious to the poor. Let us listen to the law so
our prayers will not be an abomination to You.
Do not let us lead the upright astray in an evil
way, or we will fall into our own pit.
Make us blameless, so we will inherit good.
Do not let us be wise in our own eyes;
give us understanding to see through those who are.
LORD, let the righteous triumph, so there will be great glory;
keep the wicked from rising, so men will not need to hide themselves.
We will not prosper if we conceal our transgressions;
may we find compassion as we confess and forsake them.
May we be blessed as we fear You always; do not let
us fall into calamity by hardening our hearts.

Do not let our rulers be wicked, running over poor
people like a roaring lion and a rushing bear.
Do not let our leaders be great oppressors who lack understanding;
let them prolong their days by hating unjust gain.
Do not let us be laden with the guilt of human
blood and become a fugitive until death.
Let us be delivered as we walk blamelessly;
do not let us be the crooked who fall at once.
Please give us plenty of food as we till our land;
do not let us follow empty pursuits which
create poverty in a time of plenty.
Make us faithful people who abound in blessings;
do not let us make haste to be rich and incur punishment.
Do not let us show partiality.
Remove from us an evil eye that hastens after
wealth, causing want to come upon us.
Help us to rebuke when necessary rather than flatter with the tongue.
Do not let our children rob from us and say, 'It is not a
transgression.' Do not let them become the companion of
a man who destroys. Do not let us be arrogant, stirring
up strife; let us prosper as we trust in You, LORD.
Do not let us be fools who trust in their own heart
but deliver us as we walk wisely with You.
May we never want as we give to the poor;
do not let us shut our eyes to them, incurring many curses.
May the wicked perish; let the righteous increase,
so men no longer need to hide themselves.
In Your name, Jesus~"

Please read Proverbs 29.

Meditate on verse 23.

> *A man's pride will bring him low,*
> *but a humble spirit will obtain honor.*

Pray Proverbs 29 over yourself and those for whom you stand guard as a faithful, prayerful watchman (Isaiah 62:6-7).

"LORD, please do not let _____ and me harden our necks after
much reproof; we do not want to be broken beyond remedy.
Let the righteous increase, so we can rejoice;
do not let the wicked rule, causing us to groan.
Let our children love wisdom and make us glad;
do not let them waste their wealth by keeping company with
harlots. Let our rulers bring stability to the land by justice;
do not let them take bribes, overthrowing the land.
Keep us from spreading a net for our steps by flattering our neighbor.
Do not let us be evil and ensnared by transgression.
Make us righteous so we can sing and rejoice.
Make us righteous so we are concerned for the rights of the poor.
Do not let us be wicked, not understanding such concern.
Scorners set a city aflame; make us wise people who turn away anger.
Make us wise; keep us from controversy with a foolish man,
for the foolish either rage or laugh, and there is no rest.
Keep us from men of bloodshed who hate the blameless;
make us upright, concerned for the life of the blameless.
Do not let us be fools, always losing our tempers;
make us wise, holding it back.
Do not let our rulers pay attention to falsehood,
for all their ministers become wicked.
LORD, You give light to our eyes.
Let our rulers judge the poor with truth, so
they will be established forever.

The rod and reproof give wisdom; do not let our
children get their own way, bringing shame to us.
Do not allow the wicked to increase; do not let
transgression increase; let the righteous see them fall.
Help us correct our children so they will give
us comfort and delight our souls.
Do not let us be unrestrained; we want Your vision, LORD!
Let us be happy as we keep the law. As Your bondslaves,
LORD, instruct us with Your Words.
Help us to understand and respond.
Do not let us be hasty in our words; do not let us be hopeless fools.
As we pamper our employee, may he become like a son.
Do not let us be angry, stirring up strife; do not let us
be hot-tempered, abounding in transgression.
Keep us from pride that brings us low; give us
a humble spirit that obtains honor.
Do not let us partner with a thief, hating our own life.
Keep us from making oaths to tell nothing.
Do not let us fear man, for that brings a snare.
Let us be exalted as we trust in You, LORD.
Many seek the ruler's favor, but we know that
justice comes from You, LORD.
Keep us from unjust men; they are abominable.
Keep us upright in Your Way;
make us abominable to the wicked.
For the glory of Your name, Jesus~"

July 30

Please read Proverbs 30.

Meditate on verse 5.

> *Every word of God is tested; He is a shield*
> *to those who take refuge in Him.*

Pray Proverbs 30 over yourself and those for whom you stand guard as a faithful, prayerful watchman (Isaiah 62:6-7).

> *"LORD, please do not let _____ and me be*
> *stupid. Give us Your understanding.*
> *Help us learn Your wisdom. Give us knowledge of You, the Holy One.*
> *For You ascended into heaven and descended.*
> *You gathered the wind in Your fists.*
> *You wrapped the waters in Your garment.*
> *You have established the ends of the earth.*
> *Your name is LORD Jesus Christ—surely we know!*
> *God, Your every Word is tested. You are a*
> *shield to us; we take refuge in You.*
> *Do not let us add to Your Words; we do not want Your*
> *reproof; we do not want to be proved a liar.*
> *LORD, please do not refuse us before we die.*
> *Keep deception and lies far from us. Give us neither poverty*
> *nor riches; feed us with the food that is our portion,*
> *that we may not be full and deny You and say, 'Who is the LORD?'*
> *or that we not be in want and steal and profane Your name, our God.*
> *Do not let us slander others. Do not let us curse*
> *our father; let us bless our mother.*
> *Do not let us be pure in our own eyes, yet*
> *not washed from our filthiness.*
> *LORD, do not let us be lofty in our own eyes; do*
> *not let us raise our eyelids in arrogance.*
> *Do not let our teeth be like swords and our jaw teeth like knives to*
> *devour the afflicted from the earth and the needy from among men.*
> *Do not let us be leeches who say, 'Give, give.'*

LORD, You are more than enough. Let us be satisfied with You.
Do not let our eyes mock our father or scorn our mother;
we do not want our eyes picked out by ravens and
eaten by eagles. There are things too wonderful
for us and things difficult to understand:
the way of an eagle in the sky, the way of a serpent on a rock,
the way of a ship in the middle of the sea,
and the way of a man with a maid.
Keep us from an adulterous woman who eats and wipes
her mouth and says, 'I have done no wrong.'
The earth quakes and cannot bear up when:
a slave becomes king, a fool is satisfied with food, an unloved
woman gets a husband, and a maidservant supplants her mistress.
These things are small on the earth but exceedingly wise:
ants who are not a strong people, but who prepare their food
in summer; the shephanim (small, shy, furry animals) who are
not mighty people, yet they make their houses in the rocks;
the locusts who have no king, yet all of them go out in ranks; the
lizard that you may grasp with the hands, yet it is in kings' palaces.
There are three things which are stately in their march, even
four which are stately when they walk: the lion which is mighty
among beasts and does not retreat before any, the strutting rooster,
the male goat also, and a king when his army is with him.
LORD, do not let us be foolish by exalting ourselves;
do not let us plot evil. Let us put our hand over our mouth
to keep from speaking foolishness, for the churning of milk
produces butter and pressing the nose brings forth blood.
Do not let us churn anger and produce strife.
In Your name, Jesus~"

Please read Proverbs 31.

Meditate on verses 8-9.

Open your mouth for the mute, for the rights of all the unfortunate.
Open your mouth, judge righteously, and defend
the rights of the afflicted and needy.

Pray Proverbs 31 over yourself and those for whom you stand guard as a faithful, prayerful watchman (Isaiah 62:6-7).

"LORD, please do not let our sons give their
strength to women or their ways to that
which destroys kings. Do not let our rulers
drink wine or desire strong drink,
for they will drink and forget what is decreed
and pervert the rights of the afflicted.
Strong drink is for him who is perishing, and wine is for him
whose life is bitter — he will drink and forget his poverty and
remember his trouble no more. Help us open our mouths
for the mute, for the rights of all the unfortunate.
Let us open our mouths, judge righteously, and
defend the rights of the afflicted and needy.
Make _____ an excellent wife; let her worth be far above jewels.
Let the heart of her husband trust in her; may he have no lack of gain.
Help her do him good and not evil all the days of her life.
Help her look for wool and flax and work with her hands in delight.
Make her like merchant ships; let her bring her food from afar.
May she rise while it is still night and give food to
her household and portions to her maidens.
Let her consider a field and buy it and from
her earnings plant a vineyard.
Help her gird herself with strength and make her arms strong.
May she sense that her gain is good;

do not let her lamp go out at night.
Let her stretch out her hand to the distaff (spindle);
let her hands grasp the spindle. Let her extend her hands
to the poor and stretch out her hands to the needy.
Do not let her be afraid of the snow for her household;
let all her household be clothed with scarlet.
Let her make coverings for herself; may her
clothing be fine linen and purple.
May her husband be known in the gates when
he sits among the elders of the land.
Help her make linen garments and sell them
and supply belts to the tradesmen.
Let strength and dignity be her clothing; may she smile at the future.
Let her open her mouth in wisdom and let the teaching of
kindness be on her tongue. Let her look well to the ways
of her household and not eat the bread of idleness.
May her children rise up and bless her and her husband
also; let him praise her, saying: 'Many daughters
have done nobly, but you excel them all.'
May she realize charm is deceitful, and beauty is vain.
May she fear You, LORD, and be praised.
Give her the product of her hands and let
her works praise her in the gates.
In Your name, Jesus~"

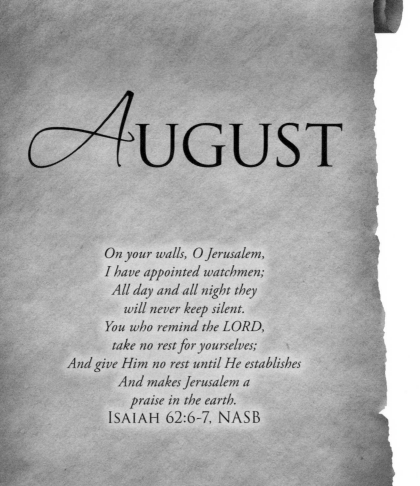

AUGUST

On your walls, O Jerusalem,
I have appointed watchmen;
All day and all night they
will never keep silent.
You who remind the LORD,
take no rest for yourselves;
And give Him no rest until He establishes
And makes Jerusalem a
praise in the earth.
ISAIAH 62:6-7, NASB

Please read Colossians 1.

Meditate on verses 3-4.

> *We give thanks to God, the Father of our LORD*
> *Jesus Christ, praying always for you,*
> *since we heard of your faith in Christ Jesus and*
> *the love which you have for all the saints.*

Imprisoned in Rome, Paul heard from Epaphras, a fellow church planter, about the faith and love of the church in Colossae. After starting this church, Epaphras visited Paul in Rome, and while there, he, too, was arrested. Tychicus brought this letter from Paul back to the Colossae Christians. God inspired Paul to write them since he was unable to meet with them. Included in the 27 books of the New Testament, this letter is also a divinely inspired message to Christians today, encouraging us to:

- Have faith in Jesus Christ (v. 4)
- Love the saints (v. 4)
- Recognize the hope laid up for us in heaven (v. 5)
- Hear and respond to the Word of Truth (v. 5)
- Help the Gospel constantly bear fruit in our communities and throughout the world (v. 6)

Pray Colossians 1:3-6 over yourself and those for whom you stand guard as a faithful, prayerful watchman (Isaiah 62:6-7).

> *"God, Father of our LORD Jesus Christ, I pray always for _____.*
> *Thank You for their faith in Christ Jesus*
> *and their love for all the saints*
> *because of the hope laid up for them in heaven,*
> *of which they previously heard in*
> *the Word of Truth, the Gospel. Let the Gospel*
> *constantly bear fruit and increase in the world.*
> *Let the Gospel constantly bear fruit and increase in _____ and*
> *me just as it has been doing since the day we heard of it*
> *and understood Your grace, O God, in truth.*
> *In Your name, Jesus~"*

Please read Colossians 2.

Meditate on verses 9-10.

> *For in Him, all the fullness of Deity dwells*
> *in bodily form, and in Him,*
> *you have been made complete, and He is the*
> *head over all rule and authority.*

The Colossae church started in the midst of the Greek and Roman god and goddess culture, where the opportunity to worship any deity was available—similar to today's world where some say it does not matter who or what you worship so long as you sincerely believe. Paul wanted the Christians to know without a doubt that Jesus Christ is fully God, and they were fully complete in Him. No god, goddess, or religious philosophy could make them more complete.

Do not be deceived by world philosophies and religions. Only in Christ, can a person be raised up (v. 12). Only in Christ, can a person have all their transgressions forgiven (v. 13). Only in Christ, can a person have their debt to God cancelled (v. 14). Only in Christ, can a person have an intimate relationship with their Creator.

If you have already been made complete in Christ, thank Him by walking wholeheartedly with Him all the days of your life. If you are trying to find completeness in the ways of the world, please stop and give yourself completely to Jesus—He promises to complete you.

Pray Colossians 2:9-10 as a commitment to Jesus Christ.

> *"LORD Jesus, I honor You as the fullness of Deity.*
> *Thank You for coming in bodily form for*
> *me. Make me complete in You.*
> *I surrender my will and authority to You, the*
> *head over all rule and authority.*
> *In Your name, Jesus~"*

Please read Colossians 3.

Meditate on verses 10-11.

> *Put on the new self who is being renewed to a true knowledge*
> *according to the image of the One who created him—a*
> *renewal in which there is no distinction between Greek*
> *and Jew, circumcised and uncircumcised, barbarian,*
> *Scythian, slave, and freeman, but Christ is all and in all.*

Imagine the relief those words brought to the Christians in Colossae who were part of the Roman empire ruled by class distinction. Slavery, gender, citizenship, religious heritage, wealth, and education all played a part in this world of status. God's renewal was stunning because none of that mattered.

Consider these other stunning realities that accompany being made new in Christ:

You are raised up with Jesus and hidden with Him in God (vs. 1, 3). Christ is your life; you set your mind on His interests (vs. 1-4).

Since Jesus is your life, you are dead to the bad things you used to do: immorality, impurity, passion, evil desire, and greed (vs. 4-5). Those things bring God's judgement and wrath; you should desire not to walk in them any longer (vs. 6-7). Like a change of clothing, put them all aside, including: anger, wrath, malice, slander, abusive speech, and lying (vs. 8-9). In the same motion of spiritually laying aside the old self clothes, put on the new self which is constantly being renewed, constantly growing in the knowledge of Jesus (v. 10).

Pray Colossians 3:10-11 over yourself and those for whom you stand guard as a faithful, prayerful watchman (Isaiah 62:6-7).

> *"LORD, thank You that _____ and I have put on the new self.*
> *Help us be renewed to a true knowledge of*
> *You, the One who created us.*
> *Thank You for a renewal in which there is no distinction*
> *because Christ, You are all and in all.*
> *In Your name, Jesus~"*

Please read Colossians 4.

Meditate on verse 3.

> *Praying at the same time for us as well, that God*
> *will open up to us a door for the Word,*
> *so that we may speak forth the mystery of Christ,*
> *for which I have also been imprisoned.*

As Paul came to the end of his letter, he had a prayer request—for God to provide opportunities, even in prison, for the Gospel to be shared. Paul knew God uses every situation for His good (Romans 8:28).

It is important to have the same perspective on your life circumstances. Perhaps you are in a bad situation in your relationships, neighborhood, school, workplace, hospital, or prison; the LORD wants you to maximize the time for the Kingdom's good. Ask Him to make you like Paul, being the best witness possible wherever you are.

Here is advice from Colossians 4 for how to be a good witness:

- ✥ Devote yourself to prayer
  - Keep alert in your prayers
  - Keep an attitude of thanksgiving (v. 2)
- ✥ Conduct yourself with wisdom toward outsiders
  - Make the most of every opportunity
  - Let your speech be with grace (as though seasoned with salt)
  - Know how to respond to each person (vs. 5-6)

Pray Colossians 4:2-6 over yourself and those for whom you stand guard as a faithful, prayerful watchman (Isaiah 62:6-7).

> *"LORD, help _____ and me devote ourselves to prayer,*
> *keeping alert in it with an attitude of thanksgiving.*
> *Open up to us a door for the Word, so we may*
> *speak forth the mystery of Christ.*

LORD, make it clear in the way we ought to speak.
Help us conduct ourselves with wisdom toward
outsiders, making the most of the opportunity.
Let our speech always be with grace, as though seasoned with salt,
so we will know how we should respond to each person.
For the sake of Your name, Jesus~"

AUGUST 5

Please read Ecclesiastes 1.

Meditate on verses 1-2.

Note: Vanity comes from the Hebrew word *hebel*. Solomon used this word 38 times in *Ecclesiastes*. *Hebel* means emptiness and unsatisfactory. It is translated as futility, fleeting, emptiness, and vanity in the New American Standard translation of *Ecclesiastes*.[1]

> *The words of the Preacher, the son of David, king in Jerusalem.*
> *"Vanity of vanities," says the Preacher,*
> *"Vanity of vanities! All is vanity."*

Ecclesiastes was written by David's son, Solomon—a king renowned for his wealth and wisdom. Yet, *Ecclesiastes* reveals him to be a human struggling with life, work, thoughts, attitudes, and relationships. Solomon's feelings, which are often negative, are honestly expressed in this book.

You may find it intriguing that God would include such a cynical book in His Holy Scripture, or perhaps you find it comforting that the Holy Spirit through Solomon put into words what your spirit may be groaning (Romans 8:23, 26). As you read *Ecclesiastes*, ask God to give you His eternal perspective and verses to pray over your life situations.

Pray Ecclesiastes 1:4-7, taking comfort in God's created consistencies.

> *"LORD, I thank You for these truths from Your Word.*
> *'A generation goes, and a generation comes,*
> *but the earth remains forever.*
> *Also, the sun rises and the sun sets; and hastening*
> *to its place it rises there again.*
> *Blowing toward the south, then turning toward the north,*
> *the wind continues swirling along; and on its*
> *circular courses the wind returns.*
> *All the rivers flow into the sea, yet the sea is not full.*
> *To the place where the rivers flow, there they flow again.'*
> *In the midst of confusion, help me remember these things.*
> *In Your name, Jesus~"*

1. Retrieved from https://www.blueletterbible.org/lang/lexicon/lexicon.cfm?Strongs=H1892&t=NASB

AUGUST 6

Please read Ecclesiastes 2.

Meditate on verse 20.

> *Therefore, I completely despaired of all the fruit of my labor*
> *for which I had labored under the sun.*

You were probably taken aback by Solomon's self-absorption in this chapter. He used the words I, me, my, and myself over 65 times. "**I** explored with **my** mind how to stimulate **my** body...**I** enlarged **my** works; **I** built houses for **myself**...**I** collected for **myself** silver and gold...**I** became great...**I** considered all **my** activities which **my** hands had done..." (vs. 3-4, 8-9, 11).

No wonder Solomon felt empty and fruitless; it is indeed vain to desire such a self-absorbed lifestyle.

Jesus did the opposite of Solomon and lived a full and fruitful life. He emptied Himself and became a bond-servant for the purpose of dying for others (Philippians 2:5-8).

As a follower of Jesus Christ, you are commanded to follow His example, doing nothing from selfishness or empty conceit, but humbly regarding others as more important than yourself (Philippians 2:3).

Examine your life. Do your words and actions mirror Solomon's, or do you try to live like Christ?

Pray Ecclesiastes 2:25-26a over yourself and those for whom you stand guard as a faithful, prayerful watchman (Isaiah 62:6-7).

> *"LORD, who can eat and have enjoyment without You?*
> *Make _____ and me good in Your sight;*
> *give us Your wisdom, knowledge, and joy.*
> *In Your name, Jesus~"*

Please read Ecclesiastes 3.

Meditate on these phrases from verses 11 and 14.

He has also set eternity in their heart.
I know that everything God does will remain forever.

Our young grandson often says, "I want to stay here **forever**" when he is someplace enjoying himself. God placed that desire for the eternal into the heart of every human, so they would turn their hearts to Him.

Ecclesiastes 3 beautifully expresses the tension between the confines of time and the freedom of eternity. "There is a time to give birth and a time to die" (v. 2). With every "There is a time to…" your heart cries out, "There is more to life than 'a time to keep and a time to throw away!'" (v. 6). You yearn for the eternal, a place where you can stay **forever**.

The world is passing away, and also its lusts;
*but the one who does the will of God lives **forever**.*
—1 John 2:17

Give your heart's desires to the LORD and seek to do His will, obtaining His eternal perspective. Pray Ecclesiastes 3:11-14 over yourself and those for whom you stand guard as a faithful, prayerful watchman (Isaiah 62:6-7).

"LORD, You have made everything appropriate
in its time. You have also set eternity
in _____ and my heart. LORD, please reveal Your work that You
have done from the beginning even to the end, so we can participate
in it. I know there is nothing better than to rejoice and do good
in our lifetime. Let us eat, drink, and see good in all our labor
— that is a gift of You, God. I know that everything You do will
remain forever; there is nothing to add to it, and there is nothing
to take from it, for You have worked that men should fear You.
May we always fear You.
In Your name, Jesus~"

Please read Ecclesiastes 4.

Meditate on verse 12b.

>   *A cord of three strands is not quickly torn apart.*

You may have heard the phrase: "A cord of three strands is not easily broken." It comes from *Ecclesiastes* and refers to the strength of a tightly twisted three-strand rope versus a one or two-strand rope. This three-strand rope is symbolic of the strength that comes from doing life with God and others.

Ecclesiastes 4:12 is sometimes used in wedding ceremonies to give the visual of a married couple becoming one with each other and with God in order to make a union that will not be broken by the world. "How blessed the two who add onto this cord that they've begun a third strand—that of God, who binds them into one."[1]

Pray Ecclesiastes 4:9 and 12 over your relationships as a faithful, prayerful watchman (Isaiah 62:6-7).

>   *"LORD, two are better than one because they*
>   *have a good return for their labor.*
>   *Help_____ and me not be overpowered. Together help us*
>   *resist one who tries to overpower us. Make us a cord of three*
>   *strands with You, so we will not be quickly torn apart.*
>   *In Your name, Jesus~"*

---

1. From the poem "Cord of Three Strands" by Jan Lutz.

Please read Ecclesiastes 5.

Meditate on verse 1.

> *Guard your steps as you go to the house of God and draw near to listen*
> *rather than to offer the sacrifice of fools; for*
> *they do not know they are doing evil.*

As a Christian, you have the privilege of being in God's presence every moment of the day. In His presence, you can talk to Him and listen to Him all the time. Examine your day. What does it look like in relation to communicating with God? Here are some questions to get you started.

1. What are the first things you do in the mornings?
2. How much of your day is in silence – no media sounds from any type of device?
3. Would you describe yourself as one who "prays without ceasing" (1 Thessalonians 5:17)?
4. Do you listen for the Holy Spirit to talk to you when you pray?
5. Do you memorize God's Word?

Ask the LORD how He would answer these questions about you. Let Him show you times in your day that need to be more wholly devoted to Him.

Pray Ecclesiastes 5:1 over yourself and those for whom you stand guard as a faithful, prayerful watchman (Isaiah 62:6-7).

> *"LORD, please help_____ and me guard*
> *our steps as we go to Your house.*
> *Let us draw near to listen rather than to offer the sacrifice of fools.*
> *LORD, please keep us from doing any form of evil.*
> *In Your name, Jesus~"*

AUGUST 10

Please read Ecclesiastes 6. Notice Solomon's questions.

Meditate on verse 1.

> *There is an evil which I have seen under the sun,*
> *and it is prevalent among men—*

Do you ever find yourself screaming, "What's the point, God!?" Solomon was in that futile place.

Let's see how God would answer some of his questions.

   ❦ Do not all go to one place (v. 6)?

> *And if anyone's name was not found written in the book of life,*
> *he was thrown into the lake of fire.*
> *We are of good courage, I say, and prefer*
> *rather to be absent from the body*
> *and to be at home with the LORD.*
> —Revelation 20:15; 2 Corinthians 5:8

   ❦ What advantage does the wise man have over the fool (v. 8)?

> *The fool has said in his heart, "There is no God."*
> *How blessed is the man who finds wisdom!*
> —Psalm 14:1a; Proverbs 3:13a

   ❦ Who knows what is good for a man during his lifetime, during the few years of his futile life (v. 12)?

> *He has told you, O man, what is good and*
> *what the LORD requires of you:*
> *to do justice, to love kindness, and to walk humbly with your God.*
> —Micah 6:8

Meditating on God's Word replaces futile thinking. Give all of your Ecclesiastes 6:1 situations to the LORD as a faithful, prayerful watchman (Isaiah 62:6-7).

> *"LORD, there is an evil which I have seen under*
> *the sun, and it is prevalent among men—*
> *LORD, I surrender what l have seen to You.*
> *In Your name, Jesus~"*

Please read Ecclesiastes 7.

Meditate on verse 9.

> *Do not be eager in your heart to be angry,*
> *for anger resides in the bosom of fools.*

Are you an angry person? Is your first reaction to get mad at situations contrary to your desires? Do people tiptoe around you, or go to great lengths to keep you happy, just so they do not have to experience your wrath?

Be honest with yourself and God. Let the Holy Spirit convict you of areas of your life where you answered "yes" to those questions. Let God's Word bring conviction, repentance, and healing to you.

> *A quick-tempered man acts foolishly.*
> —Proverbs 14:17a

> *This you know, my beloved brethren.*
> *But everyone must be quick to hear, slow to speak, and slow to anger;*
> *for the anger of man does not achieve the righteousness of God.*
> —James 1:19-20

> *Cease from anger and forsake wrath;*
> *do not fret; it leads only to evildoing.*
> —Psalm 37:8

Pray Ecclesiastes 7:9 over yourself and those for whom you stand guard as a faithful, prayerful watchman (Isaiah 62:6-7).

> *"LORD, do not let_____ and me be eager in our hearts to be angry,*
> *for anger resides in the bosoms of fools. We do not want to be fools.*
> *In Your name, Jesus~"*

Please read Ecclesiastes 8.

Meditate on verses 12-13.

> *Although a sinner does evil a hundred times and may lengthen his life,*
> *still I know that it will be well for those who*
> *fear God, who fear Him openly.*
> *But it will not be well for the evil man,*
> *and he will not lengthen his days*
> *like a shadow because he does not fear God.*

Do not grow weary and lose heart as you fear God and serve Him whole-heartedly. There may be times when it appears futile to be sold-out for God, but press on in the LORD; fight the good fight and finish the race God has called you to run with Him. The reward of running with Christ and intimately knowing Him is so worth it.

> *Say to the righteous that it will go well with them,*
> *for they will eat the fruit of their actions.*
> *Woe to the wicked! It will go badly with him,*
> *for what he deserves will be done to him.*
> —Isaiah 3:10-11

Pray Ecclesiastes 8:12-13 over yourself and those for whom you stand guard as a faithful, prayerful watchman (Isaiah 62:6-7).

> *"LORD, let it be well for _____ and me as*
> *we fear You. Let us fear You openly.*
> *LORD, make_____ stop being evil—it is not going well for them.*
> *Make them fear You, so their days can lengthen like a shadow.*
> *In Your name that is to be feared, Jesus~"*

Please read Ecclesiastes 9.

Meditate on verse 1.

*For I have taken all this to my heart and explain
it that righteous men, wise men,
and their deeds are in the hand of God.
Man does not know whether it will be love
or hatred; anything awaits him.*

Solomon understood his life was in God's hands. Knowing this truth helps you walk through your day with its good and bad, highs and lows. It helps you walk confidently in God and His ability to take you through life on earth into eternity with Him.

Whether you are in a pleasant or painful season of life, entrust your soul to the faithful Creator in doing what is right (1 Peter 4:19). Fix your eyes on eternity with Jesus and do not lose heart in doing good, for in due time, you will reap if you do not grow weary (Galatians 6:9).

Pray Ecclesiastes 9:1 over yourself and those for whom you stand guard as a faithful, prayerful watchman (Isaiah 62:6-7).

*"LORD, make_____ and me righteous and wise.
Keep our deeds and us in Your hand.
We do not know whether love or hatred awaits us,
but we trust in You.
Because of Your name, Jesus~"*

Please read Ecclesiastes 10.

Meditate on verses 12-13.

> *Words from the mouth of a wise man are gracious,*
> *while the lips of a fool consume him;*
> *the beginning of his talking is folly, and*
> *the end of it is wicked madness.*

With whom do you most relate from the meditation verses: the wise man or the fool? Are the words of your mouth pleasant and gracious or wicked and foolish? Let God's Words cleanse you of all unrighteousness.

> *Let the words of my mouth and the meditation of my heart*
> *be acceptable in Your sight, O LORD, my Rock and my Redeemer.*
> —Psalm 19:14

> *Set a guard, O LORD, over my mouth; keep*
> *watch over the door of my lips.*
> *Do not incline my heart to any evil thing.*
> —Psalm 141:3-4a

> *Then one of the seraphim flew to me with a burning coal in his hand,*
> *which he had taken from the altar with tongs. He touched my*
> *mouth with it and said, "Behold, this has touched your lips,*
> *and your iniquity is taken away, and your sin is forgiven."*
> —Isaiah 6:6-7

Thank the LORD for His ability and willingness to forgive the sins of your lips. Under His control, choose not to sin with your tongue (Psalm 39:1).

Pray Ecclesiastes 10:12 over yourself and those for whom you stand guard as a faithful, prayerful watchman (Isaiah 62:6-7).

> *"LORD, make _____ and me wise people. May*
> *the words from our mouths be gracious.*
> *Do not let us be fools with lips that consume us!*
> *In Your name, Jesus-"*

Please read Ecclesiastes 11.

Meditate on the phrase "You do not know" in verses 2 and 5-6.

> *You do not know what misfortune may occur on the earth.*
> *You do not know the path of the wind and*
> *how bones are formed in the womb.*
> *You do not know the activity of God who makes all things.*
> *You do not know whether morning or evening sowing will succeed.*

It doesn't matter how intelligent or educated you are, there are many things you do not know and things you are incapable of understanding. "However, there is a God in heaven who reveals mysteries" (Daniel 2:28), and you must choose to trust Him. When you humbly acknowledge you do not know it all and submit yourself to the God who does, you will experience inexplicable freedom and confidence for what to do and when to do it.

Pray Ecclesiastes 11:6 over yourself and those for whom you stand guard as a faithful, prayerful watchman (Isaiah 62:6-7).

> *"LORD, help _____ and me to sow our seed in the morning*
> *and not be idle in the evening, for we do not*
> *know whether morning or evening*
> *sowing will succeed, or whether both of them alike will be good.*
> *But You know, God, and we trust You.*
> *In Your name, Jesus~"*

Please read Ecclesiastes 12.

Meditate on verses 13-14.

> *The conclusion, when all has been heard, is:*
> *fear God and keep His commandments*
> *because this applies to every person.*
> *For God will bring every act to judgment,*
> *everything which is hidden, whether it is good or evil.*

Solomon addressed difficult perplexities people encounter during their journey on earth. Often sounding negative and cynical, Solomon put into words what your heart may be crying, today.

Because of what is happening in your world, obey the three commands in Ecclesiastes 12:

1. Remember your Creator (v. 1).
2. Fear God (v. 13).
3. Keep His commandments (v. 13).

Pray Ecclesiastes 12:1 and 13-14 over yourself and those for whom you stand guard as a faithful, prayerful watchman (Isaiah 62:6-7).

> *"LORD, please help _____ and me remember You, our Creator,*
> *in the days of our youth before the evil days come.*
> *May we delight in the years You give us.*
> *Help us fear You and keep Your commandments*
> *because this applies to every person.*
> *God, You will bring every act to judgment,*
> *everything which is hidden,*
> *whether it is good or evil. Please help us do*
> *acts that are good in Your sight.*
> *In Your name, Jesus~"*

Please read 1 Thessalonians 1.

Meditate on verse 5.

> *For our Gospel did not come to you in word only,*
> *but also in power and in the Holy Spirit and with full conviction;*
> *just as you know what kind of men we proved*
> *to be among you for your sake.*

Paul risked his life to share the Gospel in Thessalonica because he was fully convicted about its truth (Acts 17:1-10). Many believed, and after Paul left, he wrote this letter to encourage those Christians who lived among people who hated Jesus and His Gospel.

You still live in a world of tribulation for those who follow Christ (v. 6). Read this letter as if it were written personally to you, for the LORD certainly had you on His mind when He had Paul pen these words. Be encouraged in your walk with Jesus to imitate Him and be an example to others (vs. 6-7). Let the Word of God sound forth from you so others can hear about Jesus (v. 8).

Pray 1 Thessalonians 1:1-4 over those for whom you stand guard as a faithful, prayerful watchman (Isaiah 62:6-7).

> *"LORD, let Your grace and peace come to _____.*
> *God, I thank You always for them. Thank You*
> *for their work of faith, labor of love,*
> *and steadfastness of hope in You, our LORD Jesus Christ.*
> *Thank You for choosing them to be beloved by You.*
> *For the sake of Your name, Jesus~"*

AUGUST 18

Please read 1 Thessalonians 2.

Meditate on verse 8.

> *Having so fond an affection for you, we were well-pleased*
> *to impart to you not only the Gospel of God but also our*
> *own lives, because you had become very dear to us.*

This is a great chapter for how to share the Gospel. As you learn from the verses, pray them over yourself:

- ❧ "God, give me boldness in You to share the Gospel even amid much opposition" (v. 2).
- ❧ "Make me approved by You, God, to be entrusted with the Gospel. Let me speak to please You and not men" (v. 4).
- ❧ "Do not let me share the Gospel with flattering speech or for the glory of men" (vs. 5-6).
- ❧ "Let me be gentle in sharing the Gospel with others, as a nursing mother tenderly cares for her own children" (v. 7).
- ❧ "Give me a fond affection for others, so I will share not only the Gospel but also my life with them" (v. 8).
- ❧ "Help me behave devoutly, uprightly, and blamelessly toward others" (v. 10).
- ❧ "Let me exhort, encourage, and implore new believers as a father would his own children" (v. 11).

Now pray 1 Thessalonians 2:12-13 over those with whom you are sharing the Gospel, as their faithful, prayerful watchman (Isaiah 62:6-7).

> *"LORD, please call _____ into Your Kingdom and glory.*
> *Let them walk in a manner worthy of You. Let them receive*
> *Your Word as the Word of God, not the word of men.*
> *Let Your Word perform its work in them who believe.*
> *For the glory of Your name, Jesus–"*

Please read 1 Thessalonians 3.

Meditate on verse 8.

For now we really live, if you stand firm in the LORD.

It was a big deal to Paul for those he led to Christ to stand firm in Christ. In order for new believers to be firm in the LORD, they must be taught how to walk with Him. As you share the Gospel with others, give them the tools to walk with Jesus. Learning how to pray, read the Bible, and be part of a church are vital to standing firm in Christ. That is why Paul not only shared the Gospel with people, but his life also, so they could see and learn by example what it means to be a Christian (1 Thessalonians 2:8).

Ask God to make you a great sharer of the Gospel and a great shepherd of those you lead to Christ. You will really live, when you know that those you love are standing firm in Jesus (v. 8).

Pray 1 Thessalonians 3:12-13 over yourself and those for whom you stand guard as a faithful, prayerful watchman (Isaiah 62:6-7).

"LORD, please cause _____ and me to increase and abound
in love for one another and for all people. Establish our hearts
without blame in holiness before You, our God and Father,
at the coming of our LORD Jesus with all His saints.
In Your name, Jesus~"

We have written a workbook called *50 Steps With Jesus: Learning to Walk Daily With the Lord.* You can learn more about it at: www.Godsgreatergrace. com

You even have permission to make all the copies you need to teach new believers how to walk with Jesus.

Please read 1 Thessalonians 4.

Meditate on verse 1.

> *Finally then, brethren, we request and exhort you in the LORD Jesus,*
> *that as you received from us instruction as to how you ought to walk*
> *and please God (just as you actually do*
> *walk), that you excel still more.*

Twice in this chapter, Paul urges believers to "excel still more" in their walk with Jesus (vs. 1, 10). He didn't want them to stay as baby Christians; he wanted their walk to be abundant and excellent in Christ.

Three times in this chapter, Paul talks about the "sanctification" of believers (vs. 3, 4, 7). It is God's will for every Christian to become more and more sanctified—more and more purified—as they walk with the LORD. You cannot help but become pure and holy when you walk with Jesus—talking to Him, reading His Word, and fellowshipping with other believers. Sanctification—growing up in Christ to become more and more like Him—is a miraculous process, and it is God's will for you to excel at it.

Pray 1 Thessalonians 4:7-10 over yourself and those for whom you stand guard as a faithful, prayerful watchman (Isaiah 62:6-7).

> *"LORD, You have not called _____ and me for the*
> *purpose of impurity but for sanctification. Thank You for*
> *giving us the Holy Spirit; we will not reject You, God.*
> *Teach us how to love one another and help us to excel still more.*
> *In Your name, Jesus~"*

Please read 1 Thessalonians 5.

Meditate on verse 6.

So then let us not sleep as others do but let us be alert and sober.

Paul ends his letter with a list of exhortations for believers to be able to excel still more in their walks with Christ (1 Thessalonians 4:1). Ask the LORD to help you apply them to your walk with Him and to your relationships with others in your church:

- Be alert and sober (v. 6).
- Encourage, build up, and live in peace with one another, appreciating and esteeming those who labor among you and who teach you (vs. 11-13).
- Admonish the unruly, help the weak, encourage the fainthearted, and be patient with everyone (v. 14).
- See that no one repays another with evil for evil; always seek what is good for others (v. 15).
- Rejoice always, pray unceasingly, and give thanks in everything (vs. 16-18).
- Do not quench the Spirit and do not despise prophetic utterances (vs. 19-20).
- Examine everything carefully and hold fast to what is good (v. 21).
- Abstain from every form of evil (v. 22).

Ask the LORD to help you obey and pray 1 Thessalonians 5:23-24 over yourself and those for whom you stand guard as a faithful, prayerful watchman (Isaiah 62:6-7).

"God of peace, sanctify _____ and me entirely; may our spirit, soul, and body be preserved complete, without blame at Your coming, LORD Jesus Christ. God, You are faithful; You have called us, and You will bring it to pass. In Your name, Jesus~"

Please read 2 Thessalonians 1.

Meditate on verse 4.

> *We ourselves speak proudly of you among the*
> *churches of God for your perseverance*
> *and faith in the midst of all your persecutions*
> *and afflictions which you endure.*

Not long after writing his first letter to the believers in Thessalonica, Paul wrote a second one to encourage them as they continued to experience much persecution. Miraculously, their faith and love were growing despite affliction (vs. 3-4). Paul told them that churches around the world were being told about their faith, inspiring them to also persevere. Paul reminded the Thessalonians to keep their focus on eternity, when Christ "comes to be glorified in His saints and to be marveled at among all who believed" (v. 10). It helps to remember how the story ends when times are tough.

Take encouragement from this letter as if it were written personally to you. When your faith is enlarged and your love for others grows, you encourage others in their walk with Christ. When you are afflicted, keep your thoughts on eternity, for the LORD Jesus will deal out retribution to those who do not know God and obey His Gospel (vs. 7-8).

Pray Paul's prayer from 2 Thessalonians 1:11-12 over yourself and those for whom you stand guard as a faithful, prayerful watchman (Isaiah 62:6-7).

> *"God, count _____ and me worthy of our calling and fulfill*
> *every desire for goodness and the work of faith with power so that*
> *Your name, LORD Jesus, will be glorified in us and us in You.*
> *According to Your grace, God and LORD Jesus Christ~"*

Please read 2 Thessalonians 2.

Meditate on verses 11-13.

> *For this reason, God will send upon them a deluding influence*
> *so that they will believe what is false, in*
> *order that they all may be judged*
> *who did not believe the truth but took pleasure in wickedness.*
> ***But*** *we should always give thanks to God for*
> *you, brethren beloved by the LORD,*
> *because God has chosen you from the beginning for salvation*
> *through sanctification by the Spirit and faith in the truth.*

What a sobering contrast between those who do not believe the truth and those who are saved through faith in the Truth! Those who take pleasure in wickedness are so deceived they believe lies. But, those who receive God's love of the truth are chosen and beloved by Him. Those who do not believe God's truth will be judged; those who love the truth of God will gain the glory of the LORD Jesus Christ (vs. 10-14).

It seems like an easy choice to make. Pray for God to remove the deluding influence from those who need to be chosen and beloved by Him. Pray for them to choose to believe the truth. Pray 2 Thessalonians 2:13-17 as a faithful, prayerful watchman (Isaiah 62:6-7).

> *"God, please make _____ Your beloved. Choose them for salvation*
> *through sanctification by the Spirit and faith in the truth.*
> *Call them through the Gospel that they may*
> *gain Your glory, LORD Jesus Christ.*
> *Make _____ and me stand firm and hold*
> *to the traditions we were taught.*
> *LORD Jesus Christ and God our Father, thank You for loving us*
> *and giving us eternal comfort and good hope by grace.*
> *Please comfort and strengthen our hearts*
> *in every good work and word.*
> *In Your name, Jesus~'*

Please read 2 Thessalonians 3.

Meditate on verse 11.

> *For we hear that some among you are leading an undisciplined life,*
> *doing no work at all but acting liking busybodies.*

There were lazy people in the Thessalonian church, not working, mooching off of others, and sticking their nose in other people's business when they needed to get their own business in order to buy food (vs. 10-12). If this describes somebody you know, ask the LORD to give you the courage of Paul to speak God's truth, so they can grow-up in Christ. Do not grow weary in doing good as you disciple the undisciplined; it will yield the peaceful fruit of righteousness in their life and yours (v. 13; Hebrews 12:11).

This chapter starts with a prayer request and ends with a prayer. Pray those words from 2 Thessalonians 3:1-5, 16, and 18 as a faithful, prayerful watchman (Isaiah 62:6-7).

> *"LORD, please let Your Word spread rapidly and be glorified.*
> *Rescue _____ and me from perverse and*
> *evil men, for not all have faith.*
> *But, You are faithful; strengthen and protect us from the evil one.*
> *May we do and continue to do what You command.*
> *Direct our hearts into Your love and steadfastness.*
> *LORD of peace, continually grant us peace in every circumstance.*
> *LORD, be with us! LORD, Jesus Christ, may Your grace be with us.*
> *In Your name, Jesus~"*

Please read Micah 1.

Meditate on verses 2-3.

> *Hear, O peoples, all of you; listen, O earth and all it contains, and let the LORD God be a witness against you, the LORD from His holy temple. For behold, the LORD is coming forth from His place. He will come down and tread on the high places of the earth.*

The book of *Micah* is addressed not only to Kings Jotham, Ahaz, and Hezekiah and the people of Samaria and Jerusalem; it is addressed to you (vs. 1-3). Therefore, as you read, ask the Holy Spirit to give you ears to hear and a heart to repent concerning what God says in this book.

Notice Micah's grief over the spread of sin. Worship on the high places spread from the northern kingdom, whose capital was Samaria, to the southern kingdom, whose capital was Jerusalem (vs. 5-9).

What sin has reached the gate of your people (v. 9)? These can be generational sins passed down through your family for years: laziness, drunkenness, pornography, pride, anger, negligence, and unfaithfulness. Recognize them; confess them; ask God to miraculously cure the incurable wounds the sins have inflicted on your loved ones; be so grieved by sin and its consequences that you determine by the strength of God to stop sinning. Beg God to stop the spread of sin sickness!

Use the words from Micah 1:9 to appeal to the LORD as a faithful, prayerful watchman (Isaiah 62:6-7).

> *"O LORD, _____ and my wounds are*
> *incurable, for sin has come to our family!*
> *It has reached the gate of my people. O LORD, stop its spread!*
> *Keep us from sinning; miraculously cure us!*
> *For the sake of Your name, Jesus~"*

Please read Micah 2.

Meditate on verses 1 and 3.

> *Woe to those who scheme iniquity, who work out evil on their beds!*
> *When morning comes, they do it, for it is in the power of their hands.*
> *Therefore, thus says the LORD, "Behold, I am planning against*
> *this family a calamity from which you cannot remove your necks,*
> *and you will not walk haughtily, for it will be an evil time."*

The Hebrew words for "scheme" and "evil" in verse one are *chashab* and *ra'*.[1] They are the same Hebrew words used in verse three, where the LORD says He is planning calamity, *chashab ra'*, against the family of those who scheme evil, *chashab ra'*, on their beds.[2]

Hopefully these verses comfort you, knowing the LORD avenges those who plan evil against you. Perhaps they convict you; if so, confess any evil thoughts or plans you may have. Pray for those you love not to *chashab ra'*. Determine not to walk haughtily, so the LORD does not have to inflict calamity on your family.

Use the words from Micah 2:1, 3, and 7 to pray over yourself and those for whom you stand guard as a faithful, prayerful watchman (Isaiah 62:6-7).

> *"LORD, do not let _____ and me scheme*
> *iniquity and work out evil on our beds.*
> *Do not let us harm others just because it is*
> *in the power of our hands to do so.*
> *LORD, please do not plan calamity against my*
> *family. May we not walk haughtily.*
> *Please remove our necks from evil times.*
> *May Your Words always do good to us as we walk uprightly.*
> *In Your name, Jesus~"*

---

1. *Retrieved from www.blueletterbible.org/nasb/mic/2/1/t_conc_895001*

2. *Retrieved from www.blueletterbible.org/nasb/mic/2/1/t_conc_895003*

Please read Micah 3.

Meditate on verse 8.

> *On the other hand, I am filled with power—*
> *with the Spirit of the LORD—*
> *and with justice and courage to make*
> *known to Jacob his rebellious act,*
> *even to Israel his sin.*

The LORD spoke through the prophet Micah, addressing the leaders and prophets of Israel. Israel's leaders hated good and loved evil; they devoured the people like a bunch of piranhas (vs. 1-3). Sadly, God used these horrible leaders to punish the people for their horrific behavior (v. 4). The prophets were no better than the leaders, causing the people to wander from God because they did not speak the Word of God (vs. 5-7).

Thankfully, Micah was different. Filled with the power of God's Spirit, he boldly spoke God's Truth to people perishing for lack of it.

Let God make you a bold, Spirit-filled Micah, courageously teaching what God says about sinful rebellion (v. 8). Do not be tempted to ignore wicked behaviors in yourself and others, saying, "God is in our midst; calamity will not come upon us" (vs. 9-12). Christians must acknowledge the Truth of God's Word and live accordingly.

Pray Micah 3:8 and 11b over yourself and those for whom you stand guard as a faithful, prayerful watchman (Isaiah 62:6-7).

> *"LORD, fill _____ and me with power—with Your*
> *Spirit—and with justice and courage to make known*
> *to _____ his rebellious act, even to _____ his sin.*
> *LORD, make our rebellious acts and sin known*
> *to us before calamity comes upon us.*
> *We will repent in Your name, Jesus~"*

Please read Micah 4.

Meditate on verse 2.

> *Many nations will come and say, "Come and let us go up*
> *to the mountain of the LORD and to the house of the God*
> *of Jacob, that He may teach us about His ways and that*
> *we may walk in His paths." For from Zion will go forth*
> *the law, even the Word of the LORD from Jerusalem.*

Micah 4 contains two sets of prophecies. The Babylonian exile was prophesied in verses 9-13; its fulfillment began approximately 100 years after Micah spoke God's words. Verses 1-8 prophesy the restoration of God's Kingdom on earth.

Israel was given a glimmer of hope before their Babylonian exile; a day is coming when wars will cease, and people will come to Jerusalem to be taught by the LORD (vs. 1-3). How the people must have clung to those words as they sat in Babylon in fulfillment of prophecy, grieving their sins and hearing about the destruction of Jerusalem and their beloved temple.

These are words for you to cling to as well. As surely as the LORD fulfilled His promise concerning the exile of His people, He will fulfill His promises to come again and establish His Kingdom. "And it will come about in the last days...nation will not lift up sword against nation, and never again will they train for war" (vs. 1, 3).

Pray for God's Word to be fulfilled in your life and the lives of those you love before the last days by praying Micah 4:2 and 5 as a faithful, prayerful watchman (Isaiah 62:6-7).

> *"LORD, teach _____ and me about Your ways*
> *that we may walk in Your paths.*
> *We will walk in Your name, LORD our God, forever and ever."*

Please read Micah 5.

Meditate on verse 5a.

> *This One will be our peace.*
> *When the Assyrian invades our land....*

Micah prophesied the Babylonian takeover of Judah and Jerusalem 100 years before it happened, and he prophesied the soon approaching Assyrian destruction of the northern kingdom Israel (v. 5). (Micah prophesied from 733-701 BC. Israel was taken captive by Assyria in 722 BC. Babylon took the first wave of exiles from Judah in 605 BC.)

In the midst of the destructive prophetic visions, God gave Micah the blessed visions of Messiah—Who is from eternity—Who will rule Israel—Who will shepherd His flock—Who is our peace (vs. 2-5). What relief and hope his words were to those who would listen! Let these precious Words of God bring relief and hope to your heart as well.

Pray Micah 5:2-5 in thanksgiving to the One Who is your peace.

> *"LORD Jesus, thank You for being born in*
> *Bethlehem Ephrathah, a place too little*
> *to be among the clans of Judah. Jesus, You are*
> *the One who goes forth from God*
> *to be ruler in Israel. Your goings forth are from*
> *long ago, from the days of eternity.*
> *When You were born, Your brethren began*
> *returning to the sons of Israel.*
> *You arose to shepherd Your flock in the strength*
> *of the LORD, in the majesty*
> *of the name of the LORD Your God. And*
> *Your flock remains because You are*
> *great to the ends of the earth. Jesus, You are our peace—thank You.*
> *In Your name, Jesus~"*

Please read Micah 6.

Meditate on verses 3 and 5. The LORD is speaking.

> *"My people, what have I done to you, and how*
> *have I wearied you? Answer Me.*
> *My people, remember now what Balak king of Moab counseled*
> *and what Balaam son of Beor answered*
> *him, and from Shittim to Gilgal,*
> *so that you might know the righteous acts of the LORD."*

The LORD wants His people to remember what He has done for them, so when they are tempted to whine and complain against Him, they will instead remember—remember how He rescued—remember how He saved—remember how He provided. Then when they remember and desire to give the LORD something to thank Him for all He has done, He wants, not thousands of sacrifices, but a kind and humble soul that wholeheartedly walks with Him (vs. 6-8).

What a beautiful chapter to take personally! Always remember what God has done for you; recall His faithfulness with your thoughts, words, and actions. Remembering God's provision keeps you from discontentment and makes you a thankful person.

As you thank the LORD, give Him all of you by praying Micah 6:8 over yourself and those for whom you stand guard as a faithful, prayerful watchman (Isaiah 62:6-7).

> *"LORD, You have told _____ and me what*
> *is good and what You require of us.*
> *Help us to do justice, to love kindness, and to*
> *walk humbly with You, our God.*
> *For the sake of Your name, Jesus~"*

Please read Micah 7.

Meditate on verses 1 and 7.

> *Woe is me! For I am like the fruit pickers, like the grape gatherers.*
> *There is not a cluster of grapes to eat, or a first ripe fig, which I crave.*
> *But as for me, I will watch expectantly for the LORD;*
> *I will wait for the God of my salvation. My God will hear me.*

The first six verses of Micah 7 sound quite depressing and discouraging; they expound on the fact that life is hard. The remainder of the chapter exults in the hope of God doing the miraculous in the midst of the difficulty.

Pray Micah 7: 7-9, 14-15, and 18-20 over difficult situations in your life and the lives of those you love, as a faithful, prayerful watchman (Isaiah 62:6-7).

> *"LORD, as for _____ and me, we will watch expectantly for You;*
> *we will wait for You, God, of our salvation.*
> *My God, You will hear us!*
> *Do not let our enemy rejoice over us. Though we fall, we will rise;*
> *though we dwell in darkness, LORD, You are our light.*
> *LORD, we will bear Your indignation because we have sinned*
> *against You, until You plead our case and execute justice for us.*
> *You will bring us out to the light, and we will see Your*
> *righteousness. Shepherd us, Your people, with Your scepter,*
> *the flock of Your possession. Show us Your miracles!*
> *Who is a God like You, who pardons iniquity and passes*
> *over the rebellious act of the remnant of Your possession?*
> *You do not retain Your anger forever because You delight in*
> *unchanging love. Please have compassion on us again; tread our*
> *iniquities under foot. Cast all our sins into the depths of the*
> *sea. We desperately need Your truth and unchanging love.*
> *Because of Your name, Jesus~"*

SEPTEMBER

On your walls, O Jerusalem,
I have appointed watchmen;
All day and all night they
will never keep silent.
You who remind the LORD,
take no rest for yourselves;
And give Him no rest until He establishes
And makes Jerusalem a
praise in the earth.
ISAIAH 62:6-7, NASB

SEPTEMBER 1

Please read James 1.

Meditate on verses 14-16.

> *But each one is tempted when he is carried*
> *away and enticed by his own lust.*
> *Then when lust has conceived, it gives birth to*
> *sin; and when sin is accomplished,*
> *it brings forth death. Do not be deceived, my beloved brethren.*

James is a discipleship letter, addressing many areas of your walk with Christ. As you spend the next five days reading, meditating, and praying it, let the Holy Spirit use it to discipline you into more and more Christlikeness.

The letter starts with the reminder that life is a test. Enduring the test in the joy, strength, and wisdom of God, results in being made perfect and complete in Him (vs. 2-5).

This letter also teaches the sin path:

The Sin Path from James 1:14-15

Step 1 - Getting carried away—getting full of oneself

Step 2 - Enticed by lust

Step 3 - Lust conceives

Step 4 - Sin is birthed

Step 5 - Sin is accomplished—brought to completion

Step 6 - Death occurs—Sin ALWAYS ends in death—the death of relationships, reputation, influence, and sometimes, literal, physical death.

Sin is horrible! Learn to recognize the sin path at Step 1. As soon as you start to get carried away with yourself, get off the sin path and continue walking with Jesus.

Pray James 1:14-16 over yourself and those for whom you stand guard as a faithful, prayerful watchman (Isaiah 62:6-7).

"LORD, keep _____ and me from being tempted to sin. Do
not let us be carried away and enticed by our own lusts. Do
not let lust conceive and give birth to sin in our lives.
Do not let sin be accomplished in our lives and bring forth death.
Do not let us be deceived!
For the sake of Your name, Jesus~"

Please read James 2.

Meditate on verses 17-18.

*Even so faith, if it has no works, is dead, being
by itself. But someone may well say,
"You have faith and I have works; show me
your faith without the works,
and I will show you my faith by my works."*

Salvation is through faith in Christ alone; there are no works to earn it. After you are saved, living in and through the LORD Jesus Christ, you will want to do the work of Christ with and for Him. Doing the work of Jesus is the natural outpouring of a life eternally changed by faith in the saving work of Christ on the cross. The work of Christ will be evident in a life changed by Christ.

What about you and those you love? Is there proof of salvation in your lives? If not, is it because you need to be taught how to walk with Jesus, or is it because you need to truly believe in Him, giving your life completely to your Savior? The demons believe and are scared to death of Jesus; yet, they are not even capable of saving faith that results in salvation and the work of God (v. 19). You are created much better than the demons; you have the blessed opportunity to walk eternally with the Creator and Savior of your soul.

Commit yourself completely to Christ by praying James 2:22. Pray for those you love to do the same, as their faithful, prayerful watchman (Isaiah 62:6-7).

*"LORD, let my faith in You work with my works.
As I work with You, Jesus, perfect my faith in You.
Please draw _____ to place their faith in You.
Let me see Your work in them.
Because of Your name, Jesus~"*

Please read James 3.

Meditate on verse 8.

> *But no one can tame the tongue;*
> *it is a restless evil and full of deadly poison.*

Perhaps the first reading of the meditation verse is discouraging. You may think, "Why even try to control my tongue if it is impossible to do so?" Continue to meditate on the verse—only the Holy Spirit can control your tongue; you must give your tongue to Jesus to be used by Him for His glory. Once you allow God to control your mouth, He can bridle your whole body as well (v. 2). Even Jesus yielded His tongue to the control of the Father:

> *"The words that I say to you I do not speak on My own initiative,*
> *but the Father abiding in Me does His works."*
> —John 14:10b

Ask the LORD to tame your tongue, controlling it with the power of His wisdom by praying James 3:8 and 17-18. Pray the words over yourself and those for whom you stand guard as a faithful, prayerful watchman (Isaiah 62:6-7).

> *"LORD, I confess that no human can tame _____ and my tongue;*
> *it is a restless evil and full of deadly poison.*
> *Please control our mouths with*
> *Your wisdom from above! Make our words*
> *pure, peaceable, gentle, reasonable,*
> *full of mercy, full of good fruits, unwavering, and without hypocrisy.*
> *Let our words produce the seed whose fruit is righteousness.*
> *Make us people of peace who sow our words in peace.*
> *For the sake of Your name, Jesus~"*

Please read James 4.

Meditate on verse 9.

> *Be miserable and mourn and weep;*
> *let your laughter be turned into mourning and your joy to gloom.*

Taken out of context, the meditation verse makes Christianity sound like a real downer. However, it is written in the context of Christians lusting, murdering, envying, fighting, and quarreling (vs. 1-2). It is written in the context of God calling Christians' friendship with the world "adultery" thus making them enemies of God (v. 4). It is written in the context of Christians not allowing the Holy Spirit to move and live inside of them (v. 5). It is written in the context of Christians laughing at and finding joy in sin, and that should make Christians weep grievously (v. 9).

Sin is horrific! Christian, do not entertain the idea of indulging it, much less enjoying it. Humble yourself, confessing and repenting of everything this chapter of God's powerful Word convicts you.

Pray James 4:4-10 over yourself and those for whom you stand guard as a faithful, prayerful watchman (Isaiah 62:6-7).

> *"LORD, please forgive _____ and me for being adulteresses by being*
> *friends with the world. Make us stop being hostile to You, God! We*
> *do not want to be Your enemy. Thank You for making the Holy Spirit*
> *dwell in us; we will let the Holy Spirit live out in us. Thank You for*
> *Your greater grace that forgives us for sinning against You. Give us*
> *Your grace as we humble ourselves before You; do not let us be proud.*
> *We submit to You, God. Help us resist the devil; make him flee*
> *from us. Draw near to us as we draw near to You. We are sinners;*
> *please cleanse our hands and purify our hearts.*
> *Let us no longer be double-minded!*
> *We are miserable, mourning and weeping over our*
> *sin. We will stop laughing and being joyful because*
> *of sin. We humble ourselves in Your presence.*
> *Jesus, be exalted in our lives for the sake of Your name~"*

Please read James 5.

Meditate on verses 19-20.

> *My brethren, if any among you strays from*
> *the truth and one turns him back,*
> *let him know that he who turns a sinner from the error of his way*
> *will save his soul from death and will cover a multitude of sins.*

James is a hard-hitting, no-holds-barred letter written to Christians. It addresses many areas of life: trials, temptations, favoritism, saving faith, the tongue, God's wisdom versus worldly demonic wisdom, sinning after salvation, the power of confession and prayer. James wanted his readers to take an honest look at their walks with Christ. Some may have read the letter and accused James of being judgmental and stepping on toes, but James wrote under the divine power and inspiration of the Holy Spirit. The letter is from God, and its purpose is to convict Christians of sin, helping them grow-up in the LORD. *James* causes those who claim to be Christians to evaluate their lives and determine whether their faith actually produces good works or not. If they are really friends with the world and not friends with God, then they are not really Christians. God wants those who read this letter to humbly submit to Him, so their souls can be saved from death and their sins covered by the forgiveness of Jesus Christ (v. 20).

"The effective prayer of a righteous man can accomplish much" (v. 16b). Pray James 5:19-20 over those who need to really become Christians, as their faithful, prayerful watchman (Isaiah 62:6-7).

> *"LORD, _____ has strayed from the truth. Help me turn them back.*
> *Make them turn from the error of their way.*
> *Save their soul from death and cover a multitude of their sins.*
> *Thank You for saving my soul from death and*
> *covering a multitude of my sins.*
> *Because of Your name, Jesus~"*

SEPTEMBER 6

Please read Malachi 1.

Meditate on verse 6.

> *"A son honors his father and a servant his master. Then if I am a father, where is My honor? And if I am a master, where is My respect?" says the LORD of hosts to you, O priests who despise My name. But you say, "How have we despised Your name?"*

God spoke one more time to His people through the prophet Malachi. His message begins with, "I have loved you" (v. 2). The people's response sounds like a spoiled, disrespectful, whiny child: "How have You loved us?" (v. 2). God patiently answers their questions as the Father/child conversation continues throughout the book.

As you read *Malachi*, examine how you approach the LORD. Do you ever sound like the Israelites who insolently questioned God's motives and actions? Keep in mind you can ask the LORD anything; take some time to ask Him what He hears when you present your inquiries. Let God shape your attitudes toward Him and what He is doing in your life.

Pray Malachi 1:6, 11, and 14 in respectful honor of the LORD as His faithful, prayerful watchman (Isaiah 62:6-7).

> *"Father, I honor You. Master, I respect You, LORD of hosts.
> May I never despise Your name! For from the
> rising of the sun even to its setting,
> Your name will be great among the nations,
> and in every place, incense is going to
> be offered to Your name. May all my offerings
> be pure, for Your name will be great
> among the nations, LORD of hosts. Do not let
> me be a swindler who does not keep
> my vows. May my life be an unblemished sacrifice
> to You, for You are the great King,
> LORD of hosts, and Your name is feared among the nations.
> Because of Your name, LORD Jesus~"*

Please read Malachi 2.

Meditate on verses 13 and 17.

> *This is another thing you do; you cover the*
> *altar of the LORD with tears,*
> *with weeping and with groaning, because*
> *He no longer regards the offering*
> *or accepts it with favor from your hand.*
> *You have wearied the LORD with your words, yet you say,*
> *"How have we wearied Him?"*
> *In that you say, "Everyone who does evil is*
> *good in the sight of the LORD,*
> *and He delights in them," or, "Where is the God of justice?"*

This chapter sounds like it was written today. God's Word was not taught truthfully, causing many to stumble (vs. 6-8). People wanted God's favor without seeking His forgiveness (v. 13). Divorce was rampant (vs. 14-16). People called evil "good," and dealt treacherously with each other (vs. 14-16). As lives crumbled under unchecked sin, people questioned, "Where is God?" (v. 17).

God and His Word have not changed with the times. Times change when impacted by God and His Word; otherwise, times stay like they were when God spoke through Malachi over 2400 years ago.

Pray Malachi 2:5-7 over yourself and those you love to uphold God's Word as His faithful, prayerful watchmen (Isaiah 62:6-7).

> *"LORD, thank You for Your covenant of life*
> *and peace with _____ and me.*
> *Your Words are an object of reverence to us, so we revere You*
> *and stand in awe of Your name. May true instruction be in*
> *our mouths, and unrighteousness not be found on our lips.*
> *May we walk with You in peace and uprightness*
> *and turn many back from iniquity.*
> *May our lips preserve knowledge; let people*
> *seek instruction from our mouths.*
> *Let us be Your messengers, LORD of hosts.*
> *For the sake of Your name, LORD Jesus~"*

Please read Malachi 3.

Meditate on verses 13 and 16.

> *"Your words have been arrogant against Me," says the LORD.*
> *"Yet you say, 'What have we spoken against You?'"*

> *Then those who feared the LORD spoke to one*
> *another, and the LORD gave attention*
> *and heard it, and a book of remembrance was written before Him*
> *for those who fear the LORD and who esteem His name.*

The questioning conversation between God and His spoiled children continues into Malachi 3. Questions of: "How shall we return?" and "What have we spoken against You?" spill from the mouths of those unwilling to take responsibility for their actions (vs. 7, 13). Then suddenly the questions cease; the conversation stops, and the LORD turns His attention from the arrogant God-questioners to the humble God-fearers (vs. 16-18). As God listens to this quite different conversation, He is so touched that He has a book of remembrance written about them (v. 16). He makes those who esteem His name His own precious possession, promising to spare them from His judgment (vs. 16-17).

With whom do you most identify from *Malachi*: God-questioner or God-fearer? Ask God to make your conversations and actions pleasing to Him by praying Malachi 3:16-18 over yourself and those for whom you stand guard as a faithful, prayerful watchman (Isaiah 62:6-7).

> *"LORD, may _____ and I fear You! As we speak*
> *to one another, let our words be ones*
> *You give attention to and hear. Please write*
> *about us in Your book of remembrance,*
> *as those who fear You and esteem Your name. LORD, we want*
> *to be Yours; prepare us as Your own possession and spare us as a*
> *man spares his own son who serves him. LORD, You distinguish*
> *between the righteous and the wicked, between one who serves God*
> *and one who does not serve You. Make us Your*
> *righteous ones who serve You always.*
> *For the sake of Your name, Jesus~"*

Please read Malachi 4.

Meditate on verse 2.

> *But for you who fear My name, the sun of righteousness*
> *will rise with healing in its wings,*
> *and you will go forth and skip about like calves from the stall.*

God's final recorded Words in the Old Testament are the closing verses of *Malachi*; they describe the coming Day of the LORD (vs. 1, 5). For those who fear God's name, it holds the promise of health, youthful vitality, and restoration (vs. 2, 6). For the arrogant and wicked, it is a day for being consumed by fire (v. 1).

God gave His people 400 years to think about His sobering words. His next message came through John the Baptist, the messenger, who "in the spirit and power of Elijah" (vs. 5; Luke 1:17) declared:

> *"Behold, the Lamb of God who takes away the sin of the world!"*
> —John 1:29

Pray God's final Old Testament message from Malachi 4:1-6 over yourself and those for whom you stand guard as a faithful, prayerful watchman (Isaiah 62:6-7).

> *"LORD, do not let _____ and me be arrogant evildoers for whom the day is coming burning like a furnace. Please save us from the chaff; do not set us ablaze! Do not leave us without root or branch! Let us fear Your name, so the sun of righteousness will rise on us with healing in its wings. Let us go forth and skip about like calves from the stall. Save _____ from being the wicked who will be ashes under the soles of our feet on the day which You are preparing, LORD of hosts. Let us remember Your law of Moses, Your servant, even the statutes and ordinances which You commanded.*

*Thank You for sending Elijah the prophet in John the Baptist
before the coming of Your great and terrible day, LORD.
Continue to restore the hearts of the fathers to their children
and the hearts of the children to their fathers, so that
You will not come and smite the land with a curse.
Because You saved us from the curse, Lamb of God, Jesus Christ~"*

Please read 1 Peter 1.

Meditate on verses 1b, d and 2.

> *To those who…are chosen according to the*
> *foreknowledge of God the Father,*
> *by the sanctifying work of the Spirit, to obey Jesus*
> *Christ and be sprinkled with His blood:*
> *May grace and peace be yours in the fullest measure.*

This letter is written to **you**. Ponder the fact that God the Father chose **you**. He sprinkled **you** with the blood of Christ and purified **you** with the Holy Spirit. **You** can obey the LORD Jesus because the Father, Son, and Holy Spirit predetermined to do all this in **you**.

As you read this letter, take it very personally and take it to heart. You may even want to mark all the "you's" in your Bible. God definitely had you on His mind when He had Peter pen His Words.

Pray 1 Peter 1:3-9 over yourself and those for whom you stand guard as a faithful, prayerful watchman (Isaiah 62:6-7).

> *"Blessed are You, God and Father of our LORD Jesus Christ, who*
> *according to Your great mercy have caused _____ and me to be*
> *born again to a living hope through the resurrection of Jesus Christ*
> *from the dead, to obtain an inheritance which is imperishable*
> *and undefiled and will not fade away, reserved*
> *in heaven for us, who are protected by*
> *Your power, God, through faith for a salvation*
> *ready to be revealed in the last time.*
> *In this, we greatly rejoice, even though now for a little while, if*
> *necessary, we have been distressed by various trials. LORD, let the*
> *proof of our faith (being more precious than gold which is perishable,*
> *even though tested by fire) result in praise and glory and honor*
> *at the revelation of You, Jesus Christ.*
> *Jesus, though we have not seen You, we love You*
> *and believe in You, and we greatly rejoice with*
> *joy inexpressible and full of glory,*
> *obtaining as the outcome of our faith the salvation of our souls.*
> *Because of Your name, Jesus~"*

Please read 1 Peter 2.

Meditate on verses 9-10.

> *But you are a chosen race, a royal priesthood, a holy nation, a people*
> *for God's own possession, so that you may proclaim the excellencies*
> *of Him who has called you out of darkness into His marvelous light;*
> *for you once were not a people, but now you are the people of God;*
> *you had not received mercy, but now you have received mercy.*

Wow! It is incredible what God brought you out of and where He has placed you! You went from total darkness to being a chosen and called person of God (vs. 9-10). Amazing! Your new position in Christ as holy royalty brings with it the priestly responsibility of proclaiming the excellencies of the One who mercifully brought you into His marvelous light (v. 9). Humbling!

As you ponder your God-gifted position, heed His exhortations to stop sinning and start growing-up in Christ (vs. 1-2). Like rubbish, cast off all malice, deceit, hypocrisy, envy, and slander (v. 1). Replace the garbage of sin with God's Word, devouring it like a newborn baby devours life-giving milk, thus growing in your salvation (v. 2).

Pray 1 Peter 2:11-15 over yourself and those for whom you stand guard as a faithful, prayerful watchman (Isaiah 62:6-7).

> *"LORD, help _____ and me to abstain from fleshly lusts which*
> *wage war against the soul. Let us keep our behavior excellent*
> *among non-believers, so in the thing in which they slander us as*
> *evildoers, they may observe our good deeds and glorify You.*
> *For Your sake, help us submit to every human*
> *institution, whether kings or governors,*
> *so we will be praised for doing what is right. It is Your*
> *will for us to do what is right, so we may silence the*
> *ignorance of foolish men. Help us do what is right.*
> *For the sake of Your name, Jesus~"*

Please read 1 Peter 3.

Meditate on 1 Peter 2:13a, 18a; 3:1a and 7.

Submit yourselves for the LORD's sake to every human institution.
Servants, be submissive to your masters.
In the same way, you wives, be submissive to your own husbands.
You husbands, in the same way, live with your
wives in an understanding way,
as with a weaker vessel, since she is a woman, and show her honor
as a fellow heir of the grace of life, so that
your prayers will not be hindered.

Submission—it is a word that often gets a negative reaction, yet it is part of every facet of the Christian life. God expects every believer to submit to governing authorities, to bosses in the workplace, to His order of authority in the home, and to Him.

God calls both husbands and wives to submission. A husband proves his submission to the LORD by living with his wife in an understanding way, treating her as a "weaker vessel." In other words, a husband is to be gentle with his wife, as he would be with fine porcelain china, rather than treating her in harsh and boorish ways. A Godly husband submits to a Biblical understanding of his wife's spiritual equality, acknowledging and respecting her personal relationship with God. When a husband treats his wife in a Godly way, meeting her needs and honoring her requests, then the LORD hears and answers his prayers.

Pray 1 Peter 3:8-9 over yourself and those for whom you stand guard as a faithful, prayerful watchman (Isaiah 62:6-7).

"LORD, please make _____ and me harmonious, sympathetic,
brotherly, kindhearted, and humble in spirit.
Do not let us return evil for evil or insult for insult,
but help us give a blessing instead, for we were called
for that very purpose, that we might inherit a blessing.
In Your name, Jesus~"

Please read 1 Peter 4.

Meditate on verse 1.

> *Therefore, since Christ has suffered in the flesh, arm*
> *yourselves also with the same purpose because he who*
> *has suffered in the flesh has ceased from sin.*

Suffering can be an avoided sermon topic; however, Jesus promised that not only would He suffer, but His followers would, too (Mark 8:31; John 15:20). Jesus even taught: "Blessed are those who have been persecuted for the sake of righteousness" (Matthew 5:10). And this letter, written by the Holy Spirit and penned by Peter, says that you are blessed if you are reviled for the name of Jesus "because the Spirit of glory and of God rests on you" (v. 14). So, rather than be surprised by suffering, glorify God in it (v. 12). Let suffering bring you to the humble place of dying to sin and self and living for Jesus Christ.

This chapter is filled with exhortations from the LORD for you and those you love. Seek to be obedient to God by praying 1 Peter 4:1-2 and 7-11 as a faithful, prayerful watchman (Isaiah 62:6-7).

> *"LORD, help _____ and me cease from sin, so as to live the rest of the*
> *time in the flesh for Your will. The end of all things is near; therefore,*
> *give us sound judgment and sober spirits for the purpose of prayer.*
> *Let us keep fervent in our love for one another because love covers*
> *a multitude of sins. Help us be hospitable to one another without*
> *complaint. Help us use our gifts to serve one another as good stewards*
> *of Your grace. Let us speak Your utterances, God. Let us serve by*
> *the strength You supply, so that in all things You may be glorified*
> *through Jesus Christ, to whom belongs the glory*
> *and dominion forever and ever. Amen."*

Please read 1 Peter 5.

Meditate on verses 5b-6.

> *All of you clothe yourselves with humility toward one,*
> *for God is opposed to the proud but gives grace to the humble.*
> *Therefore, humble yourselves under the mighty hand of God,*
> *that He may exalt you at the proper time.*

Suffering and humility—God really hits on some tough topics in this letter. Here is His command to "clothe yourselves with humility" (v. 5). In order to obey that exhortation, you have to take off your pride and intentionally get dressed in humility. Ouch—that can be a painful process, but the blessed result is no longer living in opposition to God but in His grace instead.

This is another chapter filled with exhortations to heed and pray. Pray 1 Peter 5:2-12 over yourself and those for whom you stand guard as a faithful, prayerful watchman (Isaiah 62:6-7).

> *"LORD, help _____ and me eagerly shepherd the flock that*
> *You have placed among us. Let us prove to be Godly examples to*
> *them. Chief Shepherd, we want to be good shepherds for Your*
> *glory. May we always clothe ourselves with humility toward one*
> *another because You are opposed to the proud but give grace to*
> *the humble. We humble ourselves under Your mighty hand that*
> *You may exalt us at the proper time. LORD, we cast all our*
> *anxiety on You because You care for us. Give us sober spirits and*
> *keep us on the alert. Do not let the devil devour us! We resist*
> *him, firm in our faith. Strengthen us, and our brethren in the*
> *world, who experience suffering. God of all grace, You called us*
> *to Your eternal glory in Christ, and You will perfect, confirm,*
> *strengthen, and establish us. Make us stand firm in Your grace.*
> *To You be dominion forever and ever. Amen"*

Please read 2 Peter 1.

Meditate on verse 10.

> *Therefore, brethren, be all the more diligent to make*
> *certain about His calling and choosing you, for as long*
> *as you practice these things, you will never stumble.*

This chapter contains a list of eight Godly characteristics for you to practice (vs. 5-7):

- Faith
- Moral excellence
- Knowledge
- Self-control
- Perseverance
- Brotherly kindness
- Love

Believers are commanded to be diligent and increase in all eight areas in order to be useful and fruitful in the rich, intimate knowledge of the LORD Jesus Christ (vs. 5, 8). God warns that lacking in these areas makes one blind and short-sighted; while practicing the eight characteristics keeps a Christian from stumbling (vs. 9-10).

Memorize this list of eight things, asking God to help you practice and increase in them, being useful and fruitful for the sake of His eternal Kingdom (vs. 8-11).

Pray 2 Peter 1:4-8 over yourself and those for whom you stand guard as a faithful, prayerful watchman (Isaiah 62:6-7).

> *"LORD, as partakers of Your divine nature, may _____ and*
> *I apply all diligence to our faith, moral excellence, knowledge,*
> *self-control, perseverance, Godliness, brotherly kindness, and*
> *love. May these qualities be increasingly ours, so we will not*
> *be useless or unfruitful in the true knowledge of You.*
> *In Your name, LORD Jesus Christ ~"*

Please read 2 Peter 2.

Meditate on verse 19b.

> *By what a man is overcome, by this he is enslaved.*

Think about your life; what overcomes and overwhelms you? Peter warned the readers of his letter not to be overcome by: false teachers, heresy, sensuality, greed, unprincipled men, lawlessness, temptation, corruption, self-will, adultery, unrighteousness, sin, arrogance, vanity, and fleshly desires (vs. 1-3, 7-10, 14-15, 18). If you are overcome by any of those things, you are actually a slave to them.

Ask the LORD to free you from any ungodly person or thing that is overwhelming you. Repent and submit yourself to Christ as His bond-slave, being completely overcome by Him.

Pray 2 Peter 2:19-20 over yourself and those for whom you stand guard as a faithful, prayerful watchman (Isaiah 62:6-7).

"LORD, do not let _____ and me be slaves of corruption.
Let us only be enslaved by being overcome by
You. Let us escape the defilements
of the world by the knowledge of You, our
LORD and Savior Jesus Christ.
Do not let us again be entangled and
overcome by the world's defilements.
Keep us for the sake of Your name, LORD Jesus~"

SEPTEMBER 17

Please read 2 Peter 3.

Meditate on verses 11-12.

> *Since all these things are to be destroyed in this way,*
> *what sort of people ought you to be in holy conduct and*
> *Godliness, looking for and hastening the coming of*
> *the day of God, because of which the heavens*
> *will be destroyed by burning,*
> *and the elements will melt with intense heat!*

This is a sobering chapter describing the Day of LORD—the day of judgment and destruction of the ungodly (vs. 7, 10). God promises the day is coming; therefore, how should you live today? Invest your life in what is eternal—people and God's Word. Be diligent to share the Word of God with the people you love, so they will not be destroyed.

Pray 2 Peter 3:14-18 over yourself and those for whom you stand guard as a faithful, prayerful watchman (Isaiah 62:6-7).

> *"LORD, may _____ and I be diligent to be found by You in peace,*
> *spotless and blameless, regarding Your patience as salvation.*
> *LORD, in Your patience, please bring salvation*
> *to _____. Do not let us be the untaught and*
> *unstable who distort the Scriptures.*
> *LORD, teach us and make us stable in Your Word.*
> *Keep us on our guard so we are not carried away by the error of*
> *unprincipled men and fall from our own steadfastness.*
> *Let us grow in the grace and knowledge of You,*
> *our LORD and Savior Jesus Christ.*
> *To You be the glory, both now and to the day of eternity. Amen."*

Please read Jude 1.

Meditate on verse 1b.

> *To those who are the called, beloved in God*
> *the Father, and kept for Jesus Christ.*

Did you know God calls you names? Three of them are in the meditation verse: called, beloved, and kept.

- Called means invited, like to a banquet. It also means invited by God to obtain eternal salvation into the Kingdom through Jesus Christ. And, it means divinely selected and appointed.[1]
- Beloved means to be fond of, to love dearly.[2]
- Kept means to attend to carefully, take care of, to guard.[3]

Wow! You are His called. You are His beloved in God the Father. And, you are His kept for Jesus Christ. There is a lot in a name; ponder who you are in Christ, thanking Him for the names He has given you.

Pray Jude 1:1-2 and 24-25 over yourself and those for whom you stand guard as a faithful, prayerful watchman (Isaiah 62:6-7).

> *"LORD, thank You for calling _____ and me*
> *'called,' 'beloved in God the Father,'*
> *and 'kept for Jesus Christ.' Make us Your faithful bond-servants.*
> *May mercy and peace and love be multiplied to us.*
> *LORD, keep us from stumbling and make us stand*
> *in the presence of Your glory, blameless with great joy.*
> *To You, the only God our Savior, through Jesus Christ our LORD,*
> *be glory, majesty, dominion, and authority,*
> *before all time and now and forever. Amen."*

1. Retrieved from: www.blueletterbible.org/lang/lexicon/lexicon.cfm?Strongs=G2822&t=NASB
2. Retrieved from: www.blueletterbible.org/lang/lexicon/lexicon.cfm?Strongs=G25&t=NASB
3. Retrieved from: www.blueletterbible.org/lang/lexicon/lexicon.cfm?Strongs=G5083&t=NASB

Please read Psalm 101.

Meditate on verses 2b-4.

> *I will walk within my house in the integrity of my heart.*
> *I will set no worthless thing before my eyes;*
> *I hate the work of those who fall away; it*
> *shall not fasten its grip on me.*
> *A perverse heart shall depart from me; I will know no evil.*

What a great set of verses to place on your television and computer screen! What a great set of verses to write on the tablet of your heart, so they will come to your mind at the moment of temptation and keep you from sinning!

Satan wants to destroy you and your loved ones with perverse and worthless things. The LORD wants you and your loved ones devoted to Him and His Word. Declare those verses from Psalm 101 aloud—right now—as a commitment to the LORD, to your family, and to yourself:

> *"I will walk within my house in the integrity of my heart.*
> *I will set no worthless thing before my eyes;*
> *I hate the work of those who fall away; it*
> *shall not fasten its grip on me.*
> *A perverse heart shall depart from me; I will know no evil."*

Pray Psalm 101:1-4 over yourself and those you love as a faithful, prayerful watchman (Isaiah 62:6-7).

> *"LORD, I will sing of lovingkindness and justice.*
> *To You, O LORD, I will sing praises.*
> *Make _____ and me give heed to the*
> *blameless way. Come to us, LORD!*
> *Make us walk within our house in the integrity of our heart.*
> *Let us set no worthless thing before our eyes.*
> *Let us hate the work of those who fall away;*
> *do not let it fasten its grip on us.*
> *Make a perverse heart depart from us; let us know no evil.*
> *In Your name, Jesus~"*

Please read Psalm 102.

Meditate on verse18.

> *This will be written for the generation to come,*
> *that a people yet to be created may praise the LORD.*

Many of the psalms have titles such as: A Psalm of David or A Psalm of Asaph. The title of this psalm is: A Prayer of the Afflicted When He is Faint and Pours out His Complaint Before the LORD. I love it! This is my psalm—and your psalm—and every person ever created—it is our psalm!

A Prayer of the Afflicted—we have all been "the afflicted." We have all had days when we have felt so despised and reproached we could no longer speak. Thankfully, God gave the faint, afflicted soul words to cry out; then God had those precious words penned for eternity so our generation and the generations to come would have something to say to God on the days that are really, really tough.

So, we cry out to God because we have nowhere else to turn. And as we look to God, we see Him, and gradually our complaint becomes praise because He is eternal, and our children and the next generation will continue before Him (vs. 27-28). Praise the LORD!

Cry out to God with Psalm 102 as a faithful, prayerful watchman (Isaiah 62:6-7). Verses 1-2, 12, and 27-28 are printed below:

> *"Hear my prayer, O LORD! And let my cry for help come to You.*
> *Do not hide Your face from me in the day of*
> *my distress; incline Your ear to me.*
> *In the day when I call, answer me quickly.*
> *You, O LORD, abide forever, and Your name to all generations.*
> *You are the same, and Your years will not come to an end.*
> *The children of Your servants will continue,*
> *and their descendants will be established before You.*
> *Thank You, Jesus~"*

Please read Psalm 103.

Meditate on verses 1-2.

> *Bless the LORD, O my soul, and all that is*
> *within me, bless His holy name.*
> *Bless the LORD, O my soul, and forget none of His benefits.*

Psalm 103 has many treasure verses for you to pray every day over your loved ones. Verses 3-5 talk about some of the benefits that you have in the LORD. They are:

1. The LORD pardons all your iniquities.
2. The LORD heals all your diseases.
3. The LORD redeems your life from the pit.
4. The LORD crowns you with lovingkindness and compassion.
5. The LORD satisfies your years with good things, so your youth is renewed like the eagle.

That's an amazing benefits package! Thank the LORD for providing it for you and pray it over yourself and your loved ones. Pray Psalm 103:1-5 and 17-18 as a faithful, prayerful watchman (Isaiah 62:6-7).

> *"Bless the LORD, O my soul, and all that is*
> *within me, I bless Your holy name.*
> *Bless the LORD, O my soul, and I will forget none of Your benefits.*
> *You pardon all _____ and my iniquities.*
> *You heal all our diseases. You redeem our life from the pit.*
> *You crown us with lovingkindness and compassion.*
> *You satisfy our years with good things, so that*
> *our youth is renewed like the eagle.*
> *LORD, Your lovingkindness is from everlasting*
> *to everlasting on those who fear You,*
> *and Your righteous to our children's children.*
> *May we always fear You,*
> *keep Your covenant, and remember Your precepts to do them.*
> *For the sake of Your name, Jesus~"*

Please read Psalm 104.

Meditate on verse 24.

> *O LORD, how many are Your works! In*
> *wisdom You have made them all;*
> *the earth is full of Your possessions.*

Psalm 104 is a beautiful creation psalm. It is a good psalm to read when you need to refocus your attention on the LORD instead of yourself and your circumstances. Let the words soak into every fiber of your being, so when you are tempted to forget God, you say instead, "Bless the LORD, O my soul! O LORD my God, You are very great" (v. 1)! Then, step outside and find a cloud; picture God riding it like a chariot (v. 3). And when the wind is blowing so hard it gets on your nerves, imagine Him walking on the wings of that wind (v. 3).

Be amazed at your awesome God who created the heavens and the earth, the moon and the stars, the land and the seas, the plants and the animals, and you—to walk intimately with Him.

With all your heart, mind, soul, and strength, cry out Psalm 104:1-3, 24, and 33-34 to your LORD.

> *"Bless the LORD, O my soul! O LORD my God, You are very great!*
> *You are clothed with splendor and majesty, covering Yourself with*
> *light as with a cloak, stretching out heaven like a tent curtain. You*
> *lay the beams of Your upper chambers in the waters; You make*
> *the clouds Your chariot. You walk upon the wings of the wind.*
> *O LORD, how many are Your works! In*
> *wisdom You have made them all;*
> *the earth is full of Your possessions. I will sing*
> *to You, LORD, as long as I live.*
> *I will sing praise to You, my God, while I have my being.*
> *Let my meditation be pleasing to You. As for*
> *me, I shall be glad in You, LORD.*
> *In Your name, Jesus~"*

Please read Psalm 105.

Meditate on verses 4-5.

> *Seek the LORD and His strength; seek His face continually.*
> *Remember His wonders which He has done,*
> *His marvels and the judgments uttered by His mouth.*

For the next three days, you will read much of Israel's history in Psalms 105-107. It is a great way to recall those stories and learn even more about God's faithfulness.

As you observe God working on behalf of His people, ask Him to do the same for you and your loved ones. You may want to write your names next to these verses in your Bible.

- "LORD, please permit no man to oppress us. Reprove kings for our sakes, saying, 'Do not touch My anointed ones, and do My prophets no harm'" (vs. 14-15).
- "LORD, as Your people, cause us to be very fruitful and make us stronger than our adversaries" (v. 24).
- "LORD, do not let us stumble" (v. 37).
- "LORD, satisfy us with You, Bread of Heaven" (v. 40).
- "LORD, as Your people and Your chosen ones, bring us forth with joy and a joyful shout" (v. 43).
- "LORD, let us keep Your statutes and observe Your laws. Let us always praise You" (v. 45)!

Continue to pray using Psalm 105:1-4, as a faithful, prayerful watchman (Isaiah 62:6-7).

> *"LORD, I give thanks to You, calling upon Your name.*
> *I will make known Your deeds among the people.*
> *I will sing to You; I will sing praises to You*
> *and speak of all Your wonders.*
> *Let _____ and me glory in Your holy name.*
> *Let our hearts seek You and be glad.*
> *We seek You and Your strength; we seek Your face continually.*
> *In Your name, Jesus~"*

Please read Psalm 106.

Meditate on verse 23.

> *Therefore He (God) said that He would destroy*
> *them had not Moses, His chosen one,*
> *stood in the breach before Him, to turn away*
> *His wrath from destroying them.*

How important is it for you to stand in the breach before God for the sake of those you love? Moses literally begged God not to destroy the people, and God decided to have pity on them instead of wrath because of Moses' prayers (Exodus 32:9-14).

Do not grow weary in your prayer life; the lives of those you love are at stake. This psalm is full of verses for you to pray as you stand in the breach and intercede for the sake of those you are guarding as a faithful, prayerful watchman (Isaiah 62:6-7).

Pray Psalm 106:1, 4-5, and 47-48. (These are only a few of the verses we found to pray. Treasure hunt this chapter for more verses to pray specifically for your loved ones.)

> *"Praise the LORD! I give thanks to You LORD,*
> *for You are good; for Your lovingkindness*
> *is everlasting. Remember _____ and me, O LORD, in Your*
> *favor toward us; visit us with Your salvation. Please let us see*
> *the prosperity of Your chosen ones, that we may rejoice*
> *in the gladness of Your people, that we may glory in Your inheritance.*
> *Save us, O LORD our God,*
> *and gather us to give thanks to Your holy*
> *name and glory in Your praise.*
> *Blessed are You, LORD our God, from everlasting even to everlasting,*
> *Let us all say, 'Amen.' Praise the LORD!"*

Please read Psalm 107.

Meditate on verse 43.

> *Who is wise? Let him give heed to these things*
> *and consider the lovingkindesses of the LORD.*

What an incredible psalm to heed and consider!

- ✺ Wandering in the wilderness, the people cried to the LORD in their trouble, and "He delivered them out of their distresses" (vs. 4-6).

- ✺ Rebelling against God's Word, imprisoned and miserable, the people cried to the LORD in their trouble, and "He saved them out of their distresses" (vs. 10-13).

- ✺ Afflicted, rebellious fools, the people cried to the LORD in their trouble, and "He saved them from their distresses" (vs. 17-19).

- ✺ At their wits' end, the people cried to the LORD in their trouble, and "He brought them out of their distresses" (vs. 27-28).

Cry to the LORD in your trouble with Psalm 107:6, 11, 17, 20, 27, and 29-32 as a faithful, prayerful watchman (Isaiah 62:6-7).

> *"LORD, I am crying out to You in our trouble*
> *on behalf of _____ and me.*
> *Please deliver us out of our distresses! Forgive us for rebelling against*
> *Your Words and spurning Your counsel, Most High God. Forgive*
> *us for being rebellious fools, afflicted in our iniquities. Please send*
> *Your Word and heal us and deliver us from our destructions.*
> *LORD, we are reeling and staggering like*
> *drunkards; we are at our wits' end.*
> *Please cause the storm to be still, so that these waves will be*
> *hushed. We will be glad when they are quiet; guide us to*
> *our desired haven. We give thanks to You, LORD, for Your*
> *lovingkindness and for Your wonders to the sons of men!*
> *We extol and praise You in Your name, Jesus~"*

Please read Psalm 108.

Meditate on verse 1.

> *My heart is steadfast, O God; I will sing, I*
> *will sing praises, even with my soul.*

Say these words to the LORD:

> *"My heart is steadfast, O God.*
> *It is fixed, firmly established, stable, and secure in You."*

As you walk through this day with the LORD, keep those words in mind every time you hear news that would make your heart race with anxiety or pound with fear. The LORD wants you to trust Him wholeheartedly. Practice giving Him every concern that comes your way, then joyfully sing with the psalmist these words from Psalm 108:1-6 and 12-13, as His faithful, prayerful watchman (Isaiah 62:6-7).

> *"My heart is steadfast, O God; I will sing, I*
> *will sing praises, even with my soul.*
> *Awake harp and lyre; I will awaken the dawn!*
> *I will give thanks to You, O LORD,*
> *among the peoples, and I will sing praises to You among the nations.*
> *For Your lovingkindness is great above the heavens,*
> *and Your truth reaches to the skies.*
> *Be exalted, O God, above the heavens, and*
> *Your glory above all the earth.*
> *Please deliver _____ and me, Your beloveds. Save us*
> *with Your right hand, and answer us! Oh, give us help*
> *against the adversary, for deliverance by man is in vain.*
> *Through You, God, we will do valiantly, and*
> *You will tread down our adversaries.*
> *In the power of Your name, Jesus~"*

Please read Psalm 109.

Meditate on verse 4.

> *In return for my love, they act as my accusers,*
> *but I am in prayer.*

What an interesting psalm! Deeply hurt and betrayed by someone he loved, David told God what the person did to him and how he wanted that person held accountable. Perhaps the punishment section made you uncomfortable (vs. 6-20). David wanted his friend turned foe to die and be judged guilty in his sin (vs. 7-8). He wanted his children to be beggars and for no one to be gracious to them (vs. 9-12). Ouch!

Perhaps, you can relate to David. It's good to know you can be really, really honest with God—even saying, "Get them, LORD!" Hopefully, as you talk to God about your enemies, you will see them with the heart of Christ, saying: "Forgive them, Father, they do not know what they are doing" (Luke 23:34).

Pray Psalm 109:1-4 and 26 over yourself and those you love as a faithful watchman (Isaiah 62:6-7).

> *"O God of my praise, do not be silent! For they have opened*
> *the wicked and deceitful mouth against _____ and*
> *me; they have spoken against us with a lying tongue.*
> *They have surrounded us with words of hatred*
> *and fought against us without cause.*
> *In return for our love, they act as our accusers, but we are in prayer.*
> *Help us, O LORD our God! Save us according to Your lovingkindness!*
> *In Your name, Jesus~"*

Please read Psalm 110.

Meditate on verse 1.

> *The LORD says to my LORD, "Sit at My right hand until*
> *I make Your enemies a footstool for Your feet."*

Psalm 110 is a prophetic psalm about Jesus. Verse 1 could be said like this:

> *The LORD says to Jesus, "Sit at My right hand until*
> *I make Your enemies a footstool for Your feet."*

It is explained in Matthew 22:41-46 and Acts 2:34-36. The verses in Acts say:

> *For it was not David who ascended into heaven, but he himself says:*
> *"The LORD said to my LORD, 'Sit at My right hand*
> *until I make Your enemies a footstool for Your feet.'"*
> *Therefore, let all the house of Israel know for*
> *certain that God has made Him both*
> *LORD and Christ—this Jesus whom you crucified.*

Reread Psalm 110 in thanksgiving to Jesus your LORD, then pray verse 3 over yourself and those you love as a faithful, prayerful watchman (Isaiah 62:6-7).

> *"LORD, make _____ and me Your people who volunteer*
> *freely in the day of Your power. Make us go forth in the*
> *splendor of Your holiness, from the womb of the dawn.*
> *Let our young people be to You as the dew.*
> *For the glory of Your name, Jesus~"*

Please read Psalm 111.

Meditate on verses 2 and 4a.

> *Great are the works of the LORD; they are*
> *studied by all who delight in them.*
> *He has made His wonders to be remembered.*

God loves it when you notice Him, thankfully paying attention to what He is doing in your life. He wants you to observe His creation, marveling at His miraculous ways. He wants you to praise and thank Him with all your heart. Practice doing those things today, noticing what a difference it makes.

Start by praying Psalm 111 as a faithful, prayerful watchman (Isaiah 62:6-7).

> *"Praise the LORD! I give thanks to You, LORD, with all my heart, in the company of the upright and in the assembly. Great are Your works! I delight in them, and I will study them. Splendid and majestic is Your work, and Your righteousness endures forever.*
> *You have made Your wonders to be remembered—I will remember them.*
> *You are gracious and compassionate. You give food to those who fear You.*
> *May _____ and I fear You forever, for You will remember Your covenant forever.*
> *Make known to us the power of Your works. You are our heritage. The works of Your hands are truth and justice. All Your precepts are sure; they are upheld forever and ever; they are performed in truth and uprightness.*
> *You redeem us, Your people; You ordain Your covenant forever. Holy and awesome is Your name. The fear of You is the beginning of wisdom—let us always fear You. Give us good understanding as we do Your commandments.*
> *Your praise endures forever!*
> *We praise You forever in Your name, Jesus~"*

Please read Psalm 112.

Meditate on verse 1.

> *Praise the LORD! How blessed is the man who fears the LORD,*
> *who greatly delights in His commandments!*

People who fear God and delight in His commandments are blessed:

- ✺ Their descendants are the upright generation (v. 2).
- ✺ Wealth and riches are in their house (v. 3).
- ✺ Light arises in the darkness for them (v. 4).
- ✺ God maintains their cause in judgment (v. 5).
- ✺ They will never be shaken, and they will be remembered forever (v. 6).
- ✺ Their heart is steadfast, trusting in the LORD (v. 7).
- ✺ They are not afraid (v. 8).
- ✺ Their righteousness endures forever; they will be exalted in honor (v. 9).

Pray Psalm 112:1-7 over yourself and those for whom you stand guard as a faithful, prayerful watchman (Isaiah 62:6-7).

> *"Praise the LORD! Please bless _____ and me as we fear*
> *You and greatly delight in Your commandments. Make our*
> *descendants the upright generation; bless them and make them*
> *mighty on earth. Let wealth and riches be in our house; let our*
> *righteousness endure forever. Make us gracious, compassionate,*
> *and righteous; let light arise out of darkness for us.*
> *Let it go well for us when we are gracious and generous.*
> *Please maintain our cause in judgment. Let us never be*
> *shaken; let us be remembered forever. Our heart is steadfast,*
> *trusting in You, LORD; we do not fear evil things.*
> *Because of Your name, Jesus~"*

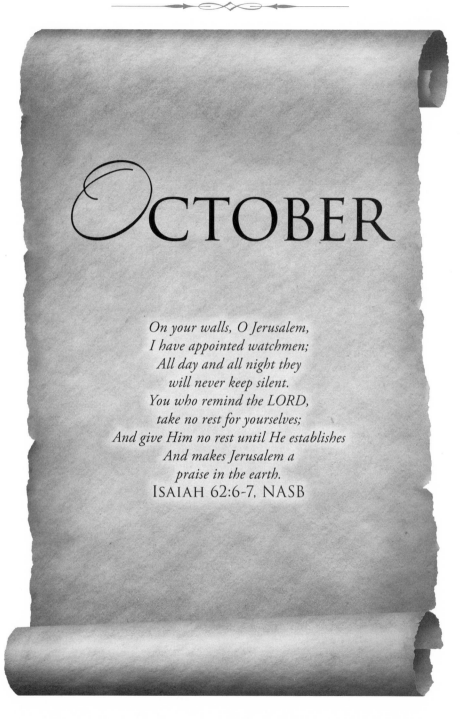

OCTOBER

On your walls, O Jerusalem,
I have appointed watchmen;
All day and all night they
will never keep silent.
You who remind the LORD,
take no rest for yourselves;
And give Him no rest until He establishes
And makes Jerusalem a
praise in the earth.
ISAIAH 62:6-7, NASB

Please read Psalm 113.

Meditate on verse 1.

> *Praise the LORD! Praise, O servants of the*
> *LORD, praise the name of the LORD.*

As a servant of the LORD, one of your sacred duties is to praise Him all day long, blessing and adoring His name forever (vs. 1-3).

Here are a few of the reasons why:

- The LORD is high about all nations, and His glory is above the heavens (v. 4).
- No one else is like Him who is enthroned on high (v. 5).
- He humbles Himself to observe what is happening in heaven and on earth (6).
- He raises up the poor and needy to sit with the princes of His people (vs. 7-8).
- He makes the barren woman abide in the house as a joyful mother of children (v. 9).

Pray Psalm 113 as a faithful, prayerful watchman (Isaiah 62:6-7).

> *"Praise the LORD! As Your servant, I will praise Your name, LORD.*
> *I will bless Your name from this time forth and forever.*
> *I will praise Your name from the rising of the sun to its setting.*
> *LORD, You are high above all nations;*
> *Your glory is above the heavens.*
> *No one is like You, LORD our God, who is enthroned on high.*
> *Thank You for humbling Yourself to behold the*
> *things in heaven and in the earth.*
> *Please raise _____ up from the dust;*
> *lift them from the ash heap.*
> *They are poor; they need You! Please let them*
> *sit with the princes of Your people.*
> *LORD, please have mercy on _____; let her abide in the house*
> *as a joyful mother of children.*
> *Praise the LORD!"*

Please read Psalm 114.

Meditate on verses 7-8.

> *Tremble, O earth, before the LORD, before the God of Jacob,*
> *who turned the rock into a pool of water,*
> *the flint into a fountain of water.*

This psalm recalls several miracles God did for Israel as part of saving them from slavery in Egypt.

- Opening of the Red Sea (Exodus 14:21)
- Opening of the Jordan River (Joshua 3:13, 16)
- Bringing water to drink from a rock (Exodus 17:6)

Can you relate to this psalm? Recall the day God brought you out of slavery to sin. Remember how the LORD miraculously opened doors for you and thank Him for working on your behalf. Never forget the day God turned your heart of flint into a heart for Him and gave you the living water of His Spirit (John 4:10; 7:37-39).

Take some time to write your own psalm of recollection to help you remember how God saved you.

Use the words from Psalm 114:1-2 and 8 to pray over those who need a psalm of salvation, as their faithful, prayerful watchman (Isaiah 62:6-7).

> *"LORD, please bring _____ forth*
> *from their slavery to sin and Satan.*
> *Free them from the strange language of the*
> *world. Jesus, please become their sanctuary*
> *and their dominion. Turn their heart that is*
> *as hard as rock into a pool of water.*
> *Make their heart of flint a fountain of living water.*
> *By Your Holy Spirit, in Your name, Jesus~"*

OCTOBER 3

Please read Psalm 115.

Meditate on verse 1.

> *Not to us, O LORD, not to us, but to Your name give glory*
> *because of Your lovingkindness, because of Your truth.*

This psalm is rich with verses to ponder and pray.

The LORD, the Maker of the heavens and the earth, is the living God. Unlike idols, He sees, hears, smells, feels, and walks (vs. 5-7). He is our God, and He does whatever He pleases (v. 3). He alone is worthy of all our trust, fear, and praise (v. 11). He helps, shields, and blesses those who fear Him (vs. 11, 13). But, those whose god is an idol become like that which they worship—mute, blind, deaf, unfeeling, immobile, and dead (vs. 4-8, 17). Those of us alive in the LORD, however, will bless Him from this time forth and forever (v. 18). Praise the LORD!

Pray Psalm 115:1, 11-15, and 18 over yourself and those for whom you stand guard as a faithful, prayerful watchman (Isaiah 62:6-7).

> *"Not to us, O LORD, not to us, but to Your name give glory*
> *because of Your lovingkindness, because of Your truth.*
> *May _____ and I fear and trust*
> *only You. Be our help and our shield.*
> *Be mindful of us and bless us as we fear You, LORD.*
> *Please give us and our children increase.*
> *LORD, Maker of heaven and earth, please bless us.*
> *We will bless You, LORD, from this time forth and forever.*
> *Praise the LORD!"*

Please read Psalm 116.

Meditate on verse 1.

I love the LORD because He hears my voice and my supplications.

Have you ever agonized in prayer for a long time over someone or something in which you desperately wanted God to do the miraculous? This psalm is a great one to cling to when you are in the midst of beseeching prayers and when you are praising the LORD for hearing and answering your cries.

Pray Psalm 116 now as His faithful, prayerful watchman (Isaiah 62:6-7).

"I love You, LORD, because You hear my voice and my supplications.
Because You incline Your ear to me, I shall
call upon You as long as I live.
The cords of death encompassed me, and the
terrors of Sheol came upon me;
I found distress and sorrow. Then I called upon Your name, LORD.
O LORD, I beseech You, save my life! You are gracious and
righteous; You are compassionate. You preserve the simple; I was
brought low, and You saved me. My soul is at rest because You
have dealt bountifully with me, LORD. You rescued my soul from
death, my eyes from tears, my feet from stumbling. I will walk before
You, LORD, in the land of the living. Thank You for saving me
from my affliction and the lies of men. Because of all Your benefits
toward me, I will lift up the cup of salvation and call upon Your
name, LORD. I will pay my vows to You, LORD; may it be in the
presence of all Your people. Precious in Your sight is the death of
Your Godly ones. O LORD, surely, I am Your servant; I am
Your servant, the child of Your handmaid; You have loosed
my bonds. To You, I shall offer a sacrifice of thanksgiving
and call upon Your name. I shall pay my vows
to You, LORD. Oh may it be in the
presence of all Your people, in the courts of Your house, LORD.
Praise the LORD!"

Please read Psalm 117.

Meditate on the second phrase of verse 2.

The truth of the LORD is everlasting.

People are quick to meditate on and claim the first phrase of verse 2—His lovingkindness is great toward us.

Most people want God's lovingkindness—they want His blessings. But sadly, many have believed Satan's lie which says that truth is relative, and truth is what is true for you; therefore, there is no absolute truth. However—the truth of the LORD is everlasting!

Speak the truth of the LORD, meditate on it, memorize it, and tell it to everyone you know. Commit your life to studying God's Word, the Bible, so you can actually know the everlasting truth of God, living it every moment of your life.

Pray Psalm 117 over yourself and those for whom you stand guard as a faithful, prayerful watchman (Isaiah 62:6-7).

> *"LORD, I look forward to the day when all nations praise You*
> *and all peoples laud You. I praise You and laud You,*
> *for Your lovingkindness is great toward* _____ *and me,*
> *and Your truth is everlasting.*
> *Praise the LORD!"*

Psalm 118 is probably the hymn Jesus and His disciples sang after drinking the last cup of wine at the Passover, the cup representing Christ's blood that would soon be "poured out for many for forgiveness of sins" (Matthew 25:28).[1] As you read Psalm 118, hear the voice of Jesus singing the words and imagine what was going through His mind as He sang.

Please read Psalm 118.

Meditate on verses 6, 17, and 24.

> *The LORD is for me; I will not fear. What can man do to me?*
> *I will not die, but live, and tell of the works of the LORD.*
> *This is the day which the LORD has made;*
> *let us rejoice and be glad in it.*

Jesus rejoiced that day because as He sang, He knew He was the fulfillment of this psalm:

- The Gate the righteous enter to come to God (v. 20; John 10:7, 9)
- Salvation (v. 21; Luke 2:25-30)
- The Stone the builders rejected who became the chief corner stone (v. 22; 1 Peter 2:6-7)
- The blessed One, coming in the name of the LORD (v. 26; John 12:12-13).
- The Light of the world (v. 27; John 8:12).
- The Passover festival sacrifice (v. 27; 1 Corinthians 5:7).

Reread Psalm 118, singing it in thanksgiving to your Savior.

> *"Thank You, LORD, for You are good; Your*
> *lovingkindness is everlasting.*
> *I fear You, LORD, and I say, 'Your lovingkindness is everlasting.'"*
> —Psalm 118:1, 4

Continue praying this psalm for the glory of Jesus' name.

1. *Retrieved from http://hallel.info/psalm-113-118-the-hallel-and-the-passover/*

Psalm 119 is an amazing psalm! Its 176 verses are divided into 22 sections, or stanzas, one for each of the 22 characters that make up the Hebrew alphabet. Each stanza contains eight verses, and in the Hebrew text (the language of the Old Testament), the eight verses of each stanza begin with the same Hebrew letter as that stanza.

You will spend the next 22 days walking slowly through this Scripture. As you read, notice the repeated words: law, testimonies, statutes, ordinances, precepts, and word, which all refer to the Bible. The LORD makes it clear through the psalmist, that to truly know and walk with Him, you must know His Word.

We will suggest a verse or two for you to meditate on and memorize each day. Feel free to choose any of the eight verses to memorize, so you can walk more closely with your Creator and LORD. Say your verse over and over all day long—silently and out loud. Speak it to the people you talk to throughout the day. Pray it over yourself, your loved ones, and the people in the car next to you. God's Word will change your world.

We pray these 22 days with be miraculous for you and your family.

Please read Psalm 119:1-8.

Meditate on and memorize verse 1.

> *How blessed are those whose way is blameless,*
> *who walk in the law of the LORD.*

The psalmist made some important observations in these eight verses. The LORD commands His precepts be kept diligently, blessing those who walk in His ways. The psalmist sincerely wanted to learn God's righteous judgments, so his ways would be established to keep God's statutes.

Does your heart's cry echo that of the psalmist? Are you ready to say, "I shall keep Your statutes" (v. 8)? As you begin this 22-day journey into Psalm 119, ask God to give you His heart for His Word.

Pray Psalm 119:1-8 over yourself and those for whom you stand guard as a faithful, prayerful watchman (Isaiah 62:6-7).

> *"LORD, let _____ and me be those who are blessed,*
> *whose way is blameless. Help us walk in Your law, LORD. Let*
> *us observe Your testimonies and seek You with all our heart.*
> *Let us do no unrighteousness and walk in Your*
> *ways. You have ordained Your precepts*
> *that we should keep them diligently. Oh, that*
> *our ways may be established to keep*
> *Your statutes! Then we shall not be ashamed when we look upon*
> *all Your commandments. We shall give thanks to You with*
> *uprightness of heart when we learn Your righteous judgments.*
> *We shall keep Your statutes. Please do not forsake us utterly!*
> *In Your name, Jesus~"*

Please read Psalm 119:9-16.

Meditate on and memorize verse 11.

> *Your Word I have treasured in my heart*
> *that I may not sin against You.*

Is there anything in your life that you do wholeheartedly? Perhaps it's your job, sport, or hobby. What about your LORD? Do you wholeheartedly pursue God and His desires?

The psalmist learned that pursuing God and His Word kept him from sinning. Wholeheartedly keeping and treasuring God's commands kept him from wandering off God's path for his life.

Ask the LORD to search your heart, revealing things you treasure more than Him. Ask Him to teach you His statutes and pray Psalm 119:9-16 over yourself and those for whom you stand guard as a faithful, prayerful watchman (Isaiah 62:6-7).

> *"LORD, help _____ and me keep our way*
> *pure by keeping it according to Your Word.*
> *Help us seek You with all our heart; do not let*
> *us wander from Your commandments.*
> *Let us treasure Your Word in our heart,*
> *that we may not sin against You.*
> *Blessed are You, O LORD, teach us Your statutes. With our*
> *lips, let us tell of all the ordinances of Your mouth. May we*
> *rejoice in the way of Your testimonies as much as in all riches.*
> *We will meditate on Your precepts and regard Your ways!*
> *We shall delight in Your statutes! We shall not forget Your Word!*
> *In Your name, Jesus~"*

Please read Psalm 119:17-24.

Meditate on and memorize verse 24.

Your testimonies also are my delight; they are my counselors.

The psalmist recognizes his citizenship is not on this earth; therefore, he needs God's commandments and counseling as he sojourns here. The world's rules and advice will not satisfy his soul; he desperately longs for God's ordinances and testimonies.

As you meditate on God's Word, let it shape your thoughts and behaviors. Even if others say negative things about you, let the LORD's statutes be what you think about. You will be amazed how different your days will be when you fix your eyes on Christ and His Word instead of the circumstances around you.

Pray Psalm 119:17-24 over yourself and those for whom you stand guard as a faithful, prayerful watchman (Isaiah 62:6-7).

*"LORD, please deal bountifully with _____ and
me, Your servants, that we may live
and keep Your Word. Open our eyes that we may behold
wonderful things from Your law. We are strangers in the
earth; do not hide Your commandments from us.
Our souls are crushed with longing after Your
ordinances at all times. Do not let us
be the arrogant, the cursed, whom You rebuke. Do not let us wander
from Your commandments! Take away reproach and contempt
from us, for we observe Your testimonies. Even though others sit
and talk against us, help us meditate on Your statutes. We are Your
servants. Your testimonies are our delight; they are our counselors.
In Your name, Jesus~"*

Please read Psalm 119:25-32.

Meditate on and memorize verse 26.

> *I have told of my ways, and You have answered me;*
> *teach me Your statutes.*

Imagine this conversation between God and the psalmist. Thinking he was doing alright, the psalmist told about his ways; when the LORD said something like, "So, do you really think your ways are pleasing in My sight?"

Whatever the LORD said caused the psalmist to ask God to teach him His statutes. A man's way is no good unless it is God's way.

> *There is a way which seems right to a man,*
> *but its end is the way of death.*
> —Proverbs 14:12

How would the LORD answer if you started telling Him about your ways? Ask Him to teach you His ways as you pray Psalm 119:25-32 over yourself and those for whom you stand guard as a faithful, prayerful watchman (Isaiah 62:6-7).

> *"LORD, my soul cleaves to the dust; revive _____ and*
> *me according to Your Word.*
> *I have told of our ways, and You have*
> *answered me; teach us Your statutes.*
> *Make us understand the way of Your precepts,*
> *so we will meditate on Your wonders.*
> *My soul weeps because of grief; strengthen us according to*
> *Your Word. Remove the false way from us and graciously*
> *grant us Your law. Help us choose the faithful way and let us*
> *place Your ordinances before us. We cling to Your testimonies;*
> *O LORD, do not put us to shame! Help us run the way of*
> *Your commandments, for You will enlarge our hearts.*
> *In Your name, Jesus~"*

OCTOBER 11

Please read Psalm 119:33-40.

Meditate on and memorize verse 33.

> *Teach me, O LORD, the way of Your statutes,*
> *and I shall observe it to the end.*

In this fifth stanza, the psalmist realizes the only way to thrive in life is to do it God's way. These are verses of total commitment to the LORD and His Word as the psalmist declares to keep God's law with all his heart, observing it to the end (vs. 33-34).

What about you? Do you crave God's Word? Do you want God to establish you in it for the purpose of walking in reverence with Him all the days of your life?

In humility, ask the Holy Spirit to show you things you long for more than Christ and His Word. In repentance, pray Psalm 119:33-40 over yourself and those for whom you stand guard as a faithful, prayerful watchman (Isaiah 62:6-7).

> *"O LORD, teach _____ and me the way of Your statutes,*
> *and let us observe them to the end. Give us understanding,*
> *that we may observe Your law and keep it with all our heart.*
> *Make us walk in the path of Your commandments; let us delight*
> *in them. Incline our hearts to Your testimonies and not to*
> *dishonest gain. Turn away our eyes from looking at vanity*
> *and revive us in Your ways. Establish Your Word to us, Your*
> *servants, as that which produces reverence for You. Turn away*
> *reproach, which we dread, for Your ordinances are good.*
> *Behold, we long for Your precepts; revive*
> *us through Your righteousness.*
> *In Your name, Jesus~"*

Please read Psalm 119:41-48.

Meditate on and memorize verse 45.

And I will walk at liberty, for I seek Your precepts.

Why was the psalmist able to walk in freedom? Because he sought to follow the LORD's commandments. Keeping the law of the LORD is the blessed secret to attaining true freedom. The lie of Satan and the world is you should do whatever you want, whatever feels right to you. God's Word calls that slavery to sin (Romans 6). In Christ, you are no longer a slave to sin; you are a child of God with the freedom to walk with God—Amazing!

Thank the LORD for the gift of walking at liberty with Him and pray Psalm 119:41-48 over yourself and those for whom you stand guard as a faithful, prayerful watchman (Isaiah 62:6-7).

"O LORD, may Your lovingkindness also come to _____ and me, Your salvation according to Your Word. Let us have an answer for him who reproaches us, for we trust in Your Word. Do not take the Word of Truth utterly out of our mouths, for we wait for Your ordinances. We will keep Your law continually, forever and ever. And we will walk at liberty, for we seek Your precepts. We will also speak of Your testimonies before kings and shall not be ashamed. We shall delight in Your commandments, which we love. We shall lift up our hands to Your commandments, which we love, and we will meditate on Your statutes. In Your name, Jesus~"

OCTOBER 13

Please read Psalm 119:49-56.

Meditate on and memorize verse 50.

This is my comfort in my affliction, that Your Word has revived me.

This seventh stanza in Psalm 119 reveals an afflicted psalmist. Surrounded by the arrogant and wicked, God and His Word are his sources of comfort and hope.

Perhaps you can relate. Have you ever been so distraught on a sleepless night that the only thing you can remember is the name of the LORD Jesus, saying it over and over? Have you ever felt stripped of everything, yet you can say, "This is mine; I observe the LORD's precepts"?

Thankfully you have the verses of this psalm to pray during difficult times. Pray them over yourself and those for whom you stand guard as a faithful, prayerful watchman (Isaiah 62:6-7).

"LORD, please remember the Word to Your servants, in which You have made _____ and me hope. This is our comfort in our affliction, that Your Word has revived us. The arrogant utterly deride us, yet we do not turn aside from Your law. Help us remember Your ordinances from of old, O LORD, and comfort us. Burning indignation has seized us because of the wicked who forsake Your law. Your statutes are our songs in the house of our pilgrimage. O LORD, we remember Your name in the night and keep Your law. This has become ours, that we observe Your precepts.
In Your name, Jesus~"

346 | *The* WATCHMAN *on the* WALL

OCTOBER 14

Please read Psalm 119:57-64.

Meditate on and memorize verse 57.

> *The LORD is my portion; I have promised to keep Your Words.*

The LORD is more than enough to meet all the needs of your life. His Word will sustain you. He gives you the privilege to seek Him with all your heart; He gives you grace and favor.

Ponder the truths from this eighth stanza of Psalm 119. Ponder your ways. What in your life needs to turn to the LORD's testimonies instead of the world's? Ask the Holy Spirit to convict you of sin and do not delay keeping His commandments. Choose to surround yourself with people who fear God and keep His precepts.

The earth is full of the LORD's lovingkindness. Look for it today as you pray Psalm 119:57-64 over yourself and those for whom you stand guard as a faithful, prayerful watchman (Isaiah 62:6-7).

> *"LORD, You are _____ and my portion;*
> *we promise to keep Your Words.*
> *We seek Your favor with all our heart; please be*
> *gracious to us according to Your Word.*
> *Help us consider our ways and turn our feet to Your testimonies.*
> *Help us hasten and not delay keeping Your commandments.*
> *When the cords of the wicked encircle us, do not let us forget Your*
> *law. At midnight we shall rise to give thanks to You because of*
> *Your righteous ordinances. Let us be a companion of all those*
> *who fear You and those who keep Your precepts. The earth is*
> *full of Your lovingkindness, O LORD; teach us Your statutes.*
> *In Your name, Jesus~"*

Please read Psalm 119:65-72.

Meditate on and memorize verse 66.

> *Teach me good discernment and knowledge,*
> *for I believe in Your commandments.*

What a great perspective on trials and afflictions! The psalmist recognizes that when life seemed to go his way, he went astray. Difficult times caused him to evaluate his life and keep God's Word. He even sees the good in being afflicted because then he learns God's statutes.

What is your perspective on affliction? When a trial comes your way, use the difficult time to come humbly before God, asking Him to show you unconfessed sins in your life. God wants trials to draw you into a deeper relationship with Him and His Word.

Pray Psalm 119:65-72 over yourself and those for whom you stand guard as a faithful, prayerful watchman (Isaiah 62:6-7).

"O LORD, you have dealt well with _____ and me, Your servants, according to Your Word. Teach us good discernment and knowledge, for we believe in Your commandments. Before we were afflicted, we went astray, but now we keep Your Word. You are good and do good; teach us Your statutes. The arrogant have forged a lie against us; with all our hearts, help us observe Your precepts. Their heart is covered with fat, but we delight in Your law. It is good for us that we were afflicted, that we may learn Your statutes. The law of Your mouth is better to us than thousands of gold and silver pieces. In Your name, Jesus~"

Please read Psalm 119:73-80.

Meditate on and memorize verse 73.

> *Your hands made me and fashioned me;*
> *give me understanding that I may learn Your commandments.*

Perhaps you have been told to use the good brain God gave you. As a Christian, you not only have a God-given brain, you have the mind of Christ; therefore, you can take every thought captive to the obedience of Him (1 Corinthians 2:16; 2 Corinthians 10:5).

This tenth stanza of Psalm 119 gives you the secret for making your thoughts pleasing to the LORD. Learn God's Word, delight in it, and meditate on it. Even if others are lying about you, ponder, speak, and pray Scripture. This holy habit will destroy speculations and vain imaginations, keeping you from wasting your day with futile thinking.

Pray Psalm 119:73-80 over yourself and those for whom you stand guard as a faithful, prayerful watchman (Isaiah 62:6-7).

> *"LORD, Your hands made and fashioned _____ and me.*
> *Give us understanding that we may learn Your commandments.*
> *May those who fear You see us and be glad because we wait for Your*
> *Word. We know, O LORD, that Your judgments are righteous and*
> *that in faithfulness You have afflicted us. O may Your lovingkindness*
> *comfort us, according to Your Word to Your servants. May Your*
> *compassion come to us that we may live, for Your law is our delight.*
> *May the arrogant be ashamed, for they subvert us with a lie,*
> *but we shall meditate on Your precepts. May those who fear*
> *You turn to us; even those who know Your testimonies.*
> *May our hearts be blameless in Your statutes,*
> *so we will not be ashamed.*
> *In Your name, Jesus~"*

OCTOBER 17

Please read Psalm 119:81-88.

Meditate on and memorize verse 88.

> *Revive me according to Your lovingkindness,*
> *so that I may keep the testimony of Your mouth.*

A distraught psalmist wrote this eleventh stanza of Psalm 119. Feeling dried up and useless, he describes himself as a wineskin in the smoke. Can you relate to him? Where do you turn in the midst of such difficulty and persecution? The psalmist knows his only source for comfort is God and His Word. His soul longs for God's salvation, not what the world offers.

These are great verses for life's difficult seasons. Use the words of Psalm 119:81-88 to pray over yourself and those for whom you stand guard as a faithful, prayerful watchman (Isaiah 62:6-7).

> *"LORD, _____ and my soul languishes for*
> *Your salvation; we wait for Your Word.*
> *Our eyes fail with longing for Your Word, while*
> *we say, 'When will You comfort us?'*
> *Though we have become like a wineskin in the*
> *smoke, we do not forget Your statutes.*
> *How many are the days of Your servants? When will You*
> *execute judgment on those who persecute us? The arrogant have*
> *dug pits for us, men who are not in accord with Your law. All*
> *Your commandments are faithful; they have persecuted us with*
> *a lie; help us! They almost destroyed us on earth, but as for us,*
> *we did not forsake Your precepts. Revive us according to Your*
> *lovingkindness, so that we may keep the testimony of Your mouth.*
> *In Your name, Jesus~"*

Please read Psalm 119:89-96.

Meditate on and memorize verse 93.

I will never forget Your precepts, for by them You have revived me.

As you continue to walk with Christ, you will experience more and more of the miraculous revitalization that comes from God's Word. The best antidote to tiredness and discouragement is resting in God and His Word.

What verses do you have tucked inside of you that come to your mind the moment you need them? Here are some to add to your Spiritual arsenal; they are short and easy to memorize:

I love You, O LORD, my strength.
—Psalm 18:1

The LORD will accomplish what concerns me.
—Psalm 138:8

Nothing is too difficult for You, LORD.
—Jeremiah 32:17

In thanksgiving for God's Word, pray Psalm 119:89-96 as a faithful, prayerful watchman (Isaiah 62:6-7).

"Forever, O LORD, Your Word is settled in heaven.
Your faithfulness continues throughout all generations;
You established the earth, and it stands.
They stand this day according to Your ordinances,
for all things are Your servants.
If Your law had not been my delight, then I
would have perished in my affliction.
I will never forget Your precepts, for by them, You have revived me.
I am Yours; save me, for I have sought Your precepts.
The wicked wait for me to destroy me; I shall
diligently consider Your testimonies.
I have seen a limit to all perfection; Your
commandment is exceedingly broad.
Because it is Your Word, Jesus~"

OCTOBER 19

Please read Psalm 119:97-104.

Meditate on and memorize verse 97.

O how I love Your law! It is my meditation all the day.

The psalmist loved God's Word so much he thought about it all day long. Pondering Scripture gave him even greater understanding than his teachers because it was the LORD Himself teaching him—amazing!

What do you think about all day long? As you love God's Word more and more, it will be your desire to dwell on it more and more. Soon you will find yourself repeating God's Words over and over in your mind, miraculously replacing negative thoughts and vain imaginations, taking every thought captive to the obedience of Christ (2 Corinthians 10:5).

Thank the LORD for giving you His Words and pray the ones from Psalm 119:97-104 over yourself and those for whom you stand guard as a faithful, prayerful watchman (Isaiah 62:6-7).

"O LORD, how I love Your law! Please let _____ love it, too. May it be our meditation all the day. Let Your commandments make us wiser than our enemies, for they are ever ours.
Give us more insight than all our teachers for
Your testimonies are our meditation.
May we understand more than the aged because
we have observed Your precepts.
Help us restrain our feet from every evil way,
that we may keep Your Word.
Please teach us Yourself, LORD. Do not let
us turn aside from Your ordinances.
How sweet are Your Words to our taste! Yes,
sweeter than honey to our mouths!
From Your precepts we get understanding;
therefore, we hate every false way.
In Your name, Jesus~"

Please read Psalm 119:105-112.

Meditate on and memorize verse 105.

Your Word is a lamp to my feet and a light to my path.

God's Word—what an incredible gift of Himself He gave to you! His Word illuminates your dark places, making clear things that are confusing. His Word sheds light on what the world calls "truth," exposing lies that desire to destroy you. His Word vivifies your life, giving you miraculous Holy Spirit power to keep going even when you are physically and mentally exhausted. His Word sheds light on every aspect of your life and gives you laser-like clarity to clearly see every step to take as you journey with Him.

Use the words from Psalm 119:105-112 as a prayer of personal commitment to Christ and His Word as His faithful, prayerful watchman (Isaiah 62:6-7).

> *"LORD, Your Word is a lamp to my feet and a light to my*
> *path. I have sworn, and I will confirm it, that I will keep Your*
> *righteous ordinances. I am exceedingly afflicted; revive me,*
> *O LORD, according to Your Word. O accept the*
> *freewill offerings of my mouth, O LORD,*
> *and teach me Your ordinances. My life is continually in my*
> *hand, yet I do not forget Your law. The wicked have laid a*
> *snare for me, yet I have not gone astray from Your precepts.*
> *I have inherited Your testimonies forever,*
> *for they are the joy of my heart.*
> *I have inclined my heart to perform Your*
> *statutes forever, even to the end.*
> *Thank You, LORD Jesus~"*

OCTOBER 21

Please read Psalm 119:113-120.

Meditate on and memorize verse 113.

I hate those who are double-minded, but I love Your law.

When you became a Christian, you were given the mind of Christ; therefore, you can think like Jesus (1 Corinthians 2:16). In Christ, you should not be double-minded, wavering between the world's opinions and what the Bible says. You can stand with unwavering confidence on Christ and His Word.

God calls a double-minded person unstable in all his ways (James 1:8). If you suffer from double-mindedness, submit to God and draw near to Him. Cleanse your hands and your heart, be grieved by sin—never joyful about it. Humble yourself before God, keeping His commandments (James 4:7-10; v. 115).

Set your mind on the things of Christ and pray Psalm 119:113-120 over yourself and those for whom you stand guard as a faithful, prayerful watchman (Isaiah 62:6-7).

> *"LORD, let _____ and me hate those who are double-minded; keep us from being double-minded and let us love Your law. Be our hiding place and our shield; we wait for Your Word. Make evildoers depart from us that we may observe Your commandments. Sustain us according to Your Word that we may live; and do not let us be ashamed of our hope. Uphold us that we may be safe, that we may have regard for Your statutes continually. You have rejected all those who wander from Your statutes, for their deceitfulness is useless. You have removed all the wicked of the earth like dross; therefore, I love Your testimonies. My flesh trembles for fear of You, and I am afraid of Your judgments. In Your name, Jesus~"*

OCTOBER 22

Please read Psalm 119:121-128.

Meditate on and memorize verse 124.

*Deal with Your servant according to Your lovingkindness
and teach me Your statutes.*

Oh, the LORD's lovingkindness! His tender regard, mercy, and favor for His own is incomparable. That He allows His servants to ask Him to deal with them according to His lovingkindness is amazing!

As you bask in these truths, thank God that He does not deal with you as your sins deserve and be even more diligent to learn His Word and walk in His ways.

Pray Psalm 119:121-128 over yourself and those for whom you stand guard as a faithful, prayerful watchman (Isaiah 62:6-7).

*"LORD, help _____ and me to do justice
and righteousness; please, do not leave us to
our oppressors. We are Your servants; be surety for us for
good; do not let the arrogant oppress us. My eyes fail with
longing for Your salvation and for Your righteous Word.
Please deal with Your servants according to Your lovingkindness
and teach us Your statutes. We are Your servants; give us
understanding that we may know Your testimonies.
LORD, it is time for You to act, for they have
broken Your law. Therefore, we love
Your commandments above gold, yes, above
fine gold. Therefore, we esteem right
all Your precepts concerning everything; we hate every false way.
Because of Your name, Jesus~"*

Please read Psalm 119:129-136.

Meditate on and memorize verse 133.

> *Establish my footsteps in Your Word,*
> *and do not let any iniquity have dominion over me.*

Establish is a powerful word. It means to be stable, firm, and steadfast. Do those words describe your life in Christ and His Word?

The psalmist knew the importance of being established in God's Word, so much so, he longed for God's commandments and wanted the LORD Himself to teach him. God's Words gave the psalmist light and understanding and kept sin from dominating him because the Word of God dominated him.

Pray for God to give you the longing to be established in His Word and the willingness to take the necessary steps to make that happen. Pray Psalm 119:129-136 over yourself and those for whom you stand guard as a faithful, prayerful watchman (Isaiah 62:6-7).

> *"LORD, Your testimonies are wonderful;*
> *therefore, my soul observes them.*
> *The unfolding of Your Words gives light; it*
> *gives understanding to the simple.*
> *LORD, please give understanding to _____ and*
> *me. I am opening my mouth wide*
> *and panting, for I long for Your commandments.*
> *Please turn to me and be gracious to*
> *me, after Your manner with those who love Your*
> *name. Establish _____ and my*
> *footsteps in Your Word, and do not let any*
> *iniquity have dominion over us.*
> *Redeem us from the oppression of man,*
> *that we may keep Your precepts.*
> *Make Your face shine upon us, Your servants,*
> *and teach us Your statutes.*
> *My eyes shed streams of water*
> *because _____ does not keep Your law.*
> *Help us, in Your name, Jesus~"*

Please read Psalm 119:137-144.

Meditate on and memorize verse 142.

> *Your righteousness is an everlasting*
> *righteousness, and Your law is truth.*

You live in a world where many people say truth is relative, and right is what is right in the eyes of the individual. Both statements are false. God defines what is true and right, and you have the joy and privilege of discovering His eternal truth and righteousness as you read His Word. You become a truthful and righteous person when you live your life according to God's Words rather than according to the world's words.

Pray the eternal and righteous Words of Truth from Psalm 119:137-144 over yourself and those for whom you stand guard as a faithful, prayerful watchman (Isaiah 62:6-7).

> *"Righteous are You, O LORD, and upright are Your judgments.*
> *You have commanded Your testimonies in righteousness and*
> *exceeding faithfulness. My zeal has consumed me because my*
> *adversaries have forgotten Your Words. Your Word is very*
> *pure; therefore, _____ and I, Your servants, love it. We*
> *are small and despised, yet we do not forget Your precepts.*
> *Your righteousness is an everlasting*
> *righteousness, and Your law is truth.*
> *Trouble and anguish have come upon us, yet*
> *Your commandments are our delight.*
> *Your testimonies are righteous forever; give*
> *us understanding that we may live.*
> *Because of Your name, Jesus~"*

Please read Psalm 119:145-152.

Meditate on and memorize verse 147.

> *I rise before dawn and cry for help; I wait for Your Words.*

What do you do in the midst of crises when you awaken in the predawn hours because worries race around in your head like a killer tornado? Instead of staying in bed and rehearsing your heart's cares, get up and move to a comfortable chair; open your Bible and start reading. Let the healing salve of God's Words coat your heart and mind. Miraculously your heart will stop racing, and the mind of Christ will take control of your storm. God's Words will revive you and give you the wisdom you need to make it through the day.

The psalmist knew help came from the Word of God. He even looked forward to the night watches, for those times gave him more opportunities to meditate on Scripture.

Pray Psalm 119:145-152 over yourself and those for whom you stand guard as a faithful, prayerful watchman (Isaiah 62:6-7).

> *"I cried with all my heart; answer me, O LORD! I will observe Your statutes. I cried to You; save me, and I shall keep Your testimonies. I rise before dawn and cry for help; I wait for Your Words. My eyes anticipate the night watches that I may meditate on Your Word. Hear my voice according to Your lovingkindness; revive me, O LORD, according to Your ordinances. Those who follow after wickedness draw near; they are far from Your law. LORD, protect _____ and me from wickedness! You are near, O LORD, and all Your commandments are truth. Of old I have known from Your testimonies that You have founded them forever. Thank You, LORD Jesus~"*

Please read Psalm 119:153-160.

Meditate on and memorize verse 160.

The sum of Your Word is truth,
and every one of Your righteous ordinances is everlasting.

The sum of God's Word is the truth. Sum is a math word; it means the whole amount. God's Word in its entirety is truth. Do not believe the lie that says: "Some of God's Word is truth." Satan loves for people to exchange the truth of God for a lie, destroying their lives (Romans 1:25).

All of God's Word is truth, and truth is according to Godliness (Titus 1:1). Knowing that truth, pray Psalm 119:153-160 over yourself and those for whom you stand guard as a faithful, prayerful watchman (Isaiah 62:6-7).

"LORD, look upon _____ and my affliction and rescue us,
for we do not forget Your law. Plead our cause and redeem us; revive
us according to Your Word. Salvation is far from the wicked, for
they do not seek Your statutes. Great are Your mercies, O LORD;
revive us according to Your ordinances. Many
are our persecutors and our adversaries,
yet we do not turn aside from Your testimonies. We behold
the treacherous and loathe them because they do not keep
Your Word. Consider how we love Your precepts;
revive us, O LORD, according to Your
lovingkindness. The sum of Your Word is truth,
and every one of Your righteous ordinances is everlasting.
In Your name, Jesus~"

Please read Psalm 119:161-168.

Meditate on and memorize verse 165.

*Those who love Your law have great peace
and nothing causes them to stumble.*

I (Marsha) must confess that writing the Psalm 119 devotionals has been very convicting for me, for I thought I loved God's Word so much, yet how much do I actually love it? Psalm 119 made me really think about what I love to meditate on throughout the day. Is it something somebody said or how I feel I have been treated unfairly, or is it the next Bible verse I am memorizing? And, my wait times throughout the day—do I pull out my phone to see the latest on the weather, news, email, and social media, or do I open my Bible application and start memorizing the next verse? I truly want my actions with God's Word to line up with what I say about God's Word, so I can know His unspeakable peace, and absolutely nothing will cause me to stumble because my feet are literally planted in His Word.

What about you? Let God's Word examine your life, then pray His Words from Psalm 119:161-168 as His faithful, prayerful watchman (Isaiah 62:6-7).

*"LORD, please do not allow princes to
persecute _____ and me without cause, but even
if they do, let our heart stand in awe of Your
Words. Let us rejoice at Your Word
as one who finds great spoil. Let us hate and
despise falsehood but love Your law.
Help us praise You seven times a day because
of Your righteous ordinances.
Those who love Your law have great peace and
nothing causes them to stumble.
May we be those people, LORD! We hope for Your salvation,
O LORD, and do Your commandments. May our souls
keep Your testimonies and love them exceedingly.
Let us keep Your precepts and Your testimonies,
for all our ways are before You.
In Your name, Jesus-"*

Please read Psalm 119:169-176.

Meditate on and memorize verse 175.

Let my soul live that it may praise You,
and let Your ordinances help me.

For the past 22 days, you read the words of a psalmist who adored God's Word. He desired God's precepts to govern him to keep from sinning and to walk in God's ways. He knew to meet that goal he must know God's Word, meditate on God's Word, and keep God's Word.

We hope that taking a slow walk through this psalm gave you time to really think about what God says to you about the importance of His Word in your life. We pray you long for the Word of the LORD and its governance of your life.

Pray Psalm 119:169-176 over yourself and those you love as a faithful, prayerful watchman (Isaiah 62:6-7).

"Let my cry come before You, O LORD; give _____ and me understanding according to Your Word. Let our supplications come before You; deliver us according to Your Word. Let our lips utter praise, for You teach us Your statutes. Let our tongues sing of Your Word, for all Your commandments are righteousness. Let Your hand be ready to help us, for we have chosen Your precepts. We long for Your salvation, O LORD, and Your law is our delight. Let our souls live to praise You, and let Your ordinances help us. Please, do not let us go astray like lost sheep; seek us, Your servants; do not let us forget Your commandments. For Your name's sake, Jesus~"

OCTOBER 29

Please read Psalm 120.

Meditate on verse 1.

In my trouble I cried to the LORD, and He answered me.

Psalms 120-134 are all titled "A Song of Ascents." These fifteen psalms will take you on a 15-day journey to a higher place.

The journey begins in such a low place there is nowhere to go but up (v. 1). The psalmist is not only in trouble, he is in anguish because he lives among liars who hate peace. When he tries to talk to these lying warmongers, it only makes matters worse (v 7). So, in his distress, the psalmist cries to the LORD, and the God of peace answers him (v. 1).

Have you ever been in a similar situation? Perhaps you are there now, dwelling with people who enjoy the fight and will even tell lies to start a war. Cry out to God—tell Him everything that is happening to you or someone you love. Then look up—Psalm 121 is coming; it will take you on the next step to a higher place.

Pray Psalm 120:1-2 over yourself and those for whom you stand guard as a faithful, prayerful watchman (Isaiah 62:6-7).

"LORD, _____ and I are in trouble, and
we are crying to You. Please answer us!
Deliver our souls, O LORD, from _____ .
In Your name, Jesus~"

Please read Psalm 121.

Meditate on verse 2.

> *My help comes from the LORD, who made heaven and earth.*

Psalm 120 says the LORD answered the troubled psalmist when he cried for help (Psalm 120:1). What was His answer? Psalm 121 is God's answer when all you can see is trouble. Hear the LORD say:

> *"Look up! Look at the mountains. Your*
> *help will not come from there.*
> *Look up at Me, the LORD! I made heaven and earth.*
> *I will not allow your foot to slip; I will keep*
> *you because I never slumber.*
> *I never slumber or sleep. I keep Israel, and I will keep you.*
> *I AM the LORD, and I AM your keeper.*
> *I AM the LORD, and I AM your shade on your right hand.*
> *The sun will not smite you by day nor the moon by night.*
> *I AM the LORD, and I will protect you*
> *from all evil; I will keep your soul.*
> *I AM the LORD, and I will guard your going out*
> *and your coming in from this time forth and forever."*

Whew—what a relief! God is in control! Look up and pray Psalm 121 over yourself and those for whom you stand guard as a faithful, prayerful watchman (Isaiah 62:6-7).

> *"LORD, _____ and I need help! We lift our eyes to You!*
> *LORD, You made heaven and earth, and our help comes from You.*
> *Please do not allow our feet to slip. Please keep*
> *us. You do not slumber or sleep.*
> *LORD, You are our keeper. You are the shade on our right hand.*
> *Do not let the sun smite us by day nor the moon by night.*
> *LORD, please protect us from all evil and keep our souls.*
> *LORD, guard our going out and our coming*
> *in from this time forth and forever.*
> *In Your name, Jesus~"*

Please read Psalm 122.

Meditate on verse 1.

> *I was glad when they said to me, "Let us*
> *go to the house of the LORD."*

Can you imagine how thankful the psalmist was when someone invited him to go to church? Here he was, living among a bunch of liars (Psalm 120), looking up to the LORD for some help (Psalm 121), when suddenly, somebody said, "Let's go to the house of the LORD" (v. 1). How relieved he must have been to get away from those who hated him and go to a place of peace!

You probably know somebody right now whom you could invite to church or to your home, so they can have a moment of peace. Don't hesitate to reach out to them, because like the psalmist, they will be glad that you did.

Pray Psalm 122:1, 4, and 6-9 over yourself and those for whom you stand guard as a faithful, prayerful watchman (Isaiah 62:6-7).

> *"LORD, I love going to Your house!*
> *Let _____ be glad when I say to them,*
> *'Let us go to the house of the LORD.' We*
> *give thanks to Your name, LORD.*
> *Please bring peace to Jerusalem and peace to _____ and me.*
> *Please let us prosper. Let peace be within our*
> *walls and prosperity within our homes.*
> *For the sake of our brothers and our friends,*
> *please give us Your peace, LORD.*
> *We seek good for the sake of Your house, LORD our God.*
> *In Your name, Jesus."*

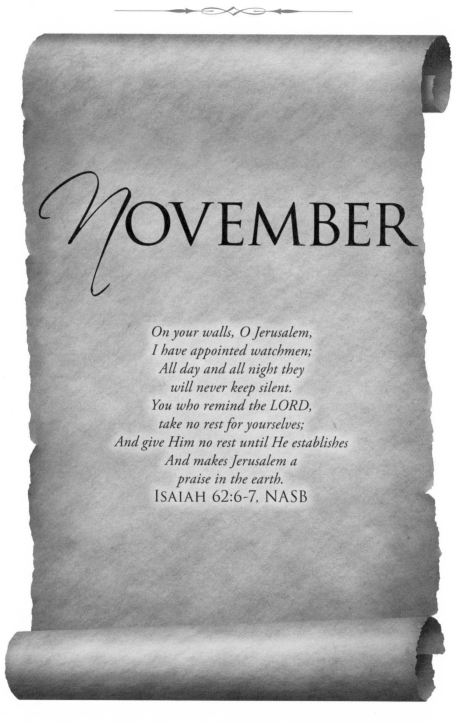

NOVEMBER

On your walls, O Jerusalem,
I have appointed watchmen;
All day and all night they
will never keep silent.
You who remind the LORD,
take no rest for yourselves;
And give Him no rest until He establishes
And makes Jerusalem a
praise in the earth.
ISAIAH 62:6-7, NASB

Please read Psalm 123.

Meditate on this phrase from verse 2.

Our eyes look to the LORD our God until He is gracious to us.

The psalmist left the dwelling place of liars and went to the house of the LORD; there he regained his focus (Psalm 120, 122, 123). Instead of lifting his eyes to the mountains, he lifted his eyes to God, focusing on Him (Psalm 121:1; 123:1-2).

It is easy to lose focus when troubles swirl around you and those you love. Satan wants you fixated on problems, worrying and fretting. This psalm tells you how to not look at your circumstances and focus on God—you do it as His servant. A faithful servant keeps their eyes on the master, watching the master's hands (v. 2). With a simple gesture, the servant obeys the master's bidding, knowing that from those same hands come what the servant needs to live for the sake of the master.

Fixing your eyes on Jesus, pray Psalm 123 over yourself and those for whom you stand guard as a faithful, prayerful watchman (Isaiah 62:6-7).

"LORD, to You I lift up my eyes. O You,
who are enthroned in the heavens!
Behold, as the eyes of servants look to the hand
of their master, as the eyes of a maid
to the hand of her mistress, so _____ and my
eyes look to You, LORD our God,
until You are gracious to us. Be gracious to
us, O LORD, be gracious to us,
for we are greatly filled with contempt. Our
soul is greatly filled with the scoffing
of those who are at ease, and with the contempt of the proud.
Help us LORD, in Your name, Jesus~"

Please read Psalm 124.

Meditate on verses 2-3a.

> *Had it not been the LORD who was on our*
> *side when men rose up against us,*
> *then they would have swallowed us alive.*

Angry people surrounded the psalmist, wanting to devour him, but God saved him. What a relief when the LORD provides a way of escape! Keep in mind the steps leading up to the rescue:

1. Cry out to God for deliverance (Psalm 120)
2. Look to God for help (Psalm 121)
3. Go to the LORD's house (Psalm 122)
4. Fix your eyes on the hand of the LORD as His faithful servant (Psalm 123)
5. Recognize God's deliverance (Psalm 124)

Thinking about these first five steps of the Ascension Psalms, be obedient to what God tells you to do to rise up from low places in your life. Pray Psalm 124 in thanksgiving for what God is doing in your life and the lives of those for whom you stand guard as a faithful, prayerful watchman (Isaiah 62:6-7).

> *"LORD, if You had not been on our side when*
> *men rose up against _____ and me,*
> *then they would have swallowed us alive, when*
> *their anger was kindled against us.*
> *The waters would have engulfed us; the stream*
> *would have swept over our soul;*
> *then the raging waters would have swept over our soul.*
> *Blessed are You, LORD, who has not given*
> *us to be torn by their teeth.*
> *Our soul has escaped as a bird out of the snare of the trapper;*
> *the snare is broken, and we have escaped.*
> *Our help is in Your name, LORD, who made heaven and earth."*

Please read Psalm 125.

Meditate on verse 2.

> *As the mountains surround Jerusalem, so*
> *the LORD surrounds His people*
> *from this time forth and forever.*

What a sharp contrast to go from being surrounded by angry people wanting to devour you to being surrounded by the LORD! Can you imagine how glad the psalmist was to have God all around him, so his enemies could not hurt him?

Bask in the security of knowing God surrounds His people. Resolve to be His righteous one who unwaveringly trusts in Him.

Pray Psalm 125 over yourself and those for whom you stand guard as a faithful, prayerful watchman (Isaiah 62:6-7).

> *"LORD, may _____ and I be those who trust*
> *in You. Make us like Mount Zion,*
> *which cannot be moved. We will abide forever*
> *in You. As the mountains surround*
> *Jerusalem, LORD, please surround us, Your*
> *people, from this time forth and forever.*
> *Do not let the scepter of wickedness rest upon our*
> *land. Keep us as Your righteous ones;*
> *do not let us put forth our hands to do wrong. Do*
> *good, O LORD, to those who are good*
> *and to those who are upright in their hearts.*
> *Please make us good and upright.*
> *But as for those who turn aside to their crooked*
> *ways, LORD, You will lead them away*
> *with the doers of iniquity. Do not let us turn aside to crooked ways;*
> *keep us from the doers of iniquity. Peace be*
> *upon Israel, and peace be upon us.*
> *In Your name, Jesus~"*

Please read Psalm 126.

Meditate on verse 3.

> *The LORD has done great things for us; we are glad.*

Can you imagine the psalmist's face as he joyfully sang this Song of Ascents? Rescue from the dwelling place of lying warmongers was merely a dream, until he looked up to the Maker of heaven and earth (Psalm 120; 121). Then, the miraculous hand of God took him back to Zion, to the mountain of God, to the place where His temple stood (Psalm 122; 123). And the psalmist rejoiced with others whom God had rescued; they rejoiced with laughter and shouting, telling about the great things the LORD had done.

If you are a Christian, this is your Song of Ascents, too. You were trapped in sin, without peace, steeped in the lies of the world. Then you looked up to the Maker of heaven and earth, the Maker of your soul, and He rescued and restored you from captivity to sin. Praise the LORD!

Pray Psalm 126 as a joyful, faithful, prayerful watchman (Isaiah 62:6-7).

> *"LORD, when You brought back _____ and me*
> *to You, we were like those who dream.*
> *Let our mouths be filled with laughter and*
> *our tongues with joyful shouting.*
> *Let it be said of us, 'The LORD has done great things for them.'*
> *LORD, You have done great things for us; we are glad!*
> *Restore us from all captivity, O LORD, as water in the streams.*
> *Let those who sow in tears reap with joyful shouting.*
> *Let those who go to and fro weeping, carrying their bag of seed,*
> *indeed come again with a shout of joy,*
> *bringing their sheaves with them.*
> *In Your name, Jesus~"*

Please read Psalm 127.

Meditate on verse 1.

> *Unless the LORD builds the house, they labor in vain who build it;*
> *unless the LORD guards the city, the watchman keeps awake in vain.*

The Hebrew word, *shav*, translated as "vain" in the meditation verse can also be translated as "falsehood" and "lying"[1] Recall Psalm 120; the psalmist knew how miserable it was to be in a place of lies. This eighth step in the Songs of Ascents acknowledges what the psalmist learned at the beginning of this upward journey—it is a waste of time to build and live apart from God. A house built without the LORD is built on a false foundation; it will topple under the weight of lies.

Commit to building your life and the life of your family on the rock-solid foundation of Christ and His Word (Luke 6:47-49). Commit your works to the LORD; let the Master Builder execute His plans for your life (Proverbs 16:3).

Ask the LORD to guard your family by praying Psalm 127 as a faithful, prayerful watchman (Isaiah 62:6-7).

> *"LORD, unless You build _____ and my*
> *house, we labor in vain who build it.*
> *Unless You guard our city, home, and family,*
> *we keep awake in vain as watchmen.*
> *It is vain for us to rise up early, to retire late,*
> *to eat the bread of painful labors;*
> *please give to us, Your beloveds, even in our sleep.*
> *Behold, children are a gift from You, LORD,*
> *the fruit of the womb is a reward.*
> *Like arrows in the hand of a warrior, so*
> *are the children of one's youth.*
> *How blessed are those whose quiver is full of them.*
> *Please bless _____ with children, LORD.*
> *Do not let us be ashamed when we speak with our enemies in the gate.*
> *In Your name, Jesus~"*

1. Retrieved from www.blueletterbible.org/lang/lexicon/lexicon.cfm?Strongs=H7723&t=NASB

Please read Psalm 128.

Meditate on verse 1.

How blessed is everyone who fears the LORD, who walks in His ways.

What a blessing it is when you start seeing more and more of your loved ones ascending from places of lies, struggles, and conflicts to the place of fearing God and walking in His ways! As you look back on your own ascension journey, do not lose heart in praying for those you love to grow closer and closer to Jesus. Take seriously your calling to be a faithful, prayerful watchman (Isaiah 62:6-7) and pray Psalm 128 over yourself and those you love.

> *"How blessed is everyone who fears You,*
> *LORD, who walks in Your ways!*
> *Please make _____ and me Your blessed ones!*
> *May we fear You and walk in Your ways, LORD!*
> *As we do, let us eat of the fruit of our hands; let*
> *us be happy, and let it be well with us.*
> *Let the wives in our family be like a fruitful vine within their*
> *homes. Let the children be like olive plants around our table.*
> *This is how we who fear You, LORD, will be blessed.*
> *LORD, please bless us! May we see the prosperity of*
> *Jerusalem and the prosperity of our family all the days of*
> *our life. Indeed, may we see our children's children.*
> *Peace be upon Israel, and peace be upon our family!*
> *Because of Your name, Jesus~"*

Please read Psalm 129.

Meditate on verse 2.

> *Many times they have persecuted me from my youth up,*
> *yet they have not prevailed against me.*

Be mindful as you ascend, there will still be times of persecution. Don't be surprised when they come and be armed with God's Word and prayer when they do.

The psalmist put well into words how persecution feels—"The plowers plowed upon my back" (v. 3). Ouch!

And, he stated truth about God to remember in the midst of persecution— "The LORD is righteous; He has cut in two the cords of the wicked" (v. 4).

The psalmist also prayed a powerful prayer against his persecutors. Keep this psalm in your arsenal of prayers for times you need it as a faithful, prayerful watchman (Isaiah 62:6-7).

Pray Psalm 129 for the sake of yourself and those you love as a faithful, prayerful watchman (Isaiah 62:6-7).

> *"LORD, many times they have persecuted _____ and*
> *me from our youth up,*
> *yet they have not prevailed against us. The*
> *plowers plowed upon our backs;*
> *they lengthened their furrows. LORD, You*
> *are righteous; You have cut in two*
> *the cords of the wicked. May all who hate Zion and who hate*
> *us be put to shame and turned backward. Let them be like*
> *grass upon the housetops, which withers before it grows up;*
> *with which the reaper does not fill his hand,*
> *or the binder of sheaves his bosom;*
> *nor do those who pass by say, 'The blessing of the LORD be upon you.'*
> *LORD, do not let us persecute others; let Your blessing be upon us.*
> *For the sake of Your name, Jesus~"*

Please read Psalm 130.

Meditate on verses 1-2a.

> *Out of the depths I have cried to You, O LORD.*
> *LORD, hear my voice!*

The LORD brought the psalmist out of the place where liars dwelled (Psalm 120; 129). Now, he needed God to bring him out of the depths of his sin (Psalm 130). The pit of one's own iniquity is more dreadful than the dread of humans wanting to harm you. Incredibly, the same LORD who can save you from human persecution can save you from the sins that persecute your soul. Thankfully, because of the sacrifice of Jesus Christ, and through faith in Him, God does not keep record of your iniquities if you belong to Him. If you are with Jesus, you dwell in abundant redemption (v. 7). Amazing!

Cry out to the LORD with the words of Psalm 130 as a faithful, prayerful watchman (Isaiah 62:6-7).

> *"Out of the depth, I am crying to You, O*
> *LORD. LORD, hear my voice!*
> *Let Your ears be attentive to the voice of my*
> *supplications. If You, LORD,*
> *should mark iniquities, O LORD, who*
> *could stand? Thank You that there*
> *is abundant forgiveness with You, that You may*
> *be feared. I wait for You, LORD,*
> *my soul does wait, and in Your Word, I hope.*
> *My soul waits for You, LORD;*
> *more than the watchmen for the morning; indeed, more*
> *than the watchmen for the morning. I hope in You, LORD;*
> *for with You, there is lovingkindness, and with You*
> *is abundant redemption. LORD, You will redeem Israel;*
> *please redeem _____ and me from all our iniquities.*
> *In Your name, Jesus~"*

Please read Psalm 131.

Meditate on verse 2.

> *Surely I have composed and quieted my soul; like a weaned child rests against his mother, my soul is like a weaned child within me.*

Psalm 131 is a sigh of relief. After dealing with bad guys, persecution, and personal sin, the psalmist ascends to the step of realization. Those things are part of living in a fallen world, and rather than get all huffy or defensive or anguished over so many difficulties, he simply rests in God.

> *"Come to Me, all who are weary and heavy-laden, and I will give you rest."*
> —Matthew 11:28

Perhaps you, too, are tired of dealing with the bombardments of a sin-riddled world. Snuggle into the Savior and let Him deal with things too difficult for you, which will probably be everything.

As you abide with Jesus, pray Psalm 131 as a faithful, prayerful watchman (Isaiah 62:6-7).

> *"O LORD, my heart is not proud, nor my eyes haughty; nor do I involve myself in great matters, or in things too difficult for me. Surely I have composed and quieted my soul; like a weaned child rests against his mother, my soul is like a weaned child within me. O LORD, I hope in You from this time forth and forever. O LORD, let Israel hope in You from this time forth and forever. O LORD, let _____ hope in You from this time forth and forever. Because You are our only hope, Jesus~"*

Please read Psalm 132.

Meditate on verse 1.

Remember, O LORD, on David's behalf, all his affliction.

As the psalmist took the last few steps upward, he remembered David and his affliction (v. 1). He recalled David's tenacity to make certain the house of God was built (vs. 2-5). The psalmist saw the fulfillment of David's dream as he had the privilege to enter the temple along with the priests and the ark of God (vs. 7-9).

Seeing a vision fulfilled is glorious! However, it is not an easy journey. As you ascend toward the goal, remember faithful ones who persevered on their ascension journeys and be encouraged as you step upward with Christ. Beware of persecutors along the way and your own temptation to sin (Psalm 120; 129-130). Fix your eyes on the LORD and His vision for you (Psalm 121). Approach the climb as a faithful servant, keeping your eyes on the hands of the Master (Psalm 123). Trust the LORD for every step of the way (Psalm 125).

Pray Psalm 132:9-10 and 16 over yourself and those for whom you stand guard as a faithful, prayerful watchman (Isaiah 62:6-7).

> *"LORD, make _____ and me Your priests;*
> *clothe us with Your righteousness.*
> *Make us Your Godly ones; let us sing for joy.*
> *Make us Your servants, Your anointed ones;*
> *do not let our faces turn from You.*
> *As Your priests, clothe us with salvation,*
> *and as Your Godly ones, let us sing aloud for joy.*
> *Because of Your name, Jesus~"*

Please read Psalm 133.

Meditate on verse 1.

Behold, how good and pleasant it is for
brothers to dwell together in unity!

As the psalmist nears the summit, he finds himself at the top with others who love the LORD. These precious ones ascended from the world's pit to the glorious heights attained by walking with God. This sacred journey cannot be made without the anointing of God, for it is impossible to climb to such a holy elevation without the favor of the LORD. The prize awaiting all who complete the ascent is the blessing of God—His eternal life.

Praise and petition God with the fourteenth Song of Ascents, Psalm 133, as His faithful, prayerful watchman (Isaiah 62:6-7).

"Behold, how good and pleasant it is for
brothers to dwell together in unity!
LORD, please let _____ and me dwell together in unity.
Anoint us, LORD, with Your Spirit.
Let our unity be like the precious oil upon the
head, coming down upon the beard,
even Aaron's beard, coming down upon the edge of his robes.
Let our unity be like the dew of Hermon, coming
down upon the mountains of Zion,
positively affecting others. LORD, command
for us the blessing—life forever.
In Your name, Jesus~"

Please read Psalm 134.

Meditate on verse 1.

> *Behold, bless the LORD, all servants of the LORD,*
> *who serve by night in the house of the LORD!*

Step 15 in the Song of Ascents ends as a servant in the house of God, pulling night-duty. Could there be any higher place—in the still of the night, with the LORD, serving Him? Have you committed your life to God as His servant?

Use this day to remember your journey with God. From where did He you pluck you out? What are your earliest memories of going to the house of the LORD? How has God sustained you on your journey with Him? How has the LORD protected you from persecutors? Do you rest in Him? Are you His servant with your eyes fixed on Him?

Psalms 120-134 can be your personal Songs of Ascents, putting into words your upward journey with God. Pray Psalm 134 in thanksgiving and devotion to the LORD as His faithful, prayerful watchman (Isaiah 62:6-7).

> *"Behold, bless the LORD, all servants of the LORD,*
> *who serve by night in the house of the LORD!*
> *LORD, may _____ and I be Your servants*
> *who serve You by night in Your house.*
> *We bless You, LORD! We lift up our hands to*
> *Your sanctuary and bless You, LORD!*
> *LORD, You made heaven and earth; please*
> *bless us. Bless us from Zion.*
> *For the sake of Your name, Jesus~"*

Please read Psalm 135.

Meditate on verse 1.

> *Praise the LORD! Praise the name of the LORD;*
> *praise Him, O servants of the LORD.*

This psalm is addressed to you and gives you a command: "Praise the LORD, O servants of the LORD. You who revere the LORD, bless the LORD" (vs. 1, 20). (Bless means to praise, glorify, magnify, and extol.)

This psalm tells you why you are to bless and praise the LORD:

- ⌘ He is good, and His name is lovely (v. 3).
- ⌘ He is great, and He is above all gods (v. 5).
- ⌘ He does whatever He pleases (v. 6).

The psalm tells about some of the great things the LORD did for Israel that should cause them to praise Him (vs. 8-14). What has the LORD done on your behalf that deserves your praise?

As a servant of the LORD, praise the LORD. Start with the words from Psalm 135:1 and 3-7.

> *"Praise the LORD! I praise Your name, LORD.*
> *I praise You for You are good, LORD.*
> *I sing praises to Your name, for it is lovely.*
> *LORD, You have chosen me for Yourself.*
> *Please choose _____ for Your own possession.*
> *I know You are great, and You are above all gods.*
> *LORD, You do whatever You please, in heaven*
> *and in earth, in the seas and in all deeps.*
> *LORD, do whatever You please in _____ and my life.*
> *You cause the clouds to ascend from the ends of the earth;*
> *You make lightnings for the rain; You bring*
> *forth the wind from Your treasuries.*
> *(Continue to praise the LORD for what He*
> *has done for you and those you love.)*
> *Praise the LORD!"*

Please read Psalm 136.

Meditate on verse 1.

Give thanks to the LORD, for He is good, for
His lovingkindness is everlasting.

Lovingkindness—it is a Scriptural word rooted in the tender regard and mercy of God for His people. The fact that His lovingkindness is everlasting is amazing.

The psalmist recognized God's lovingkindness as a catalyst in his life, and he praised Him for it. Pray Psalm 136:1-9 and 23-26 in acknowledgment and thanksgiving of God's lovingkindness as His faithful, prayerful watchman (Isaiah 62:6-7).

"I give thanks to You, LORD, for You are good,
for Your lovingkindness is everlasting.
I give thanks to You, the God of gods, for
Your lovingkindness is everlasting.
I give thanks to You, LORD of lords, for
Your lovingkindness is everlasting.
You alone do great wonders, for Your lovingkindness is everlasting.
You made the heavens with skill, for Your
lovingkindness is everlasting.
You spread out the earth above the waters, for
Your lovingkindness is everlasting.
You made the great lights, for Your lovingkindness is everlasting.
You made the sun to rule by day, for Your
lovingkindness is everlasting.
You made the moon and stars to rule by night,
for Your lovingkindness is everlasting.
You remembered us in our low estate, for
Your lovingkindness is everlasting.
You have rescued us from our adversaries, for
Your lovingkindness is everlasting.
You give food to all flesh, for Your lovingkindness is everlasting.
I give thanks to You, God of heaven, for
Your lovingkindness is everlasting."

Please read Psalm 137.

Meditate on verse 4.

> *How can we sing the LORD'S song in a foreign land?*

This psalm gives insight into the hopelessness of the Jews forced to leave Israel and go to Babylon. Their captors wanted them to sing temple songs for the purpose of making fun of them. The Israelites defiantly hung up their instruments, refusing to play and sing. Their despair even took them to the wretched place of hoping Babylonian babies would be dashed against rocks (vs. 8-9). What a horrible situation!

The Jews probably should have ignored their persecutors and sung a song to the LORD to quiet their tormented souls. Thanking and praising God in the midst of difficulties is the best antidote to hopeless despair. In fact, the LORD commands it:

> *Rejoice always; in everything give thanks,*
> *for this is God's will for you in Christ Jesus.*
> —1 Thessalonians 5:16, 18

Psalm 137 may describe how you or someone you love feels today. Pray for God to help you sing to Him by giving you the answer to the question in verse 4.

> *"LORD, how can _____ and I sing Your song in a foreign land?*
> *Please help us sing for the sake of Your name, Jesus~"*

What is a song for God that comes to your mind? Do not hesitate; sing it to Him.

Please read Psalm 138.

Meditate on and memorize verse 8a to pray the moment you need it.

The LORD will accomplish what concerns me.

This is my go-to verse when I need desperate prayers for desperate situations. There are days those are the only words my faint heart and quivering lips can form:

"The LORD will accomplish what concerns me;
the LORD will accomplish what concerns me; the
LORD will accomplish what concerns me...."

I have said them literally hundreds of times—"The LORD will accomplish what concerns me...." And, He absolutely does accomplish what concerns me. "Thank You, LORD!"

Pray Psalm 138 over yourself and those for whom you stand guard as a faithful, prayerful watchman (Isaiah 62:6-7).

"LORD, I give thanks to You with all my heart;
I sing praises to You before the gods.
I bow down toward Your holy temple and give thanks to Your name
for Your lovingkindness and Your truth; for You have magnified
Your Word according to all Your name. LORD, I am calling
to You on behalf of _____ and me. Please answer me.
Make us bold with strength in our souls. May all
the kings of the earth give thanks to You,
O LORD, when they hear the Words of Your
mouth. Let them sing of Your ways,
for great is Your glory, LORD. LORD, You
are exalted, yet You regard the lowly,
but the haughty

You know from afar. Do not let us be haughty, LORD.
We walk in the midst of trouble; please revive us.
Stretch forth Your hand
against the wrath of our enemies; let Your right hand save us.
LORD, You will accomplish what concerns
me; Your lovingkindness, O LORD,
is everlasting; do not forsake the works of Your hands.
For the sake of Your name, Jesus~"

November 17

Please read Psalm 139.

Meditate on verse 1.

O LORD, You have searched me and known me.

The LORD is intimately acquainted with you. Let that thought soak in—the LORD intimately knows everything about you. He knows when you sit down and when you get up (v. 2). He knows and understands what you are thinking (v. 2). He knows what you are going to say before you say it (v. 4). He intricately put every cell of your body together, wonderfully the way He wanted you (vs. 13-15). He knew the exact day of your birth, and He knows the exact day of your death; everyday of your life has already been written in His book (v. 16). These are amazing truths about you from God's Word! Knowing these truths, you can walk in confident, constant intimacy with your Creator—incredible!

As you continue in intimate conversation with God, say these words from Psalm 139:17-18 and 23-24 to Him as His faithful, prayerful watchman (Isaiah 62:6-7).

*"How precious are Your thoughts to me, O
God! How vast is the sum of them!
If I should count them, they would outnumber the sand.
When I awake, I am still with You. Search
me, O God, and know my heart;
try me and know my anxious thoughts; and
see if there be any hurtful way in me
and lead me in the everlasting way.
In Your name, Jesus~"*

Please read Psalm 140.

Meditate on verse 6.

> *I said to the LORD, "You are my God; give ear, O LORD,*
> *to the voice of my supplications."*

This psalm contains really strong verses to pray over really difficult situations. Pray it with discretion when you need the LORD's protection from slanderous and violent people who want to harm you and those you love.

Pray Psalm 140 on behalf of those in desperate situations.

> *"Rescue _____ and me, O LORD, from evil*
> *men; preserve us from violent men*
> *who devise evil things in their hearts; they continually stir up wars.*
> *They sharpen their tongues as a serpent;*
> *poison of a viper is under their lips.*
> *Keep us, O LORD, from the hands of the wicked; preserve*
> *us from violent men who have purposed to trip up our*
> *feet. The proud have hidden a trap for us and cords;*
> *they have spread a net by the wayside; they have set snares for us.*
> *LORD, You are our God; give ear, O LORD,*
> *to the voice of my supplications!*
> *O God the LORD, the strength of our salvation, You have covered*
> *our head in the day of battle. Do not grant, O LORD, the desires*
> *of the wicked; do not promote their evil device, that they not*
> *be exalted. As for the head of those who surround us, may the*
> *mischief of their lips cover them. May burning coals fall upon*
> *them; may they be cast into the fire, into deep pits from which*
> *they cannot rise. May a slanderer not be established in the earth;*
> *may evil hunt the violent man speedily. LORD, I know that You*
> *will maintain the cause of the afflicted and justice for the poor.*
> *LORD, keep us righteous; we will give thanks to Your name.*
> *Keep us upright; let us dwell in Your presence.*
> *For the sake of Your name, Jesus"*

Please read Psalm 141.

Meditate on and memorize verse 3.

> *Set a guard, O LORD, over my mouth;*
> *keep watch over the door of my lips.*

Have you ever said something and wished you could take it back? If so, you know it is impossible to do, and sadly, can cause irreparable damage. The meditation verse is a good one to memorize and pray before opening your mouth. It can keep you from saying the regrettable, giving you the opportunity to engage in conversations knowing the Holy Spirit, instead of your flesh, is controlling what you say.

Call to the LORD on behalf of yourself and those for whom you stand guard with Psalm 141:1-4 and 8, as a faithful, prayerful watchman (Isaiah 62:6-7).

> *"O LORD, I call upon You; hasten to _____ and me!*
> *Give ear to our voice when we call to You!*
> *May our prayers be counted as incense before You;*
> *the lifting up of our hands as the evening offering.*
> *Set a guard, O LORD, over our mouths; keep*
> *watch over the door of our lips.*
> *Do not incline our hearts to any evil thing,*
> *to practice deeds of wickedness*
> *with men who do iniquity; and do not let us eat of their delicacies.*
> *Our eyes are toward You, O God, the LORD;*
> *in You we take refuge; do not leave us defenseless.*
> *In Your name, Jesus~"*

Please read Psalm 142.

Meditate on verses 1-2.

> *I cry aloud with my voice to the LORD;*
> *I make supplication with my voice to the LORD.*
> *I pour out my complaint before Him; I*
> *declare my trouble before Him.*

Ponder the privilege you have to cry out, literally, to shriek in anguish to the God of the universe. You have the precious opportunity to beseech your Creator for His favor on you and your loved ones. He will not strike you dead for pouring out your complaints to Him and telling Him all your troubles; on the contrary, He desires a relationship with you where you have the intimate freedom to tell Him everything. Amazing!

Cry aloud to God with Psalm 142 as a faithful, prayerful watchman (Isaiah 62:6-7).

> *"I cry aloud with my voice to You, LORD;*
> *I make supplication with my voice to You, LORD.*
> *I pour out my complaint before You; I declare my trouble to You.*
> *My spirit is overwhelmed within me; You know my path.*
> *In the way where I walk, they have hidden a trap for _____ and me.*
> *LORD, look to the right and see, for there is no one who regards us.*
> *There is no escape for us; no one cares for our*
> *souls. LORD, please regard us*
> *and provide a way of escape because You care for*
> *our souls. I cry out to You, O LORD!*
> *You are our refuge, our portion in the land*
> *of the living. Give heed to my cry,*
> *for we are brought very low; deliver us from*
> *our persecutors, for they are*
> *too strong for us. Bring our souls out of prison, so*
> *that we may give thanks to Your name.*
> *The righteous will surround us, for You will deal bountifully with us.*
> *For the sake of Your name, Jesus-"*

Please read Psalm 143.

Meditate on verse 10.

Teach me to do Your will, for You are my God.

Crushed and overwhelmed in the middle of serious trials, David cried out to God, not only begging Him to come to his aid, but wanting God to teach him, so the hard time could be a productive time. Are you or someone you love in the midst of difficult days? What is God teaching you? He doesn't allow these seasons for naught. As you walk through trying times with the LORD, your faith increases, and you are made perfect and complete in Him (James 1:2-4).

Pray Psalm 143:1 and 3-12 over yourself and those you love as a faithful, prayerful watchman (Isaiah 62:6-7).

"Hear my prayer, O LORD, give ear to my supplications!
Answer me in Your faithfulness, in Your righteousness!
The enemy has persecuted _____ and my soul;
he has crushed our life to the ground;
he has made us dwell in dark places, like
those who have long been dead.
Therefore, my spirit is overwhelmed within
me; my heart is appalled within me.
I remember the days of old; I meditate on all Your doings;
I muse on the work of Your hands. I stretch out my hands
to You; my soul longs for You, as a parched land.
Answer me quickly, O LORD; our spirits
fail; do not hide Your face from us,
or we will become like those who go down to the
pit. Let us hear Your lovingkindness
in the morning, for we trust in You; teach us
the way in which we should walk;
for to You we lift up our souls.

*Deliver us, O LORD, from our enemies; we take refuge
in You. Teach us to do Your will, for You are our God; let
Your good Spirit lead us on level ground. For the sake of
Your name, O LORD, revive us. In Your righteousness,
bring our souls out of trouble. And in Your
lovingkindness, cut off our enemies
and destroy all those who afflict our souls, for we are Your servants.
In Your name, Jesus~"*

Please read Psalm 144.

Meditate on verse 1a.

Blessed be the LORD, my Rock.

David had such a personal relationship with the LORD that he knew God as:

- ∞ my Rock
- ∞ my Lovingkindness
- ∞ my Fortress
- ∞ my Stronghold
- ∞ my Deliverer
- ∞ my Shield (vs. 1-2)

How do you know the LORD? Continue the list from Psalm 144 with your own, saying, "God, You are:

- ∞ my _____
- ∞ my _____
- ∞ my _____…

Continue talking to the LORD your God with the words from Psalm 144:1-2 and 12-15 as a faithful, prayerful watchman (Isaiah 62:6-7).

*"LORD, **my** Rock, **my** Lovingkindness, **my** Fortress, **my** Stronghold, **my** Deliverer, **my** Shield, **my** Refuge, let our sons in their youth be as grown-up plants and our daughters as corner pillars fashioned as for a palace. Let our garners be full, furnishing every kind of produce, and our flocks bring forth thousands and ten-thousands in our fields; let our cattle bear without mishap and without loss. Let there be no outcry in our streets! How blessed are the people who are so situated; how blessed are the people whose God is the LORD! Please make us Your blessed people! In Your name, Jesus~"*

Please read Psalm 145.

Meditate on verse 19a.

He will fulfill the desire of those who fear Him.

What an encouraging psalm of praise for those who love and fear God! Pray it now over yourself and those for whom you stand guard as a faithful, prayerful watchman (Isaiah 62:6-7).

"LORD, I extol You, my God, O King, and
I bless Your name forever and ever!
Everyday I bless You and praise Your name forever and ever!
LORD, You are great and highly to be praised.
Your greatness is unsearchable.
Let my generation praise Your works to another
and declare Your mighty acts.
I meditate on the glorious splendor of Your
majesty and on Your wonderful works.
Let _____ and me speak of the power of Your
awesome acts and tell of Your greatness.
We eagerly utter the memory of Your abundant goodness and
shout joyfully of Your righteousness. LORD, You are gracious
and merciful, slow to anger and great in lovingkindness. LORD,
You are good to all, and Your mercies are over all Your works.
May all Your works give thanks to You, O LORD, and Your
Godly ones bless You. Let us speak of the glory of Your kingdom
and talk of Your power. Let us make known Your mighty acts
and the glory of the majesty of Your kingdom.
Your kingdom is an everlasting kingdom,
and Your dominion endures throughout all generations. LORD,
sustain us when we fall and raise up all who are bowed down. Our
eyes look to You; please give us our food in due time. Open Your hand
and satisfy the desire of every living thing. LORD, You are righteous
in all Your ways and kind in all Your deeds. LORD, You are near to
all who call upon You, to all who call upon You in truth. LORD, we
fear You; fulfill our desire and hear our cry and save us. LORD, we
love You; please keep us. We will speak Your praise with our mouth.
May all flesh bless Your holy name forever and ever, LORD Jesus~"

Please read Psalm 146.

Meditate on verse 5.

> *How blessed is he whose help is the God of Jacob;*
> *whose hope is in the LORD his God.*

The psalmist knew he should trust in the LORD instead of trusting in people to save him (v. 3). As he recalled who God is, his confidence grew strong in Him.

Pray Psalm 146 and let the words increase your confidence in God as you trust Him more and more as His faithful, prayerful watchman (Isaiah 62:6-7).

> *"Praise the LORD! Praise the LORD, O my soul!*
> *I praise You, LORD, while I live; I sing praises*
> *to You, my God, while I have my being.*
> *I do not trust in princes, in mortal man,*
> *in whom there is no salvation.*
> *His spirit departs; he returns to the earth; in*
> *that very day, his thoughts perish.*
> *How blessed are _____ and I whose help is You, the God of Jacob;*
> *our hope is in You, LORD our God! You made heaven and*
> *earth, the sea and all that is in them. You keep faith forever; You*
> *execute justice for the oppressed; You give food to the hungry.*
> *LORD, You set prisoners free. LORD, You open the eyes of the*
> *blind. LORD, You raise up those who are bowed down. LORD,*
> *You love the righteous. LORD, You protect the sojourners. You*
> *support the fatherless and the widow, but You thwart the way of*
> *the wicked. LORD, You will reign forever to all generations.*
> *Praise the LORD!"*

Please read Psalm 147.

Meditate on verse 1.

Praise the LORD! For it is good to sing praises to our God;
for it is pleasant, and praise is becoming.

It is proper and fitting to praise the LORD, and this psalm tells you why.
Praise the LORD with Psalm 147, telling Him why He alone is worthy of
your praise.

"Praise the LORD! It is good to sing praises to You, God.
It is pleasant, and praise is becoming, so let _____ and me
praise You forever. LORD, You build up Jerusalem; You
gather the outcasts of Israel. You heal the brokenhearted and
bind up their wounds. You count the number of the stars;
You give names to all of them. Great are You, LORD, and
abundant in strength. Your understanding is infinite.
LORD, You support the afflicted; You bring down the wicked to the
ground. We sing to You with thanksgiving; we sing praises on the lyre.
You cover the heavens with clouds; You provide rain for the
earth and make grass grow on the mountains. You give to
the beast its food and to the young ravens which cry.
You do not delight in the strength of the horse; You
do not take pleasure in the legs of a man.
LORD, You favor those who fear You, those
who wait for Your lovingkindness.
LORD, let that be our family! LORD, You strengthen the bars of
our gates; You bless our sons; You make peace within our borders;
You satisfy us; You send forth Your commands; Your Word runs
very swiftly; You give snow like wool; You scatter the frost like ashes;
You cast forth You ice as fragments; You send for Your Word; You
cause Your wind to blow and the waters to flow; You declare Your
Words, Your statutes, and Your ordinances to Israel and to us.
Praise the LORD!"

Please read Psalm 148.

Meditate on verses 12-13.

> *Both young men and virgins, old men and children,*
> *let them praise the name of the LORD,*
> *for His name alone is exalted; His glory is above earth and heaven.*

Psalm 147 told you why you praise the LORD. Today's psalm tells you who is to praise him—everything in the heavens, and everything and everyone on the earth. Every created person, animal, and thing is to praise the Creator. Interestingly, scientists have learned that planets and stars do actually emit sounds. Here is one of many websites where you can actually listen to planets praising the LORD: http://canyouactually.com/nasa-actually-recorded-sound-in-space-and-its-absolutely-chilling/

Jesus even said that if the people didn't cry out in praise of Him, the rocks would (Luke 19:40). Praise the LORD with Psalm 148 as His faithful, prayerful watchman (Isaiah 62:6-7).

> *"Praise the LORD! LORD, You are to be praised*
> *from the heavens and in the heights.*
> *May all Your angels praise You. May all Your hosts praise You.*
> *May the sun and moon praise You. May all the stars of light praise*
> *You. May the highest heavens and the waters that are above the*
> *heavens praise You! Let them praise Your name, LORD, for You*
> *commanded and they were created. You also established them forever*
> *and ever; You made a decree which will not pass away. LORD,*
> *You are to be praised from the earth. Sea monsters and all deeps*
> *praise You. Fire and hail, snow and clouds, stormy*
> *wind, fulfilling Your Word; mountains*
> *and all hills; fruit trees and all cedars; beasts and all cattle;*
> *creeping things and winged fowl; kings of the earth and all peoples;*
> *princes and all judges of the earth; both young men and virgins;*
> *old men and children, let them praise Your name, LORD, for*
> *Your name alone is exalted; Your glory is above earth and heaven.*
> *You have lifted up a horn for Your people, praise for all Your*
> *Godly ones, even for the sons of Israel, a people near to You.*
> *Praise the LORD!"*

Please read Psalm 149.

Meditate on verses 5-6.

*Let the Godly ones exult in glory; let them sing for joy on their beds.
Let the high praises of God be in their mouth
and a two-edged sword in their hand.*

Psalms 147 and 148 tell why and who are to praise the LORD. Psalm 149 tells when and how to praise Him. With spoken and singing words, dancing and musical instruments, praise the LORD (vs. 1-3, 5). Praise Him when you are with other believers; praise Him when you are alone or with your spouse on your bed; praise Him when you are fighting for the sake of His name (vs. 1, 5-6). In other words, all the time, with everything you have, in every circumstance, praise the LORD!

Praise the LORD with Psalm 149 as His faithful, prayerful watchman (Isaiah 62:6-7).

*"Praise the LORD! LORD, I sing to You a new song; I
sing Your praise in the congregation of the Godly ones.
Let Israel, _____, and me be glad in You, our Maker. Let
the sons of Zion, _____, and me rejoice in You, our King. Let
us praise Your name with dancing. Let us sing praises to You
with timbrel and lyre. LORD, take pleasure in us, Your people;
beautify the afflicted ones with salvation. We are Your Godly
ones; we will exult in glory and sing for joy on our beds.
The high praises of You, our God, will be in our mouths and
a two-edged sword, Your Word, in our hand (Hebrews 4:12).
By Your Word, let us execute vengeance on the nations and
punishment on the peoples, to bind their kings with chains
and their nobles with fetters of iron, to execute on them the
judgment written; this is an honor for all Your Godly ones.
Praise the LORD!"*

Please read Psalm 150.

Meditate on verse 1a.

Praise the LORD!

It is fitting that this book of 150 psalms ends with four praise psalms. Recall many of the psalms are desperate cries for God's help and deliverance. Some are prayers for God's vengeance on enemies. Some are questioning psalms asking God, "Why?" Ending the 150 psalms with praise is the perfect benediction; for at the end of it all, it should be praise to the LORD for His sustaining grace and mercy on you, no matter what and despite all.

Praise the LORD one more time with Psalm 150 as His faithful, prayerful watchman (Isaiah 62:6-7).

"Praise the LORD!
God, I praise You in Your sanctuary; I praise
You in Your mighty expanse.
I praise You for Your mighty deeds; I praise You
according to Your excellent greatness.
I praise You with trumpet sound; I praise You with harp and lyre.
I praise You with timbrel and dancing.
I praise You with stringed instruments and pipe.
I praise You with loud cymbals; I praise
You with resounding cymbals.
Let everything that has breath praise You, LORD.
Praise the LORD!"

The Psalms are not the only songs in the Bible. For the next 23 days, you will read and pray those other songs, scattered throughout Scripture. We hope it is an amazing time with the LORD, during this season of Advent—the days leading up to the celebration of Jesus' birth.

Please read Exodus 15:1-18 and 21.

The Song of Moses and Miriam

Meditate on Exodus 14:31-15:1a.

> *When Israel saw the great power which the*
> *LORD had used against the Egyptians,*
> *the people feared the LORD, and they believed*
> *in the LORD and in His servant Moses.*
> *Then Moses and the sons of Israel sang this song to the LORD.*

The LORD acted in such a miraculous way on behalf of His people that the immediate response was singing a song, declaring His amazing attributes. As the men sang the story of God's victory (vs. 1-18), the women danced and played timbrels (tambourines), singing the chorus:

> *Sing to the LORD, for He is highly exalted;*
> *the horse and his rider He has hurled into the sea.*
> —Exodus 15:21

This can become one your songs of victory. Use the words from Exodus 15:1-18 to praise the LORD.

> *"I will sing to the LORD, for He is highly exalted.*
> *(Tell what the LORD has done for you.)*
> *The LORD is my strength and song, and He has become my salvation.*
> *This is my God, and I will praise Him; my*
> *father's God, and I will extol Him.*
> *The LORD is a warrior; the LORD is His name.*
> *(Tell what the LORD has done for you.)*
> *Your right hand, O LORD, is majestic in power;*
> *Your right hand, O LORD, shatters the enemy.*

And in the greatness of Your excellence, You
overthrow those who rise up against You;
You send forth Your burning anger, and it consumes them as chaff.
(Tell what the LORD has done for you.)
Who is like You among the gods, O LORD?
Who is like You, majestic in holiness, awesome
in praises, working wonders?
(Tell what the LORD has done for you.)
The LORD shall reign forever and ever."

Please read Deuteronomy 32:1-43.

Song of Moses, Joshua, and God

Meditate on verses 2-3.

> *Let my teaching drop as the rain, my speech distill as the dew,*
> *as the droplets on the fresh grass and as the showers on the herb,*
> *for I proclaim the name of the LORD; ascribe greatness to our God!*

On the day Moses died, he spoke this song to the children of Israel, with his successor, Joshua, by his side (Deuteronomy 32:44-52). Moses starts the song with a prayer request that his words will distill (purify) the hearers. Then Moses immediately condemns the people for being corrupt toward God their Father (vs. 5-6). After elaborating on their abominations (vs. 5-18), the LORD takes over the song, warning the people of His coming judgment, but also reassuring them of His mercy and compassion (vs. 19-43).

What a treasure—the final words of Moses that are the eternal Words of God! Take them to heart, letting them distill you.

Appeal to the LORD with His Words by praying Deuteronomy 32:20, 28-29, 31, 36, and 39 over yourself and those for whom you stand guard as a faithful, prayerful watchman (Isaiah 62:6-7).

> *"LORD, please do not hide Your face from _____ and me.*
> *Do not let us be a perverse generation; make us Your faithful ones.*
> *Make us a nation guided by Your counsel and understanding.*
> *Make us wise, so we can understand and discern our future.*
> *Jesus, You are our Rock, and there is no other rock like You—*
> *let even our enemies know this. LORD, vindicate us, Your people,*
> *and have compassion on us, Your servants,*
> *when You see that our strength is gone.*
> *You are God! There is no god besides You!*
> *You put to death and give life.*
> *You wound, and You heal, and there is no one*
> *who can deliver from Your hand.*
> *In the name of our Rock, Jesus~"*

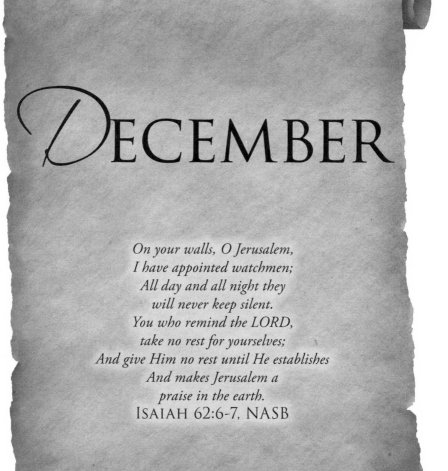

DECEMBER

On your walls, O Jerusalem,
I have appointed watchmen;
All day and all night they
will never keep silent.
You who remind the LORD,
take no rest for yourselves;
And give Him no rest until He establishes
And makes Jerusalem a
praise in the earth.

ISAIAH 62:6-7, NASB

Please read Judges 5.

Song of Deborah and Barak

Meditate on verse 13b.

> *The people of the LORD came down to me as warriors.*

Deborah and Barak sang this song after God gave the Israelites victory over the Canaanites who had severely oppressed them for 20 years (Judges 4:1-3). It declares victory in so many areas of their lives. After 20 years of doing evil in the sight of the LORD and being punished severely for it, finally:

- ❧ the leaders led in Israel (v. 2).
- ❧ the people volunteered (v. 2).
- ❧ the people of the LORD showed up to fight as warriors (v. 13).
- ❧ there were great resolves of heart (v. 15).
- ❧ there were great searchings of heart (v. 16).

Do not stop praying for those you love to finally follow Christ. Pray for your leaders to lead and be Godly. Pray for God's people to volunteer. Pray for the people of the LORD to fight as warriors. Pray for God's people to search their hearts and resolve to do what's right in His sight.

Pray Judges 5:31 as a faithful, prayerful watchman (Isaiah 62:6-7).

> *"O LORD, let all Your enemies perish,*
> *but let those who love You be like the rising of the sun in its might.*
> *Please let our land be undisturbed.*
> *In Your name, Jesus~"*

Please read 1 Samuel 1:24-2:10.

Hannah's Prayer Song.

Meditate on this sentence from 1 Samuel 2:1.

My heart exults in the LORD.

Imagine how Hannah felt as she prayed these words. As promised, Hannah gave her beloved little boy Samuel to God, leaving him at the tabernacle to live with Eli the priest. She could easily have sung a begging prayer, asking God to let her out of her commitment. Instead, she worshiped, acknowledging God's supreme holiness and power.

Pray Hannah's song, 1 Samuel 2:1-10, as a faithful, prayerful watchman (Isaiah 62:6-7).

> *"My heart exults in You, LORD; my horn is exalted in You, LORD.*
> *My mouth speaks boldly against my enemies because I rejoice*
> *in Your salvation. There is no one holy like You, LORD; indeed,*
> *there is no one besides You, nor is there any rock like You, God.*
> *Let _____ and me boast no more so very*
> *proudly; do not let arrogance*
> *come out of our mouths, for LORD, You are*
> *a God of knowledge, and with You*
> *actions are weighed. Shatter the bows of the*
> *mighty but gird the feeble with strength.*
> *Let those who are hungry cease to hunger.*
> *Let the barren give birth to seven.*
> *LORD, You kill and make alive; You bring*
> *down to Sheol and raise up.*
> *LORD, You make poor and rich; You bring low; You also exalt.*
> *You raise the poor from the dust; You lift the needy from the ash heap*
> *to make them sit with nobles and inherit a seat of honor,*
> *for the pillars of the earth are Yours,*

LORD, and You set the world on them.
You keep the feet of Your Godly ones, but the
wicked are silenced in darkness,
for not by might shall a man prevail. Shatter
those who contend with You, LORD;
thunder against them in the heavens. You
will judge the ends of the earth,
and You will give strength to Your king and
will exalt the horn of Your anointed.
For Your name's sake, Jesus~"

DECEMBER 3

Please read 2 Samuel 1:17-27.

The Song of the Bow

Meditate on verse 24.

> *O daughters of Israel, weep over Saul, who*
> *clothed you luxuriously in scarlet,*
> *who put ornaments of gold on your apparel.*

David sang this funeral dirge for Saul and Jonathan after they were killed by the Philistines (1 Samuel 31). Saul spent the last years of his life hunting and trying to kill David. David had every reason to rejoice over his death, yet he genuinely laments the loss of both his best friend, Jonathan, and his archenemy, Saul. What a powerful testimony to David not allowing bitterness to overcome his thoughts and emotions!

Bitterness is an incredibly destructive emotion. It defiles you and keeps you from taking every thought captive to the obedience of Christ (Hebrews 12:15; 2 Corinthians 10:5). That is why God commands you to get rid of it:

> *Let all bitterness and wrath and anger and clamor and slander*
> *be put away from you, along with all malice.*
> —Ephesians 4:31

Ask the LORD to search your heart for bitterness; let Him remove it, so you can speak about the mighty things God has done in your life and how He brought beauty out of difficulty (v. 19).

Use the last phrase from this lament (2 Samuel 1:27b) to ask God to remove the bitter thoughts that are warring in your heart and mind.

> *"LORD, the weapons of war perished with*
> *the deaths of Saul and Jonathan.*
> *Let the weapons of war of my bitter thoughts and attitudes*
> *perish as I surrender them to You.*
> *In Your name, Jesus~"*

Please read 2 Samuel 22.

David's Song of Deliverance

Meditate on verses 2-3.

> *He said, "The LORD is my rock and my fortress and my deliverer;*
> *my God, my rock, in whom I take refuge, my*
> *shield and the horn of my salvation,*
> *my stronghold and my refuge; my Savior, You save me from violence."*

Years ago, I wrote "David and God" in my Bible as a theme for 2 Samuel 22. Today, I wrote "Marsha and God" next to these incredibly intimate words written by an adorer of the One to be adored. I love that God's Word can be read as if it were personally written for the reader; that is how I approach it every time I open the precious pages of Holy Scripture— "LORD, what do You want to tell me, today?"

You can reread this entire chapter, personally saying it to your LORD. Here are some of the verses to get you started—2 Samuel 22:2-4, 29, 47, and 50-51.

> *"LORD, You are my rock and my fortress and*
> *my deliverer; my God, my rock,*
> *in whom I take refuge, my shield and the horn of*
> *my salvation, my stronghold and my refuge;*
> *my Savior, You save me from violence. I call upon*
> *You, LORD, who is worthy to be praised,*
> *and I am saved from my enemies. You are my lamp,*
> *O LORD; You illumine my darkness.*
> *LORD, You live! And blessed are You, my Rock, and exalted*
> *are You, God, the Rock of my salvation! Therefore, I will*
> *give thanks to You, O LORD, among the nations,*
> *and I will sing praises to Your name. You are a tower of*
> *deliverance to me, and You show lovingkindness to Your*
> *anointed, to (your name), and my descendants forever.*
> *Thank You, in Your name, Jesus~"*

Please read Song of Solomon 1.

Meditate on verse 2.

> *May he kiss me with the kisses of his mouth!*
> *For your love is better than wine.*

Song of Solomon is a love story. There are different interpretations of this book. The literal interpretation is the love between a husband and wife. Symbolic interpretations are of Israel's relationship with God, the church's relationship with Jesus, and an individual's devotion to Christ.[1] As you read and pray the book, ask the Holy Spirit to show you the interpretation in which He wants you to gain understanding. For these devotions, we will focus on the literal interpretation of a love story between a husband and wife, praying the prayers over existing marriages and marriages yet to be.

In this chapter, the bride and bridegroom acknowledge the surpassing value of each to the other. His love is better to her than wine; she is the most beautiful of all women to him, and they do not hesitate to tell each other those truths. Do not hesitate to tell those you love how special they are to you.

Pray Song of Solomon 1:15-17 over the marriages you are guarding as a faithful, prayerful watchman (Isaiah 62:6-7).

> *"LORD, may _____ say to his bride:*
> *'How beautiful you are, my darling, how beautiful*
> *you are! Your eyes are like doves.'*
> *May _____ say to her bridegroom:*
> *'How handsome you are, my beloved, and so pleasant!'*
> *Make their (our) couch luxuriant! Let the beams*
> *of their (our) home be made of cedars*
> *and their (our) rafters of cypresses.*
> *Because their (our) home and marriage are built on You, Jesus~"*

1. Retrieved from *The New Inductive Study Bible* @2000 Precept Ministries International, pgs. 1078-1079

Please read Song of Solomon 2.

Meditate on verse 15.

> *Catch the foxes for us, the little foxes that are ruining the vineyards,*
> *while our vineyards are in blossom.*

The couple is thriving in this chapter, taking great delight in each other, pursuing and embracing each other (vs. 3, 5, 8-9). But while their vineyard blossoms, little foxes come to destroy it (v. 15). These rascals must be caught before they can damage this fabulous vineyard.

Destructive foxes can quickly crawl into a marriage. Be aware of them and remove them immediately, before they hurt the relationship. Unforgiveness, bitterness, unkindness, and jealousy are just a few of the foxes' names that want to ruin your marriage. If they have already crept in, do not be tempted to throw your hands up in defeat; the damage can always be repaired with God's help.

Talk to your spouse about the foxes that have been allowed to enter; then prayerfully purpose to throw them out. Fox-proof your home and marriage in the strength and love of Christ and His Word.

Pray Song of Solomon 2:15-16 over the marriages you guard as a faithful, prayerful watchman (Isaiah 62:6-7).

> *"LORD, catch the little foxes for us, the little foxes*
> *that are ruining the vineyard of _____. Let our*
> *vineyards blossom with no foxes to ruin them.*
> *Let _____'s beloved be hers alone and let her belong to him.*
> *May he faithfully pasture his flock among the lilies.*
> *For the sake of Your name, Jesus~"*

Please read Song of Solomon 3.

Meditate on verse 4.

> *Scarcely had I left them when I found him whom my soul loves;*
> *I held on to him and would not let him go until*
> *I had brought him to my mother's house,*
> *and into the room of her who conceived me.*

This woman wants her husband! Leading up to the wedding night, she desperately wants him to be with her; nothing and no one else can meet her needs (v. 1). He is the one whom her soul loves—there is no other (vs. 1-4).

If you are married, say these words, putting your spouse's name in the blank:

> *"On my bed at night, I seek _____, whom my soul loves.*
> *No matter where I go, I only seek _____, whom my soul loves.*
> *I inquire about and seek the wellbeing of _____,*
> *whom my soul loves.*
> *I have found _____, whom my soul loves;*
> *I only hold on to and will not let go of _____."*

Now, pray Song of Solomon 3:1-4 over the marriages you guard as a faithful, prayerful watchman (Isaiah 62:6-7).

> *"LORD, on their bed night after night, let _____ only seek _____.*
> *Let their souls only love each other. Let them seek and find each other.*
> *Let their souls only love each other. Let them*
> *inquire about and find each other.*
> *Let their souls only love each other. Let them*
> *hold on to each other and never let go.*
> *Let their souls only love each other.*
> *Because of Your love, Jesus~"*

Please read Song of Solomon 4.

Meditate on verse 9.

> *You have made my heart beat faster, my sister, my bride;*
> *you have made my heart beat faster with a single glance of your eyes,*
> *with a single strand of your necklace.*

What an incredibly holy and passionate chapter in God's Word! Marital intimacy is so important to the LORD; it is part of: "God saw all that He had made, and behold, it was very good" from Genesis 1 and 2 (Genesis 1:31). Marital intimacy is a gift from God and the ability to return to the perfection of the Garden of Eden. Savor the gift; do not neglect it or take it for granted.

Husband, say these words to your wife:

> *"How beautiful you are, my darling, how beautiful you are!*
> *You are altogether beautiful, my darling,*
> *and there is no blemish in you."*
> —Song of Solomon 4:1, 7

Wife, when you are blessed to hear your husband say words similar to these, receive them with joy and love. Do not say or do anything that would hurt your husband in the giving of such precious words to you.

Pray Song of Solomon 4:16 over the marriages you guard as a faithful, prayerful watchman (Isaiah 62:6-7).

> *"LORD, awake the north wind, and let the wind of the south come.*
> *Make the garden of _____ breathe out fragrance.*
> *Let its spices be wafted abroad.*
> *May _____ come into his garden as the beloved of _____.*
> *May they eat its choice fruits.*
> *For the glory of Your name, Jesus~"*

Please read Song of Solomon 5.

Meditate on verses 2-3.

> *I was asleep, but my heart was awake. A*
> *voice! My beloved was knocking:*
> *"Open to me, my sister, my darling, my dove, my perfect one!*
> *For my head is drenched with dew, my locks*
> *with the damp of the night."*
> *"I have taken off my dress; how can I put it on again?*
> *I have washed my feet, how can I dirty them again?"*

Excuses, excuses, excuses. Everyone is guilty of making them— "I'm too tired." "I'm too busy." "I don't feel well." "I don't want to...". Here, in God's Holy Word, is a wife making excuses for not letting her husband into the house and engaging in marital intimacy—she doesn't want to get her feet dirty! Before you judge the woman, ask the Holy Spirit to reveal excuses you are making for not obeying His will for your life.

When the bride came to her senses and got out of bed to open the door for her man, he was gone. Ugh—delayed obedience is disobedience—with consequences that follow! What could have been a lovely evening spent with her husband turns into a wretched night of being beaten by street thugs as she searches for him. She ends up wistfully telling the daughters of Jerusalem all about her husband instead of intimately whispering those words to him (vs. 8-16). Oh, how different the night could have been, if only....

Live your life without regrets. Stop making excuses. Love wholeheartedly. Follow the LORD completely. Let Him make your marriage all He wants it to be.

Pray Song of Solomon 5:1b over the marriages you guard as a faithful, prayerful watchman (Isaiah 62:6-7).

> *"LORD, let _____ and _____ hear You say,*
> *'Eat, friends; drink and imbibe deeply, O lovers.'*
> *For the sake of their (our) marriage*
> *and for the glory of Your name, Jesus~"*

Please read Song of Solomon 6.

Meditate on verse 5a. The bridegroom is talking to his bride.

"Turn your eyes away from me, for they have confused me."

The lovers' spat from chapter 5 lingers into chapter 6. The groom went to his garden (v. 2). The bride wants her groom; he is her beloved, and she is his (v. 3). The groom can't look her in the eyes, yet, but he is thinking about her, thinking about all her positive qualities (vs. 4-9).

This couple gives a good example to follow when marriage is tough—and there will be tough times—let the tough times strengthen your marriage. Do not allow Satan to use the tough times to destroy your marriage. When you are in the midst of difficulty with your spouse, say these words over and over:

"I am my beloved's, and my beloved is mine.
I am my beloved's, and my beloved is mine...."

If you need to, go to a quiet place, perhaps a garden, and recall all the positive things about your spouse. Say them aloud; write them down; think about them. Dwell on what is true, honorable, right, pure, lovely, admirable, excellent, and praise-worthy about your spouse (Philippians 4:8).

Let God get glory from your tough times.

Pray Song of Solomon 6:13a over the marriages you guard as a faithful, prayerful watchman (Isaiah 62:6-7).

"LORD, please let _____ come back, come
back, come back, come back,
for the sake of their marriage and their family.
For the sake of Your name, Jesus~"

Please read Song of Solomon 7.

Meditate on verse 10. The bride is talking about her groom.

> *"I am my beloved's, and his desire is for me!"*

Oh the joy of reconciliation! After pondering the positives of his bride, the groom returns, wooing and romancing his wife into blessed intimacy. "How beautiful and how delightful you are, my love, with all your charms" (v. 6)! He is captivated with her, and despite past difficulties, their relationship is in the springtime of intimate passion.

How amazing is God who wrote this book into His Holy Word! God loves marriage—the union of one man and one woman. God wants marriages to thrive, so He wrote *Song of Solomon* to intimately show the amazing power of marital love that keeps pursuing in the midst of heart-wrenching difficulty, resulting in a fruitful and passionate relationship.

Nothing is too difficult for the LORD (Jeremiah 32:17). Give Him the marriages you guard as a faithful, prayerful watchman (Isaiah 62:6-7), asking Him to bless them with Song of Solomon 7:13.

> *"LORD, the mandrakes have given forth*
> *fragrance; may all choice fruits,*
> *both old and new, be over the doors of _____ .*
> *Let them (us) save those fruits only*
> *for each other. May they (we) only be beloved to each other.*
> *For the sake of Your name, Jesus~"*

Please read Song of Solomon 8.

Meditate on verses 13-14. Notice how the bride answers her groom.

"O you who sit in the gardens, my companions
are listening for your voice—
Let me hear it!"
"Hurry, my beloved, and be like a gazelle or a young stag
on the mountains of spices."

The groom wanted to hear his bride call for him to come into her. His companions had no right to hear that call; it was only for the groom.

A marriage between one man and one woman is such a sacred thing. Satan and the world want to destroy that holy union because ultimately, it is the amazing picture God gave for intimacy between Christ and His church (Ephesians 5:31-32).

If you are blessed to be in a marriage, take care of it, for your marriage is precious in the sight of God. Encourage others to stay faithful to their spouse and not grow weary and lose heart.

Continue to pray *Song of Solomon* over marriages and use it to encourage married couples.

Pray Song of Solomon 8:6-7 over the marriages you guard as a faithful, prayerful watchman (Isaiah 62:6-7).

"LORD, let _____ put _____ as a seal over their (our) heart,
like a seal on their (our) arm. Let their
(our) love be as strong as death.
Make them (us) jealous for their (our) marriage.
Let their (our) passion be flashes of fire,
the very flame of You, LORD. Let no waters quench their (our) love,
nor rivers overflow it. If a man were to give
them (us) all the riches of his house
for their (our) love, his riches would be utterly despised.
Because their (our) marriage is for the glory of Your name, Jesus-"

Please read Lamentations 1.

Meditate on these phrases from verses 5 and 9.

> *For the LORD has caused her grief because of*
> *the multitude of her transgressions.*
> *She did not consider her future; therefore, she has fallen astonishingly.*

Earlier this year (January 22-April 25), you read the *1 & 2 Kings* and *Ezekiel* devotionals, which helped you understand why God punished Judah and Jerusalem by exiling the people to Babylon. *Lamentations* is another book, written in a more poetic style, clearly revealing the consequences of unchecked and unrelenting sin. God, the righteous judge, reveals His fierce anger in His condemnation of sin.

As you observe this chapter, notice the people of Jerusalem trying to restore their lives on their own (v. 11). Their futile attempts leave them hopeless, desperately needing a comforter (vs. 16-17, 21).

Thankfully, through Jesus Christ, you are saved from the wrath of God and delivered into His eternal comfort and hope (Romans 5:9; 2 Thessalonians 2:16-17). Take time to consider God's incredible gift of salvation, thanking Him for saving you from His fierce anger and for giving you the Comforter, the Holy Spirit.

Pray Lamentations 1:5 and 9 over yourself and those for whom you stand guard as a faithful, prayerful watchman (Isaiah 62:6-7).

> *"LORD, do not let _____ and my adversaries become our masters.*
> *Do not let our enemies prosper. Keep us from*
> *a multitude of transgressions;*
> *we do not want to grieve because of sin in our lives. Do not let*
> *our little ones be taken away as captives before the adversary.*
> *Let us consider our future so we do not fall astonishingly.*
> *LORD, You are our Comforter; see our affliction;*
> *do not let the enemy magnify himself!*
> *In Your name, Jesus~"*

Please read Lamentations 2.

Meditate on verse 14.

> *Your prophets have seen for you false and foolish visions;*
> *and they have not exposed your iniquity so*
> *as to restore you from captivity,*
> *but they have seen for you false and misleading oracles.*

Israel's prophets preached what the people wanted to hear, leading them to believe that God would not punish their sin and idolatry. The results were deadly as God poured out His wrath on His sinful nation, condemning the false prophets for leading the people astray.

> *"My hand will be against the prophets who see*
> *false visions and utter lying divinations.*
> *They will have no place in the council of My people."*
> —Ezekiel 13:9a

Sadly, some preachers and teachers still tickle people's ears instead of proclaiming all of God's Word (2 Timothy 4:3-4). Examine your teachers. For example, when was the last time you heard a sermon on God's anger and wrath? God's wrath is mentioned in the New Testament as well as the Old. Romans 1:18; Ephesians 5:6; Colossians 3:6; Revelation 6:16-17 and 19:15 are a few of the many New Testament verses that talk about the wrath of God and Jesus.

God's wrath was poured out on the people of Judah over 2500 years ago, and He promises to pour it out again on those who refuse to obey Christ (John 3:36). The need is urgent! "Arise and cry aloud in the night; pour out your heart like water before the presence of the LORD; lift up your hands to Him for the life of your little ones" (v. 19). Start by pouring your heart out to God with Lamentations 2:20a as His faithful, prayerful watchman (Isaiah 62:6-7).

> *"See, O LORD, and look!*
> *Please look at _____.*
> *(Tell God about those who need to be saved from His wrath.)*
> *For the sake of Your name, Jesus~"*

Please read Lamentations 3.

Meditate on verses 55-56.

> *I called on Your name, O LORD, out of the lowest pit.*
> *You have heard my voice, "Do not hide Your ear*
> *from my prayer for relief, from my cry for help."*

While many Bible scholars believe Jeremiah penned *Lamentations*, you do not see his name in the text. God did that on purpose, so the book is not the lamenting of any one person. They can be your lamentations, too, on hard days, when you want to put difficult feelings into words.

So, when you feel torn to pieces and it seems God is using you for target practice, tell Him about it (vs. 11-13). Then, use the words from Lamentations 3:21-25 and 55-58 to appeal to Him as a faithful, prayerful watchman (Isaiah 62:6-7).

> *"LORD, this I recall to mind; therefore, I have hope. Your*
> *lovingkindnesses indeed never cease, for Your compassions never*
> *fail. They are new every morning; great is Your faithfulness.*
> *LORD, You are my portion; therefore, I have hope in You.*
> *LORD, You are good to those who wait for You, to the person*
> *who seeks You. I am waiting for and seeking You! I call on Your*
> *name, O LORD, out of the lowest pit. Hear my voice! Do not*
> *hide Your ear from my prayer for relief, from my cry for help!*
> *Draw near when I call on You; I hear You say, 'Do not fear!'*
> *O LORD, plead my soul's cause and redeem my life.*
> *In Your name, Jesus~"*

Please read Lamentations 4.

Meditate on verse 11.

> *The LORD has accomplished His wrath; He*
> *has poured out His fierce anger,*
> *and He has kindled a fire in Zion, which*
> *has consumed its foundations.*

God's punishment of Jerusalem for relentless sin was fierce, and no one was left unscathed. Lamentations 4 vividly describes how absolutely horrific the circumstances were inside the walls of the city, so horrendous that even compassionate mamas were boiling and eating their own children because of starvation (v. 10).

You may have a variety of emotions toward this chapter of the Bible. Perhaps you are crying out, "How could God allow such a thing?" Keep in mind: sin is lamentable, its consequences grievous, and God's wrath for it completely justifiable and righteous. God warned the Jews over and over of what would happen if they refused to obey Him, but they loved their sinful lifestyles more than they loved the LORD, so the events recorded in *Lamentations* were some of the results.

As you take *Lamentations* to heart, ask God to help you see sin the way He does, no longer taking it lightly or considering it to be no big deal. Sin is a huge deal to God, and one proof of your salvation is that sin no longer lords over you; Jesus does.

Come to the LORD, humbly repenting and begging Him not to have to do Lamentations 4:11 and 16 to you and those you are guarding as a faithful, prayerful watchman (Isaiah 62:6-7).

> *"LORD, please forgive _____ and me.*
> *May we obey You, so You do not*
> *have to accomplish Your wrath and pour out Your fierce anger on us.*
> *Let us follow You so You do not kindle a fire and consume us.*
> *We do not want to be scattered from Your presence.*
> *Please continue to regard us.*
> *For the sake of Your name, Jesus~"*

Please read Lamentations 5.

Meditate on verses 15-16.

> *The joy of our hearts has ceased; our dancing*
> *has been turned into mourning.*
> *The crown has fallen from our head; woe to us, for we have sinned!*

The Israelites learned the hard way that sin has serious consequences. Thankfully, they acknowledged that it was indeed their sins that caused their horrific circumstances; they were responsible for the punishment inflicted by God on them and their children.

Quickly recognizing and admitting personal sin is an important step to take as you mature in Christ. Confessing your sins and asking for God's forgiveness is the next step. Desiring to never commit those sins again is the third step. And, walking obediently with the LORD is the joy-filled fourth step.

Let *Lamentations* be a good reminder of how lamentable sin is and how much God hates it. And if you find yourself lackadaisical towards sin and its consequences, reread the book; then fall on your face before God, confessing and repenting. The lives of so many are at stake.

Pray Lamentations 5:1, 15-16, and 19-22 over yourself and those for whom you stand guard as a faithful, prayerful watchman (Isaiah 62:6-7).

> *"Remember, O LORD, what has befallen _____ and*
> *me. Look and see our reproach!*
> *The joy of our hearts has ceased; our dancing*
> *has been turned into mourning.*
> *The crown has fallen from our head; woe to us, for we have sinned!*
> *You, O LORD, rule forever; Your throne is*
> *from generation to generation.*
> *Please do not forget us forever! Please do not forsake us so long!*
> *Restore us to You, O LORD, that we may be*
> *restored; renew our days as of old.*
> *Please do not utterly reject us and be exceedingly angry with us.*
> *Because we belong to You, Jesus~"*

DECEMBER 18

Please read Habakkuk 3.

Habakkuk's Song

Meditate on verses 17-18.

> *Though the fig tree should not blossom and*
> *there be no fruit on the vines,*
> *though the yield of the olive should fail and the fields produce no food,*
> *though the flock should be cut off from the fold*
> *and there be no cattle in the stalls,*
> *yet I will exult in the LORD; I will rejoice*
> *in the God of my salvation.*

Habakkuk wrote this prayer for the choir to sing while waiting for God to fulfill a vision He had given him (Habakkuk 2:2-3; 3:19b). Waiting is difficult, and because Habakkuk wanted a choir to sing about it, you know that Habakkuk's was a public waiting, where people probably questioned if God would even fulfill His Word for the vision.

Let this song encourage you in the midst of the wait. Observe how Habakkuk waited. He stayed focused on the LORD. He recalled God's faithfulness in the past; he waited, expecting God's faithfulness in the future. And, no matter what happened, Habakkuk rejoiced in God (v. 18).

While you are waiting, let the LORD take you to His Spiritual high place, fixing your thoughts and joy on Him (vs. 18-19).

Pray Habakkuk 3:17-19 with wholehearted faith, as God's faithful, prayerful watchman (Isaiah 62:6-7).

> *"Though the fig tree should not blossom and*
> *there be no fruit on the vines,*
> *though the yield of the olive should fail and the fields produce no food,*
> *though the flock should be cut off from the fold*
> *and there be no cattle in the stalls,*
> *yet I will exult in You, LORD, I will rejoice*
> *in You, God of my salvation.*
> *LORD GOD, You are my strength, and You*
> *have made my feet like hinds' feet,*
> *make me walk on Your high places.*
> *For the glory of Your name, Jesus-"*

Please read Luke 1:26-55. The Song of Mary is found in verses 46-55.

Meditate on verses 46b-47a.

> *My soul exalts the LORD, and my spirit*
> *has rejoiced in God my Savior,*
> *for He has had regard for the humble state of His bondslave.*

How excited Gabriel must have been to receive God's order to announce to Mary that she was to be the mother of Jesus! For 4,000 years, every Old Testament believer had put their faith in the coming of Messiah, and now Mary was to be the human vessel through whom God would put on flesh to be the perfect, sinless sacrifice for the sinfulness of all mankind.

Bask in the CHRISTmas story like never before this year, asking God to reveal new insights into His miracles of Christ's birth. Give yourself to God saying: "Behold, the bondslave of the LORD; may it be done to me according Your Word" (v. 38).

After making that commitment to Christ, Mary's song can be your song, too (vs. 46-55). Say/sing it to Him as His faithful, prayerful watchman (Isaiah 62:6-7).

> *"My soul exalts You, LORD, and my spirit*
> *rejoices in You, God, my Savior.*
> *For You have regard for the humble state of Your*
> *bondslave; for behold, from this time on,*
> *all generations will count me blessed. For You,*
> *the Mighty One, have done great things*
> *for me, and holy is Your name. Your mercy*
> *is upon generation after generation*
> *toward those who fear You.*
> *You have done mighty deeds with Your arm;*
> *You have scattered those who are proud in the thoughts of their heart.*
> *You have broken down rulers from their thrones, and You have*
> *exalted those who were humble. You have filled the hungry with*
> *good things and sent away the rich empty-handed. You have given*
> *help to Israel, Your servant, in remembrance of Your mercy,*
> *as You spoke to our fathers, to Abraham and his descendants forever.*
> *Thank You, Jesus Messiah~"*

Please read Luke 1:57-79.

Zacharias' Song (vs. 68-79)

Meditate on verses 68-69a.

> *Blessed be the LORD God of Israel, for He has visited us*
> *and accomplished redemption for His people*
> *and has raised up a horn of salvation for us.*

These were the first words Zacharias spoke since questioning Gabriel in Luke 1:18. Zacharias had at least nine months to ponder how his words would be different should he ever be allowed to speak again. When his tongue was finally loosed, he spoke the praise of God (v. 64).

Do you ever have a "loose tongue," talking too much about things you shouldn't? Ask God to loose your tongue for praising Him. What a difference it will make in the lives of those you love!

Filled with the Holy Spirit (v. 67), pray Zacharias' words, making them your own (vs. 68-79).

> *"Blessed are You, LORD God of Israel and of*
> *my family, for You have visited us*
> *and accomplished redemption for Your people.*
> *You have raised up a horn of salvation for us*
> *in the house of David Your servant—*
> *as You spoke by the mouth of Your holy prophets from of old—*
> *Salvation from our enemies and from the hand of all who hate us;*
> *to show mercy toward our fathers and to*
> *remember Your holy covenant,*
> *the oath which You swore to Abraham our father, to grant us that we,*
> *being rescued from the hand of our enemies,*
> *might serve You without fear,*
> *in holiness and righteousness, before You all our days.*
> *LORD, make us Your people who go with You to give Your people*
> *the knowledge of salvation by the forgiveness of their sins,*
> *because of Your tender mercy, with which the*
> *Sunrise from on high has visited us,*
> *to shine upon those who sit in darkness and the shadow of death,*
> *to guide our feet into the way of peace.*
> *Because of Your name, Jesus–"*

Please read Luke 2:25-32.

Simeon's Song (vs. 29-32).

Meditate on verse 30.

My eyes have seen Your salvation.

As Simeon held Jesus in his arms, he knew God had fulfilled His promise that he "would not see death before he had seen the LORD's Christ" (v. 26). Can you imagine his joy, knowing his soul would leave this earth in peace because he saw God's salvation? Simeon's incredible encounter with Messiah, must be yours as well. In order to depart this life in peace, you must see God's salvation, Jesus Christ, holding Him in your arms as God's gift of Messiah to you.

Thank the LORD for His indescribable gift of Jesus! Pray for those you love who still need to see the LORD's Christ, accepting Him as God's gift of salvation.

Bless God with Simeon's words, making them your own (vs. 28-32).

"Now LORD, You can release me, Your bond-
servant, to depart in peace,
according to Your Word, for my eyes have seen Your salvation,
which You have prepared in the presence of all peoples,
a Light of Revelation to the Gentiles and
the glory of Your people Israel.
LORD, let _____ see Your salvation.
In Your name, Jesus~"

DECEMBER 22

Please read Ruth 1.

Meditate on verse 19.

> *So they both went until they came to Bethlehem.*
> *And when they had come to Bethlehem, all*
> *the city was stirred because of them,*
> *and the women said, "Is this Naomi?"*

Naomi and Ruth were in a hopeless situation. Their husbands were dead; they had no children, and they lived during a time when women relied heavily on husbands and sons to provide for them. They needed a savior! Ruth insisted on staying with her beloved mother-in-law, entering into a covenant relationship by committing to never leave God or Naomi. The promises made by Ruth led her to Bethlehem where the Almighty would perform the miraculous on behalf of her, Naomi, and all of humanity.

As you continue reading the beloved book of *Ruth*, you will be reading the Christmas story. You, too, will journey with Naomi and Ruth to Bethlehem, being stirred by the hand of the Almighty. As you spend these next four days of the CHRISTmas holy days, in Bethlehem, be filled with hope for what the Almighty will miraculously do in your life, too.

Start your journey to Bethlehem, recommitting yourself to God by praying Ruth 1:16-17.

> *"LORD, I will never leave You or turn back from*
> *following You, for where You go, I will go,*
> *and where You lodge, I will lodge. Your people will*
> *be my people because You are my God.*
> *LORD, thank You that not even death will part me from You.*
> *Because of You, LORD Jesus~"*

Please read Ruth 2.

Meditate on verse 1.

> *Now Naomi had a kinsman of her husband, a man of great*
> *wealth, of the family of Elimelech, whose name was Boaz.*

Boaz was a Godly man and a close relative of Naomi's deceased husband, Elimelech, making him her kinsman-redeemer. A kinsman-redeemer had the right to marry his deceased relative's widow in order to beget a child for him and redeem his land.

Boaz was from Bethlehem, and he had fields in that same region. It is possible the fields where Ruth gathered grain are the same fields that Luke wrote about saying:

> *In the same region there were some shepherds staying out in the fields*
> *and keeping watch over their flock by night.*
> —Luke 2:8

As you continue reading the story of Naomi, Ruth, and Boaz, notice how Boaz foreshadows the coming Messiah. Jesus Christ is your kinsman-redeemer who delivers you from hopelessness and death. He is your protector, giving you everything you need to live. He extends His favor and kindness to you.

Pray Ruth 2:12-13 over yourself and those for whom you stand guard as a faithful, prayerful watchman (Isaiah 62:6-7).

> *"LORD, please reward the work of _____ and me.*
> *May our wages be full from You, LORD, under*
> *whose wings we have taken refuge.*
> *Let us find favor in Your sight, our LORD, for You have comforted us*
> *and indeed have spoken kindly to Your bond-servants.*
> *Because You are our kinsman-redeemer, Jesus Christ~"*

Please read Ruth 3.

Meditate on verse 9.

> *He said, "Who are you?"*
> *And she answered, "I am Ruth your maid. So*
> *spread your covering over your maid,*
> *for you are a close relative (redeemer)."*

Redeem and redeemer (translated as "close relative" in the NASB) are the same Hebrew word, *ga'al*, and repeated several times in this chapter (vs. 9, 12, 13).[1] Naomi and Ruth needed a redeemer, someone to save them from their hopeless situation.

Covering is a Hebrew word that also means "wings."[2] The meditation verse (v. 9) could be translated from Hebrew (the original language of the Old Testament) as:

> *He said, "Who are you?" And she answered, "I am Ruth your maid.*
> *So spread your wings over your maid, for you are a redeemer."*

The psalmist made a similar plea to His Redeemer in Psalm 61:4:

> *"Let me dwell in Your tent forever; let me take*
> *refuge in the shelter of Your wings."*

Jesus was born 2000 years ago for the purpose of redeeming you from your hopeless situation, covering you with His love and forgiveness. Fall at the feet of your Savior, praying Ruth 3:9.

> *"LORD, I am _____, Your servant.*
> *Spread Your covering over me, for You are my Redeemer.*
> *Thank You, LORD Jesus~"*

---

1. *Retrieved from www.blueletterbible.org/lang/lexicon/lexicon.cfm?Strongs=H1350&t=NASB*

2. *Retrieved from www.blueletterbible.org/lang/lexicon/lexicon.cfm?Strongs=H3671&t=NASB*

Please read Ruth 4.

Meditate on verse 14.

> *Then the women said to Naomi, "Blessed is*
> *the LORD who has not left you*
> *without a redeemer today, and may his*
> *name become famous in Israel."*

What an amazing story of God's redemption! Boaz's redemption of Naomi and Ruth set into motion the lineage of Jesus Christ, whose name would indeed become famous in Bethlehem and Israel. As Naomi held her beloved baby, Obed, who was born to Boaz and Ruth in Bethlehem, she was holding the great-great-great-great…grandfather of her Redeemer Jesus Christ.

> *The record of the genealogy of Jesus the Messiah… Salmon*
> *was the father of Boaz by Rahab, Boaz was the father*
> *of Obed by Ruth, and Obed the father of Jesse.*
> *Jesse was the father of David the king.*
> —Matthew 1:1, 5-6

It's Christmas, and as you think about Jesus being born in Bethlehem, 2000 years ago, think about Naomi, Ruth, and Boaz, too. Think about these faithful ancestors of Christ, following God wherever He led them, in good times and bad. Thank God for faithful legacies, asking Him to help you give your family the gift of faithfulness this Christmas.

Pray Ruth 4:14-15 in thanksgiving to your LORD and Savior Jesus Christ.

> *"Blessed are You, LORD, who has not left*
> *us without a Redeemer today.*
> *May Your name become famous in Israel*
> *and in the lives of my loved ones.*
> *Jesus, You are the Restorer of life and*
> *Sustainer of us, even in our old age.*
> *You are better to us than anyone.*
> *Happy Birthday, Jesus. I love You~"*

DECEMBER 26

Please read Ephesians 1.

As you read, notice what God does because of "His will" and for "the praise of His glory."

Meditate on verses 5-6.\

> *He predestined us to adoption as sons through Jesus Christ to Himself,*
> *according to the kind intention of His will, to*
> *the praise of the glory of His grace,*
> *which He freely bestowed on us in the Beloved.*

The Truths of God in this chapter are like waves of the ocean on a beach—they keep miraculously coming. Ponder these waves of glorious truth:

- God has blessed you with every spiritual blessing (v. 3).
- God chose you before the foundation (creation) of the world (v. 4).
- God predestined you to adoption as His child (v. 5).
- God gave you His redemption and forgiveness (v. 7).
- God lavished His rich grace on you (vs. 7-8).
- God sealed you in Jesus with the Holy Spirit (v. 13).

And those are only a handful of the waves in this incredible chapter! Spend time today praising God for all He has done and is doing in your life. Ask Him to make you more aware of who He is and what He is doing as you walk with Him.

Pray Ephesians 1:17 over yourself and those for whom you stand guard as a faithful, prayerful watchman (Isaiah 62:6-7).

> *"God of our LORD Jesus Christ, the Father of glory,*
> *give _____ and me a spirit of wisdom*
> *and of revelation in the knowledge of You.*
> *In Your name, Jesus-"*

Please read Ephesians 2.

Meditate on verse 13.

> *But now in Christ Jesus, you who formerly were far off*
> *have been brought near by the blood of Christ.*

In this chapter, Paul teaches amazing things about God's love for you and the power of Jesus' work in your life.

Despite being a dead, disobedient child of wrath, God in His rich mercy and great love, makes you alive and seated with Jesus in heaven (vs. 1-6).

Ponder these truths applied to your life:

- Jesus saves you by grace through faith—it is God's gift (vs. 8-9).
- You are His workmanship, created in Christ Jesus for good works (v. 10).
- You were separate from Christ, far off with no hope, but now, you are brought near to Him (vs. 11-13).
- No longer a stranger and alien, now a fellow citizen with the saints of God's household, you are part of the family of God built upon Jesus your cornerstone (vs. 19-20).

Take advantage of this treasure and treasured life. The Creator of the universe went to all this trouble, so you can draw near to Him and walk with Him.

Pray Ephesians 2:1 and 13 over yourself and those for whom you stand guard as a faithful, prayerful watchman (Isaiah 62:6-7).

> *"LORD, _____ is dead in their trespasses and sins;*
> *please bring them near to you.*
> *I was formerly far off from you;*
> *thank You for bringing me near by the blood of Christ.*
> *In Your name, Jesus~"*

Please read Ephesians 3.

Meditate on verses 4 and 6.

> *By referring to this, when you read you can understand my*
> *insight into the mystery of Christ, to be specific, that the Gentiles*
> *are fellow heirs and fellow members of the body, and fellow*
> *partakers of the promise in Christ Jesus through the Gospel.*

There is a popular global craze for a new kind of adventure. It is a physical puzzle game that combines thinking, solving clues, and beating the clock to get yourself or your group out safely. The craze is known as "Escape Rooms." "Escape Rooms" certainly describe Paul's prison experiences, but they are also a good illustration of Paul's revelation that he received from the LORD—that Gentiles are fellow heirs in Christ.

Paul, who is in prison writing this letter, says not to worry about his troubles; they are no big deal because he knows the clues to the escape room. Paul is not asking the Christians to pray for his escape from prison. He is only concerned that the Church of Ephesus know and tell others the mystery that God wants them to be His children. All people can escape their spiritual prison and break out into an intimate relationship with Jesus.

Ephesians 3:16-21 is a prayer Paul prayed for the Church of Ephesus. Pray it over yourself and those for whom you stand guard as a faithful, prayerful watchman (Isaiah 62:6-7).

> *"LORD, grant _____ and me, according to the riches of Your glory,*
> *to be strengthened with power through Your Spirit in our inner man.*
> *Christ, dwell in our hearts through faith. Root us*
> *and ground us in love. Let us be able to comprehend*
> *the breadth and length and height and depth*
> *and know Your love which surpasses knowledge.*
> *Fill us up to all the fullness of You, God!*
> *You are able to do exceedingly abundantly*
> *beyond all that we ask or think,*
> *according to Your power that works within us.*
> *To You be the glory in the church*
> *and in Christ Jesus to all generations forever and ever. Amen"*

Please read Ephesians 4.

Meditate on verse 1.

> *Therefore I, the prisoner of the LORD,*
> *implore you to walk in a manner*
> *worthy of the calling with which you have been called.*

The word calling is a very important part of Christian life. Calling is used to describe those going into full-time ministry or missions. For example, "He received a calling to preach."

In a much broader sense, calling is used to describe the activity of God drawing people to become Christians. It is the purposeful action of God who calls you to come to Him (Ephesians 1:18). Calling is not accidental like when you dial someone without knowing it on your cell phone. It is very intentional.

Ephesians 4 gives a great picture of being intentionally called by God to salvation, to ministry, and to living a life consistent with the reputation of being part of God's family.

You have been recruited—called—to be on God's team as a member of His family. This is the highest calling a person can have.

Pray Ephesians 4:1-6 over yourself and those you love to be faithful to the calling of God.

> *"LORD, help _____ and me walk in a manner worthy*
> *of the calling with which You have called us—with all*
> *humility and gentleness, with patience, showing tolerance*
> *for one another in love, being diligent to*
> *preserve the unity of the Spirit*
> *in the bond of peace. There is one body of*
> *Christ and one Spirit, just as we were*
> *called in one hope of Your calling; there is one*
> *LORD, one faith, and one baptism.*
> *You are one God and Father who is over*
> *all and through all and in all.*
> *In Your name, Jesus~"*

DECEMBER 30

Please read Ephesians 5.

Meditate on verses 22, 25, and 33.

> *Wives, be subject to your own husbands, as to the LORD.*
> *Husbands, love your wives, just as Christ also loved*
> *the church and gave Himself up for her.*
> *Each individual among you also is to love*
> *his own wife, even as himself,*
> *and the wife must see to it that she respects her husband.*

In Ephesians 5, you see how the church, as the Bride of Christ, and the relationship of marriage between a man and a woman, are divinely related (vs. 25, 32). The purpose of marriage is to emulate the relationship of the church to the LORD.

Therefore, there is great responsibility for husbands to offer themselves unselfishly for their wives to care for and protect them. They are to give their wife all she needs to be the best Christian she can be, just like Christ gave everything for people to be followers of Him. Husband, put your wife's needs above your own and help her grow in the faith.

Wives are to honor their husband and his responsibility for leading the home. Wives are to respect and follow their husband just like the church should respect and follow Christ. Wife, respect your husband and let him lead your family.

Ask the LORD to make you a Godly completer for your spouse, to bring oneness to your marriage, and for you both to be more like Jesus.

Pray Ephesians 5:22, 25, and 33 over marriages you guard as a faithful, prayerful watchman (Isaiah 62:6-7).

> *"LORD, help wives be subject to their own*
> *husband, as to You, LORD.*
> *Help husbands love their wife, just as You, Christ,*
> *also loved the church and gave Yourself up for her.*
> *Let each individual love his own wife even as himself,*
> *and let the wife see to it that she respects her husband.*
> *In Your name, Jesus~"*

DECEMBER 31

Please read Ephesians 6.

Meditate on verses 1-4.

> *Children, obey your parents in the LORD, for this is right.*
> *Honor your father and mother (which is the*
> *first commandment with a promise),*
> *so that it may be well with you, and that*
> *you may live long on the earth.*
> *Fathers, do not provoke your children to anger, but bring them up*
> *in the discipline and instruction of the LORD.*

This passage is full of vital information for families, starting with children obeying and honoring (valuing) their parents. When a child is obedient, they do their parents' will and understand the world does not revolve around them. They learn to submit to proper authorities, preparing them for relationships with authorities at school, work, church, and most importantly with God, which require unselfishness and obedience to be successful. Constant, Godly parenting develops these characteristics, so children are good citizens of their family and community.

Fathers are singled out in this passage to build character and behaviors that emulate God, so their children have as accurate a picture of God from their earthly fathers as possible. Father, be a Godly example by leading a consistent, stable home, where love and rules do not vacillate, and your children have a foundation to become successful in their walk with God. Strive for these goals so when they graduate high school, they have a relationship with the LORD that is real and the desire and ability to discern His will for their lives.

Pray Ephesians 6:1-4 over yourself and those for whom you stand guard as a faithful, prayerful watchman (Isaiah 62:6-7).

> *"LORD, help _____ bey their parents, for this is right.*
> *Help _____ and me honor our father and*
> *mother. Fulfill Your promise, LORD,*
> *that it may be well with us, and that we may live long on the earth.*
> *Help _____ be a good father, to not provoke his children to anger,*
> *but bring them up in the discipline and instruction of You, LORD.*
> *In Your name, Jesus~"*

SCRIPTURE INDEX

HABAKKUK 3	December 18
MALACHI	September 6 – September 9
LUKE 1	December 19 – December 20
LUKE 2	December 21
JOHN	January 1 - 21
ROMANS	April 26 - May 11
GALATIONS	May 26 - May 31
EPHESIANS	December 26 – December 31
PHILIPPIANS	June 14 - June 17
COLOSSIANS	August 1 – August 4
1 THESSALONIANS	August 17 – August 21
2 THESSALONIANS	August 22 – August 24
TITUS	June 28 – June 30
JAMES	September 1 – September 5
1 PETER	September 10 – September 14
2 PETER	September 15 – September 17
JUDE	September 18

TOPICAL INDEX

CHURCH
April 26, June 11, June 15, June 28,
October 31, November 11, December 28

DISCIPLESHIP
January 8, January 15, May 7, May 22, May 30, May 31, August 1,
August 3, August 20, August 21, August 22, August 28,
August 30, September 2, September 4, December 29

FEAR GOD
February 8, April 15, June 7, June 20, July 9, July 23, August 12,
August 16, September 6, September 8,
September 9, October 3, October 21

GOD'S WILL
January 26, January 28, January 30, February 13, February 21,
April 17, April 24, June 14, June 27, July 16, July 19, August 7

GOD'S WORD

February 7, February 12, February 15, March 5, March 6, March 11, March 20, April 7, April 10, June 8, June 10, September 7, October 9, October 13, October 18, October 19, October 20, October 23, October 27, October 28

HELP! DELIVERANCE AND RESTORATION

February 18, February 19, February 23, March 2, May 10, May 12, May 17, June 21, June 24, June 25, June 26, August 24, August 31, September 20, September 21, September 25, September 26, September 27, October 17, October 25, October 29, October 30, November 1, November 2, November 7, November 8, November 15, November 16, November 18, November 20, November 21, December 3, December 17

HOLINESS

February 6, February 14, March 28, April 1, April 3, April 12, April 19, April 21, May 20, August 9, September 3, September 15, September 16, September 19, November 19, December 1

HOME AND FAMILY

January 22, January 23, February 20, June 29, July 14, July 31, August 17, August 25, September 30, November 5, November 6, December 13, December 31

INTIMACY WITH GOD

January 13, April 18, June 16, June 22, September 10, November 3, November 9, November 17, November 22, November 29, December 4

JESUS

January 1, January 18, January 20, February 16, March 12, March 25, August 2, August 29, September 28, December 23, December 24, December 25

LORDSHIP

January 4, January 12, February 5, March 9, March 10, March 27, March 29, May 9, May 26, September 18, October 7, October 8, October 10, November 12, December 19, December 22,

LOVINGKINDNESS

March 8, March 24, June 13, October 6, October 14, October 22, November 14, December 15,

MARRIAGE

June 18, July 21, August 8, September 12, December 5, December 6, December 7, December 8, December 9, December 10, December 11, December 12, December 30

OBEDIENCE

January 2, January 3, January 11, January 21, January 27, January 29, February 1, February 2, February 3, February 4, February 9, February 10, February 28, February 29, March 1, March 4, May 8, July 7, September 11, September 13, October 11, October 12, October 16

PRAISE

April 20, April 29, May 6, May 11, June 12, September 22, September 29, October 1, November 4, November 13, November 23, November 24, November 25, November 26, November 27, November 28, December 2, December 20

PRAYER

January 14, March 30, May 3, June 17, August 4, September 24, October 4

Pride and Humility

February 24, March 3, April 2, April 4, April 5, April 6, April 8,
April 9,May 18, June 19, June 23, July 6, July 8,
July 11, July 22, July 27, July 29

Repentance

February 25, February 26, March 7, March 16, March 19,
March 22, March 26, March 31, April 13, May 16, May 19,
May 23, May 24, May 25, June 1, June 9, December 16

Righteousness

January 16, April 22, April 28, May 4, May 21, July 10, July 12,
July 15, July 18, July 20, July 28, October 24, November 10

Salvation

January 5, January 6, January 7, January 9, January 10, January 17,
February 17, March 13, March 14, March 15, March 18, April 14,
April 16, April 23, April 25, April 27, May 1, May 2, May 5, May 13,
May 14, May 28, May 29, June 30, August 18, August 23, September 5,
September 17, October 2, December 14, December 21, December 27,

Shepherd God's Flock

April 11, August 19, September 14

Sin

February 11, February 22, February 27, March 17,
August 10, August 11, August 26, August 27, September 1

Strength

June 2, June 3, June 4, June 6, September 23

TRUST AND FAITHFULNESS

March 23, April 30, June 5, July 25, August 13,
August 15, November 30, December 18

TRUTH

January 19, March 21, May 27, August 5, October 5, October 26

WISDOM AND DISCERNMENT

January 24, January 25, January 31, May 15, July 1, July 2, July 3, July 4,
July 5, July 13, July 17, July 24, July 26, July 30,
August 6, August 14, October 15, December 26

ABOUT THE AUTHORS

MARSHA HARVELL

Marsha Harvell has a passion for the LORD and treasures His Word. She has led more than 100 Bible studies. As an international trainer for Precept Ministries, she has taught hundreds of people in Germany, France, Qatar, Bahrain, India, Malaysia, and Japan how to study the Bible and lead Bible studies. Marsha is dedicated to helping others discover the promises found in Scripture.

Marsha is a missionary to the military as a chaplain's wife, appointed by the North American Mission Board (1991). She and her husband, Ron, recently returned to the States after serving for five years in Europe and the Middle East. They now minister to the military community from Washington, D.C.

With a Bachelor of Education degree from Hardin-Simmons University and a Masters in Gifted and Talented Education from Texas Women's University, Marsha Harvell has taught in both public and private schools. She has helped plant churches and served as a worship leader and a women's ministry director. She is also a conference speaker; some of her favorite topics include: The Covenant Maker, Godly Relationships, Being a Godly Wife and Mother, Hearing and Heeding God, Being Complete in Christ, Knowing God, and How to Pray.

She is the author of *The Covenant Maker: Knowing God and His Promises for Salvation and Marriage*, co-author with Ron of *The Watchman on the Wall: Daily Devotions for Praying God's Word over Those You Love (Volumes 1, 2, and 3)* and co-author with Ron and Wendy K. Walters of *50 Steps with Jesus: Learning to Walk Daily with the Lord (New Believer's and Shepherd's Guides)*.

Marsha and Ron have been married since 1984 and have two grown children, Stephanie (married to Jonathan) and Steven (married to Rachel). Both families serve the LORD overseas. They have seven grandchildren: Nathan, Adilynn, Kik, Daniel, Kyro, Caleb, and Abigail.

Dr. Ron Harvell is the Deputy Chief of Chaplains for the United States Air Force where he is responsible for supporting the Air Force Chief of Chaplains for ministry to all Air Force personnel. Previously he was the Command Chaplain for Air Force Mobility Command, Air Force Global Strike Command, and Air Force Central Command, caring for all Air Force personnel serving in the 22 countries of the Middle East.

Ron felt called to ministry when he was 17 years old. After being licensed to the Gospel Ministry by Circle Drive Baptist Church in Colorado Springs, he attended college where he met and married Marsha (1984). In June of 1985, he was ordained by Friendship Baptist Church in Weatherford, Texas. Following seminary, he pastored Northside Baptist Church in Kermit, Texas for four-and-a-half years. Since 1991, Ron and Marsha have lived in 15 locations around the world, serving as endorsed ministers of the North American Mission Board to the Air Force Active Duty Chaplain Corps.

He is an award-winning church growth pastor in both civilian and military organizations and a visionary leader serving God in His transformation of individuals, communities, and institutions. He is the co-author with Marsha of *The Watchman on the Wall: Daily Devotions for Praying God's Word over Those You Love (Volumes 1, 2, and 3)* and co-author with Ron and Wendy K. Walters of *50 Steps with Jesus: Learning to Walk Daily with the Lord (New Believer's and Shepherd's Guides)*.

Ron has earned a Bachelor of Arts degree from Hardin-Simmons University in Bible and History, a Master of Divinity from Southwestern

Baptist Theological Seminary, and a Doctor of Ministry from Asia Graduate School of Theology with a focus in Transformational Leadership for the Global City. He also has a Master of Science in National Security Strategy from National War College at the National Defense University and a Master of Arts in Organizational Management from The George Washington University. These academic experiences help to shape ministry opportunities and capacities for where his gifts and passions are: preaching, teaching, discipleship, church planting, and church growth.

Marsha and Ron have been married since 1984 and have two grown children, Stephanie (married to Jonathan) and Steven (married to Rachel). Both families serve the LORD overseas. They have seven grandchildren: Nathan, Adilynn, Kik, Daniel, Kyro, Caleb, and Abigail.